By the Same Author

BLACK ENGLISH
Its History and Usage in the United States

ALL-AMERICAN ENGLISH

ALL-AMERICAN ENGLISH

ENGLISH

J.L. DILLARD

Random House
New York

Library of Congress Cataloging in Publication Data

Dillard, Joey Lee, 1924-
All-American English

Bibliography: p.
Includes index.
1.   English language in the United States—History.
I.   Title.
PE2809.D54   420'.9   74-26995
ISBN 0-394-48965-9

The material contained in Chapter II first appeared
in slightly different form in the *Kansas Journal of
Sociology*, Vol. IX, No. 2 (Fall 1973) .

Manufactured in the United States of America

9 8 7 6 5 4 3 2

FIRST EDITION

CONTENTS

PREFATORY NOTE

IN THE SIXTEENTH AND SEVENTEENTH CENTURIES, THE ENGLISH language took the first steps toward becoming a world language by acquiring a large group of nonnative speakers.[1] Almost imperceptibly at first, it began spreading beyond the British Isles, along the oceanways of the world. At about the same time it came to be spoken on the North American continent. Obviously, both these developments are part of the same spread. But histories of the language have never betrayed any awareness of the connection between the two. In fact, the first has gone almost unnoticed in historical treatments, with a brief mention conventionally inserted somewhere after the section on the distribution of American "regional" dialects.

The reason for this seems to be that language histories have been based on the attempt to reconstruct Proto-Indo-European, the still hypothetical ancestor of most European languages and some Asian. This "parent" language has been presumed to exist because of the similarities in "daughter" languages like Sanskrit and the Germanic languages, which in nonhistorical terms are quite dissimilar. This reconstruction, the big triumph of nineteenth-century historical lin-

ix

guistics, sketched a putative overland migration route from somewhere in the Caucasus region to various parts of the Eurasian land mass. *Overland* and *land mass* are the key words here. The historical (as distinct from reconstructed) migrations that were used for comparative purposes were overland migrations. But what began happening in the sixteenth century for the English, French, Portuguese, Spanish, and Dutch were seaborne migrations. Furthermore, the participants were polyethnic and multicultural rather than the theoretically homogeneous tribal groups in such re-created migrations as the Germanic *Völkerwanderung*.

The earliest stage of the maritime language "migration" was only slightly better chronicled than the prehistoric migrations of the Indo-Europeans and the Germanic tribes—which were not chronicled at all—and certainly not so well as the historic contacts of English with Norse in the Danelaw and with Norman French after the Conquest. European maritime language contacts, of which there may have been many, were not nearly so well recorded as was the spread of Latin on the continent of Europe; but they may have been as important in the subsequent development of the languages of the world. The reason for the discrepancy is simple: Latin and to some extent the "standard" European languages were used by scholars, who got little from life beyond publicity and recognition; the trade varieties, on the other hand, were spoken by merchants, who made money and didn't care whether they got recognition or not.

The variety of English that went along with English—and later American—maritime expansion, colonialism, and imperialism was Pidgin English. It is still well known, in only slightly distorted form, from old movies, novels, and other accounts. Roughly accurate renditions have even appeared in the comic strips and on television programs. Its land locus was the islands, seaports, and coastal areas where the English Navy put in. It changed somewhat as it moved from one locale to another. The forms spoken in several different locales have been described by several professional linguists who specialize in pidgin languages. None of these is, however, well known to the general public. Popularizers of linguistics have made some terrible blunders when they have tried to present information on Pidgin English to the public; and professional liberals have mistaken the language that accompanied the exploitation of minority groups for the exploitation itself and have denounced even the recognition of Pidgin English in print. But Pidgin English figured in the continental colonies that later became the United States, since migration to those areas was part of the same process that brought migration to many other areas around the world.

For those Englishmen who went to North America (and later to Australia) almost exclusively in the company of other Englishmen, another process related to the use of pidgin was involved. This process, too, involved what it is convenient to think of as "simplification," although in an absolute sense language use is never really simple. But whatever simplicity English may have acquired in its two kinds of migratory relationships, it soon lost in the contact with other languages in the Americas and elsewhere.

This book is about the development of those two forms of "simplicity" and the new kind of complexity that made American English recognizably different from British English, even when the many different varieties or "dialects" of both are taken into account.

One of the first to recognize the significant differences between British and American English was H. L. Mencken, whose book *The American Language* was first published in 1919. As its title shows, Mencken believed that "British" (or "English") and "American" should no longer be called the same language. Subsequent writers on the language have generally rejected Mencken's major thesis, although every last one of them has owed a great debt to the data that he provided. They have tried to find—as Mencken did not—the origins of American English in the "regional" dialects of British English, and have generally underplayed Mencken's attribution of the differences to the many immigrant groups that came to the alleged "Land of Freedom." Mencken himself, in his three later editions and two supplements, tended to abandon his position to some degree, while the 1963 "edition" of *The American Language* prepared by McDavid and Maurer remade the work into a book on dialect geography. Since dialect geography is part of the discipline of internal reconstruction,[2] Mencken's original insight was in effect submerged in the tradition that, ironically, Mencken had rejected when he accused American language scholars of knowing more about Sanskrit and the older stages of the Germanic languages than they did about the language spoken around them.

With recent discoveries and improvements in the study of language varieties used primarily in contact situations (prominent among which are pidgins), it seems time to reexamine Mencken's original thesis—not just to reshuffle his data. Although British English and American English may not be different "languages," they are obviously different. Recent work on linguistic typology should provide us with at least more satisfactory terms. And there are sources of data that neither Mencken nor his followers and advisors ever thought to consult. With the vast amount of historical documentation available, it should be possible to examine *how* the English of the United States and the English of Great Britain came to be different. This book presents a theory of that process.

A history of American English cannot, however, justifiably limit itself to tracing the differences from British English. There are too many differences among Americans themselves—so many that linguist William A. Stewart has urged me to entitle this book *American Englishes.* The fact that many Americans say *truck, gas(oline), hood, drugstore, elevator, apartment, mad, sick, molasses, baby carriage,* and *radio* whereas the majority of British speakers of equivalent status would say *lorry, petrol, bonnet, chemist's, lift, flat, angry, ill, treacle, pram,* and *wireless* is interesting enough. But the legitimate aim of a history of American English cannot be simply to detail how these differences from British arose—even if it includes the manner in which the Americanisms have recently found their way into British use.

Even though some British influence continued, once English was in the Americas there was a basic change. Mencken thought that what resulted was a new language. Peter Finley Dunn's Mr. Dooley expressed another American insight when he said that the English language, when the Americans got through with it, would look as if it had been run over by a musical comedy. Linguists, however, have not been willing to attribute that much influence to show business; and they have been almost unanimous in rejecting Mencken's classification of American English as a new language. But perhaps a neo-Mencken-Dooley may be permitted to give it the compromise term—a new act in a new theater.

ALL-AMERICAN ENGLISH

I
MARITIME ENGLISH
AND THE
AMERICAN COLONISTS

———◆◆◆———

IN *American English* (1958), ALBERT H. MARCKWARDT WROTE:

> In considering the history and development of American English we must remember that the courageous bands who ventured westward into the unknown with Captain John Smith or on board the *Mayflower*, as well as those who followed them later in the seventeenth century, were speaking and writing the English language as it was currently employed in England.[1]

While this statement is at one level as self-evidently true as the assertion that the sun of England shines on Englishmen, at another level it leaves out most of what turns out to be of basic significance in the history of American English. For John Smith and his followers, like the crew of the

3

Mayflower, operated in the medium of the sea; and at the time of their expeditions, the sea nourished varieties of English almost completely unknown to landlocked Englishmen, and to the hidebound scholars who have dealt with the history of the language thereafter.[2] To the extent that all the colonists were exposed to some degree to that kind of sea change (to be discussed in detail later),[3] they were not exclusively speakers of British varieties that happened to have been transferred to the New World. Thus, in a real sense it may be said that the history of American English has never been written.[4]

Marckwardt and others make a great deal of the American use of English at a time when Shakespeare was still writing. As a means of chronological orientation, this emphasis may be very useful. But there is not all that much resemblance between the speech to be found in the records of the early colonies and that of Shakespeare's plays. For example, impersonal constructions like *it dislikes me, it yearns me*, and *methinks* (meaning "It seems to me," not "I think") are not found in the American records, although they abound in the works of Shakespeare and his contemporaries.[5] In fact, language historians have been as landbound as Shakespeare himself, whose *Tempest* is a masterpiece of writing about what a Caribbean island of the early seventeenth century was *not* like.

At sea Englishmen, like other Europeans involved in the great maritime and colonial expansion of the time, did not find the simple linguistic and cultural situation they had left behind at home. In England they had lived in a country with one dominant language (although, it is true, with a multiplicity of dialects) and occasional bilingualism in the rural areas to which the Welsh, Cornish, and Irish remnants of a once-great Celtic civilization[6] had been banished. But in the ports they now visited they were faced with the many tongues and cultures of peoples whose languages and origins were not even related to those Europeans knew.

The strangeness of the languages they encountered was almost too much for the European travelers and immigrants. They desperately needed to find some trace of the familiar, to be able to interpret the unknown in terms of some known. It is amusing, in the light of modern knowledge about the genetic relationships of Asian and African languages, to read the early attempts to link all these previously unknown languages to Hebrew. The analogy was slight: Hebrew was strange to the European, even to the scholar in most cases, and the "new" languages were also strange to him—therefore these languages must be like Hebrew. This strained analogy at least made it possible to relate new material to familiar lore. Even for those few Englishmen, like Roger Williams, who learned the languages of American Indians, the theory that they had come upon the long-lost Ten Tribes of Israel was almost irresistible.

It was impossible for the sailor to speak the languages of all the Africans and Asians with whom he had to deal. He had to find a radical solution to the linguistic problem that threatened to overwhelm him. It is now pretty clear that he drew upon the only experience he knew of that corresponded at all to these new polyglot contacts: he utilized Sabir, the Lingua Franca or trade language developed in the Mediterranean in the medieval period or earlier, famed as the "Frank Tongue" of the Crusades.[7] Based, in its early form, on the Italian of the great city-states, which dominated Mediterranean shipping in the twelfth and thirteenth centuries, it came to include words and phrases from all the Romance languages, with a smattering from the languages of the Turks and Arabs, two of the early non-Indo-European language groups with whom it was intended to be used. When the Portuguese began to achieve dominance in the world's sea routes around the time of Marco Polo, the Lingua Franca began to take on an especially Portuguese cast insofar as vocabulary was concerned. By the seventeenth century any sailor who expected to be able to ply his trade in a respectable fashion had to be able to handle the Portuguese Trade Pidgin—which in all probability was an offshoot of the Lingua Franca.[8]

As the English became more and more dominant at sea, particularly in such highly lucrative enterprises as the West African slave trade, they began to exert their own dominion over the Lingua Franca, remaking the Portuguese Trade Pidgin into Pidgin English in certain areas, although not destroying the original in the process.[9] A good deal of Portuguese remained in English sailor talk of the eighteenth, nineteenth, and even twentieth centuries: *pickaninny* (and the related *pickin*, 'small'), *savvy*, *palaver*, *mas que* (which became *maskie*, 'Never mind!') ; all the pidgins[10] easily picked up vocabulary and turns of expression from the languages with which they came into contact.

The experience in coping with complexity was not, of course, entirely one-sided. The "new populations" the Europeans began to deal with had a corresponding problem. Most of them had had no previous experience of European languages and were just as puzzled by the Europeans as vice versa, although it is not reported that they thought the Europeans were speaking Hebrew. In the case of impossibly mixed language contact situations like that of the West Africans who became involuntary "immigrants" to the Americas in the course of the slave trade, the pidgin languages became a necessity.[11] Since the slave traders deliberately mixed up tribal and language groups in order to minimize the possibility of revolts, no one West African language was usable by any New World slave community on record. The pidgin languages tended, then, to become the first language of a generation of children. The process that we call *creolization*, with a great deal of African borrowing in vocabulary, syntax, and phonology, was in progress.

The West Africans, wrenched from their own tribes, cultures, and languages, picked up the pidgin auxiliary languages out of harsh necessity as they waited on the west coast of Africa for transportation to the New World, as they sweltered in the holds of slave ships with little to remind them of their human status except the attempt to establish communication with neighbors who came from different tribes and cultures, or as they found themselves on the plantations of the Caribbean islands or in North or South America. Since the slaves used the pidgin languages primarily to establish communication with other slaves, they mixed in West African linguistic forms freely. (An expression like *nyam nyam*, to eat, was intelligible to Africans from many diverse tribal backgrounds.) In the whole Lingua Franca-pidgin tradition, communication was what counted. There were no schoolteachers and no grammar books, and those who spoke the trade languages would have been surprised to learn that they had internalized very complex syntactic structures, which are characteristic of all human languages.

The pidgin and creole languages spread along the oceans, the coasts and the islands. A good indication of their history can be gained from Plate 1.

The trade languages were not taught formally in schools, and almost no one bothered to write them down. The more affluent Europeans who learned them were businessmen who got their compensations from the wealth they amassed, not by impressing their friends with their polyglot accomplishments. But European culture was essentially literate at that time—in historical perspective the group moving to the New World was highly literate—and the contact languages did find their way into the records. Probably the most famous example is the scene in French-lexicon Sabir in Molière's *Le Bourgeois Gentilhomme*.[12]

Slave dealers like William Smith, John Atkins, and Hugh Crow recorded Pidgin English utterances in passing, and often in the context of relating something done by an African that they regarded as funny.[13] A British sea captain not in the slave trade, William Fitzwilliam Owen, and his lieutenant Boteler recorded long conversations in that variety in

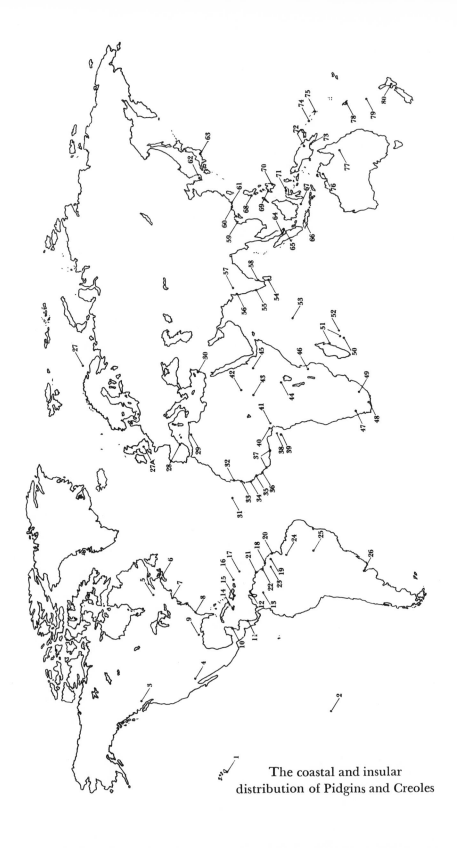

The coastal and insular
distribution of Pidgins and Creoles

LIST OF LANGUAGES

(From Hancock, "A Survey of the Pidgins and Creoles of the World," in Hymes, *Pidginization and Creolization of Languages,* Cambridge University Press, 1971, pp. 509–523)

1. Hawaiian Pidgin/Creole English
   Hawaiian Island Dialect
2. Pitcairnese Creole English
3. Chinook Jargon
   Pidgin Eskimo
4. Pachuco, or Pochismo
   Trader Navaho
5. Franco-Amerindian contact vernacular
6. Souriquoien
7. New Jersey Amerindian Trade Pidgin
   Mogilian
   American Indian Pidgin English
8. Gullah, or Geechee
9. Louisiana French Creole, or Gumbo
10. Creole English of British Honduras
11. Pidginized variety of Caribbean Creole English
    Creolized Nahuatal-Spanish
12. Papiamentu
    Cuban Spanish (*Habla Bozal Antillana*)
13. Pidgin Spanish
    Palenquero
14. Jamaican Creole (English)
15. Haitian Creole (French)
16. Virgin Islands Dutch Creole
17. Antillean French Creole
18. Sranan Tongo
19. Djuka
20. French Creole of French Guiana
21. English Creole of Trinidad and Tobago
    English Creole of Antigua
22. Guyana Creole English
    Portuguese Contact Variety
    Pidgin Dutch
23. Saramaccan
    Matuwari
24. Brazilian Creole Portuguese
25. Lingoa Gêral
26. Cocoliche
    Franco-Spanish contact vernacular
27. Russenorsk
    Anglo-Romani
    Shelta
28. Inglés de Escalerilla
29. Petit Mauresque
30. Sabir
31. Portuguese Creole of Cape Verde Islands
32. Senegal Creole Portuguese
33. Creole English of Bathurst, the Gambia
34. Guine Creole Portuguese
35. Krio
36. Americo-Liberian
    Kru
37. Petit-Nègre

38. Fernando Po Creole
39. Gulf of Guinea Portuguese
    Creoles
40. Cameroons Pidgin/Creole
    English
41. Ewondo Populaire
    Pidgin Hausa
42. Pidgin Arabic
    Sudan-Arabic
43. Sango
44. Pidginized African lan-
    guages
45. Asmara Pidgin Italian
46. Swahili
47. Pidginized Afrikaans
48. Afrikaans
49. Fanagalo
    Town Bemba
50. Reunion French Creole
51. Mauritian French Creole
    Swahili-Malgasy contact
    language
52. Rodrigues French Creole
53. Seychelles French Creole
54. Creole Portuguese of Ceylon
    Semi-creolized form of
    Dutch
55. Goanese
56. Creole Portuguese of Diu and
    Daman
57. Babu English

58. Butler English
59. Tay Boi (Pidgin French)
60. Portuguese-derived Creole
    of Macao
61. China Coast Pidgin English
    Pidginized Chinese
62. Korean Pidgin English
    ("Bamboo English")
63. Japanese Pidgin English
64. Papia Kristang
65. Singapore Portuguese
    Creole
66. Portuguese Creole of
    Jakarta
67. Bazaar Malay
68. Caviteño
    Ermitano
69. Zamboangueño
70. Davaueño
71. Ternateño
72. New Guinea Pidgin English
73. Police Motu
74. Melanesian Pidgin English
75. Neosolomonic
76. Bagot Creole English
77. Australian Pidgin English
78. New Caledonia Pidgin
    French
79. Norfolkese
80. Maori Pidgin English

the nineteenth century. Fictional representations of Pidgin English appear in stories set in many parts of the world, notably in the works of Daniel Defoe, the one British literary figure who as historian of trade and of pirates was likely to have a good command of the seaborne varieties. Such American writers as Cotton Mather and Benjamin Franklin observed its use by the slave population before the end of the eighteenth century. American Indians, who probably learned it from the West African slaves with whom they mixed,[14] also became users of Pidgin English in the complex language contact situation into which American imperialism, disguised as "Manifest Destiny," forced them as they were pushed farther and farther west.[15]

The chief mistake made in dealing professionally with the pidgin languages has been to regard them as local developments.[16] (For special reasons, historical linguistics has regularly been forced into giving geographic factors and local matters greater weight than they deserve.) Pidgin English, to take only the variety with which this discussion is most directly concerned,[17] very quickly spread as far as China and Melanesia.[18] And Americans in the China trade—good New Englanders from Massachusetts—were clearly learning Chinese Pidgin English as early as 1784.

In that year a Chinese was reported as saying to a Bostonian trader:

> You and I olo flen; you belong honest man only no get chance . . . Just now have settee counter. All finishee; you go, you please.[19]

In the same year another is reported as saying:

> Too muchee strong gale; sea all same high mast head—no can see sky.[20]

That the enclitic vowel (*-ee* of *settee*) is inconsistently represented is probably the fault of the transcriber; *all same* in the second quotation is undoubtedly the same phrase as the one

11

in the famous statement of "Sammy," the Chinese laundry-man: "No tickee, no washee; allee samee to me."

Another prominent historian, Foster Rhea Dulles, gives no examples but specifically reports the American use of pidgin in the China trade:

> During this period [again, about 1784] the sole medium of communication between the Chinese and their visitors was that queer jargon known as Pidgin English.[21]

Dulles's footnote is even more revealing:

> The dialect largely made up of English words with some Portuguese and Chinese embellishments.[22]

In view of the laggard nature of linguistic histories of the pidgins, Dulles can hardly be blamed for failing to see that Portuguese was, if anything, basic and English an embellishment; for his own time, his statement is astonishingly perceptive.

The Chinese were not the only linguistically complex group the early American maritime trade had to deal with. New England-based ships began engaging in the slave trade as early as 1643, when an American ship coming from the Canary Islands stopped off at Barbados and bought tobacco "in exchange for Africoes, which she carried from the Isle of Maio."[23] Thus the Americans entered the infamous "triangular slave voyage" pattern, engaged in by Hugh Crow and others (see below). There, they apparently learned terms like *caboodle* ('the whole lot'), called by Leland and Barrere a "New England expression originally used by coasting sailors" and compared by Hancock to the Krio *kabudu*. Leland and Barrere trace it to the Spanish *cabildo* ('meeting' or 'assembly', which may have had the meaning 'the whole lot' in nautical use), which as a source would produce some problems; but a Lingua Franca source is more likely. The same can be said of *galoot* (Krio *galut*), perhaps from a Romance word for galley slave (Italian *galeotto*, Spanish *galeoto*).

It may have been about this time, and probably in the African slave trade, that the rugged Americanism *kick the bucket* came in use. The expression, considered to be of unknown origin by all the dictionary makers who have dealt with it, is at least somewhat like

KICKERAPOO   Dead. *Negro Word.*[24]
KICKATAVOO.   Killed, or Dead.[25]

Today Krio, the English-based creole of Sierra Leone, has kɛkrɛbu or kɛkɛrɛbu, 'dead' or 'to wither' (as of fruit or leaves). Gã, a West African language, has *kekre*, 'dry, stiff', and *bu*, 'to befall, end'. The rudely formed oral tradition of recording West African words may account for the spelling variations, which go even further, recorded by folklorist Hans Nathan:

> One of Didbin's [Charles Didbin, an eighteenth-century British author of stage works which often involved creole-like speech for Negro characters] Negro songs is "Kickera-boo," which was interpolated . . . The title seems to be the equivalent of the modern colloquialism "kicking the bucket." In the song the death of a Negro is described as something ludicrous, revealing an attitude that was per-petuated in American blackface minstrel songs until about the middle of the nineteenth century.[26]

And Nathan (my admiration for whose work has influenced my willingness to accept his informally proposed etymology) gives one more spelling variant:

> All your friend drop one tear when you Kickaraboo.[27]

The change from *boo* to *bucket* can probably best be explained as folk etymology, the process by which foreign words are made to sound like forms of one's own language. Folk etymology played a big part in the complex linguistic adaptation of the English immigrants to the Americas, from the early days in which they made American Indian words into quasi-English forms like *woodchuck* (from the Cree *wuchak* or *otchuck*). Traces of the process can be found everywhere the Europeans had to cope with "exotic" new languages.

The surprising thing to most observers, including some historians of language, is that the contact varieties of English came to "belong" to the other populations, that Americans and Englishmen who use Pidgin English are not automatically authorities on it. If they want to use it, they must learn to do so from the Africans, Indians, Chinese, and others who are expert (if, by definition, not native) speakers. Usually, the native speakers of English are quite clumsy in their attempts to use Pidgin; they are often objects of mockery to more proficient users.[28]

Although in some sense the first impetus for Pidgin English must have come from the British sailors, "ownership" soon passed to other hands—or mouths. We have little record of the reaction of sailors to the use of Pidgin English by other populations. They seem to have accepted as a matter of course the fact that it would be used by Africans, Asians, and Polynesian islanders. But missionaries (who by profession are somewhat more likely to seek explanations for phenomena) were often puzzled, like those who wrote of the African "repatriation" settlement at Regents Town in Sierra Leone:

> Natives of twenty-two different nations were here collected together; and a considerable number of them had been but recently liberated from the holds of Slave Vessels; they were greatly prejudiced against one another, and in a state of common hostility, with no common medium of intercourse but a little broken English.[29]

The emergency type of language contact in which a pidgin is a happy solution afflicted no other group so much as the African slaves; no other group was so completely uprooted and so definitively torn away from its cultural heritage. The

European intervention in Africa did not take the form of enslavement alone, however; many of those who remained in West Africa saw "things fall apart," in the brilliant allusion of Nigerian author Chinua Achebe. And, by the mid-nineteenth century, Pidgin English had established itself along the West African coast.[30] (The first traces go back as far as 1590.) In 1824 "Grandy King George" of Old Calabar wrote letters to the British Crown in Pidgin English, and texts have survived. A "New Testament translated into Blackman's English" was reported.[31] So important was West African Pidgin English and its Caribbean and continental American derivatives that German missionaries in Bautzen prepared a *Kurzgefaste Negerenglische Grammatik*, ostensibly for use by their members in the field.

But the Africans were by no means the only non-European users of Pidgin English, as the records of the missionaries show. Especially in insular and coastal areas, people all around the now-encircled globe were beginning to be exposed to multicultural and multilingual contacts. Between the African attestations in *The Religious Intelligencer* for 1821, there are letters dictated by Hawaiian King Tamoree of Atooi, who had "for many years been able to speak broken English," and his queen, who signed herself (by proxy) Charlotte Tapoolee. The queen's letter is quoted below:

Atooi, July 28, 1820

Dear Friend,

    I am glad your daughter came here. I shall be her mother now, and she be my daughter. I be good to her; give her tappa; give her mat; give her plenty eat. By and by your daughter speak Owhyee [Hawaiian]: then she learn me how to read, and write, and sew; and talk of that great Akooah, which the good people of America love. I begin spell little: read come very hard, like stone. You very good, send your daughter great way to teach

15

the heathen. I am very glad I can write you a short
letter, and tell you that I be good to your daughter. I
send you my *aloha,* and tell you I am

> Your friend
> CHARLOTTE TAPOOLEE
> *Queen of Atooi*

If some of this ("teach the heathen") reads like "Letters
We Doubt Ever Got Dictated," the presence of the missionary transcriber should be remembered. That same transcriber
would also be responsible for "de-pidginizing" the language:
by and by would have been more accurately rendered
bimeby;[32] *your daughter* by *you daughter,* and so forth.
But some reality shows through even the normalizing recti-
tude of the missionary. Syncretism in language can be as all-
pervading as syncretism in religion, of which the "Sandwich
Islanders" practiced not a little in the early days of Christian influence.

The 1821 attestations from *The Religious Intelligencer*
probably do not represent the beginning of full-scale utiliza-
tion of Pidgin English in the Hawaiian Islands. The persons
quoted are royalty, interested in international communication. The early missionaries made an earnest attempt to
preach in Hawaiian; some of the early traders also attempted
to use that language. The result was something called "Hapa
Haole" ("Half-Foreigner" or "Half-American"), understood
by the Hawaiians but obviously not mistakable for their own
language.

As long as the language contact situation was a relatively
simple bilingualism, "Hapa Haole" (like "Spanglish" in
Puerto Rico) was perfectly adequate. Later in the nineteenth century, when Chinese, Japanese, Filipinos, Portuguese from the Azores, and even Puerto Ricans joined the
Hawaiians and Americans, Pidgin English spread rapidly. A
book entitled *Me Speak English* was circulated to help teach
it. Today, not only Pidgin but a creolized version and a

slightly decreolized variety (called Island Dialect by Reinecke) coexist with Standard English, and a few linguistically talented islanders can manage all three, in addition to an "ethnic" home language like Chinese, Japanese, or Hawaiian.

American seamen like Richard Henry Dana, who wrote *Two Years Before the Mast*, came into close and extensive contact with Pidgin English in the Hawaiian Islands in the nineteenth century. Dana quotes "Kanakas" (Hawaiians):

> Now, got plenty money; no good, work. Mamule, money pau—all gone. Ah! very good, work!   (*p. 118*)

The Pidgin English is mixed with what Dana and others called "the Sandwich Island language." Very likely, this is a kind of carry-over from the contact function of "Hapa Haole." We get a great deal of:

> Aye! Me know that. By-'em'by money *pau*—gone; then Kanaka work plenty.   (*p. 118*)

> Me no eatee Cap'nee Cook! Me pickaninny—small—so high—no more! My fader see Cap'nee Cook! me—no (*p. 121*)

> New Zealand Kanaka eatee white man; Sandwich Island Kanaka—no. Sandwich Island Kanaka *ua like pu na haole* —all 'e same a' you.   (*p. 121*)

Perhaps the linguistic pride of the American sailors, who wanted to show off their store, however small, of Hawaiian, had something to do with the frequent use of Hawaiian words and phrases in the pidgin. But influences from other languages remain in Hawaiian Pidgin English, and today one can identify Japanese- and Filipino-tinged Hawaiian Pidgin English. Hawaiian Pidginist John Reinecke reports anecdotes like that of the Japanese evangelist who sang: "Yes, Jesus Rub Me,"[33] in what obviously represents the Japanese substitution of *r* for *l*.

Hawaiian Pidgin English began to be commonplace toward the middle of the nineteenth century. Joseph G.

Clark tells us of an 1840 Hawaiian ("Sandwich Islander") who "could speak a little English tolerably well," which is a typical naïve observer's reaction to Pidgin English. The islander is reported to have used phrases like "fall into some of the holes and kill his neck."[34] *Kill one's neck* is still in use in Hawaii today. It is an interesting and complicated study to try to separate what is "direct translation" from an ethnic language and what is general pidgin. *Brokum-up* ('demolish'), in use in the Islands today, has a direct parallel in Cameroonian Pidgin English and is therefore probably of Maritime Pidgin transmission. But only a small part of the research needed to establish the complete pattern of such relationships has been done.

One must accept some strange notions to believe that Pidgin English "sprang up" spontaneously wherever it is reported. For example, the earliest reported Hawaiian user of Pidgin English was actually recorded while he was in Connecticut. An early convert to Christianity named Henry Obookiah, who died in Connecticut in 1818, is extensively quoted by his biographers, who explicitly indicate their intention to represent, as closely as possible, his exact words. They wrote that he had said

> Owhyhee gods! They *wood*, burn; Me go home, put 'em in
> a fire, burn 'em up.—They no *see*, no *hear*, no *anything*.
> . . . We make them—Our God. . . . *He* make *us*.[35]

But the reader of the complete Beecher and Harvey *Memoir* soon learns that Henry Obookiah had traveled at sea extensively before coming to Connecticut and getting religion. It was at sea that he learned Pidgin English, which was Maritime and neither "Hawaiian" nor "Connecticut."

Although its history has been so sloppily written that its every migration has been taken as a new birth, Pidgin English spread over all the maritime routes at a very early period. It must have come to Australia and New Guinea almost as soon as the British reached those shores. And with their complex, multilingual "aboriginal" populations, both areas provided the conditions for the rapid spread of a pidgin. Baker estimates that about five hundred "aboriginal" languages were spoken in Australia in the early period of contact with Englishmen.[36]

In the few historical treatments that exist, there are such statements as:

> New Guinea Pidgin, or Neo-Melanesian, is a regional variety of a large group of pidgin languages spread by traders through the Pacific.[37]

Statements like this have their value for the historian of pidgin and maritime varieties, but it may be necessary to discount further statements like this:

> Some of its vocabulary, e.g., *pikinini* 'small', *save* 'know', reminds us of its origin in regions where Portuguese and Spanish Pidgin languages were already formed.[38]

There is no real evidence of a genuinely Spanish-based Pidgin language (the Portuguese Trade Pidgin being close enough to satisfy Spanish contact language requirements), and no real reason to refer to Spanish in this context.

There is now general recognition that the languages with which Pidgin English came into contact added positive features to it; the "simplification" beloved of those who have not really studied pidgins applies only to a few superficial features, like personal endings of verbs and the "loss" of irksome (for foreign speakers) gender agreement between nouns and adjectives.

> The use of a general numeral and adjective suffix seems to have its origin in the Chinese classifiers or 'itemizers.' Chinese Pidgin used to distinguish animates, e.g., *wan fela man* from inanimates, e.g., *wan pisi tebal*, but in later Chinese Pidgin and in Neo-Melanesian *-fela* or *-pela* alone is used.[39]

The Chinese, who may well have had Pidgin English before the Australians, could have been a great influence in spreading it.[40] Turner points out that "a large number of Chinese gold-diggers came to Australia in that continent's Gold Rush of the 1860's." (See below, Chapter III, for Chinese in the American Gold Rush of 1848 and after.) But the Chinese were hardly the only factor in spreading the Pidgin. In places like New Guinea, where there is "a multiplicity of peoples, divided by language, belief, and custom,"[41] Pidgin English still plays a most important role. Read, who gives no actual quotations in the language, refers at least twelve times in his book to the relative proficiency of members of the Gahuku tribes in Pidgin English.

It is easy to forget that the Europeans' dealings with the West Africans in the slave trade were of essentially the same type as in other commerce. When Black identity movements today adopt Swahili, now essentially an inland language, and when the landlocked Congo, Rwanda, and Burundi, from which few if any slaves were ever taken, figure in international news, one can easily forget that early relations between the Africans and the Europeans were largely confined to coastal and port areas. European sailors who operated there brought the cultural and linguistic adaptations of the maritime trade to West Africa just as surely as they carried them to the China coast and to New Guinea. And the Africans just as surely exerted their own subtle influence on the international contact languages, as did the Chinese and the Melanesians.

The chief impression that emerges from some years of study of the pidgin languages is of their essential unity despite a degree of "local" variation. This unity, which stems from a characteristically European lumping-together of West Africans from vastly diverse tribes, and from the harsher necessities of the slave trade, is the great prerequisite for understanding the process that produced Black American English and related varieties like the creole dialects of the West Indies and Surinam.

The slave traders, slave masters, and sailors of slave ships did not bother to report on the unity of their practices; they were too busy making money buying and selling human cargo. But some of them—such as John Atkins, William Smith, and Hugh Crow—did eventually write memoirs of their experiences. And early explorers not tainted with the slave trade (as, for example, John Barbot) provided rather elaborate descriptions of what caught their eyes about West Africa. From these sources, the historian can piece together a great deal of the language chronicle of the slave trade. The reporters were not, of course, professional linguists; no such professionals existed at the time. But there is a positive side to that limitation: they were not biasing their data to prove a pet theory about language. Thus, there is a kind of stand-off as far as the reliability of the observers is concerned. They had neither the skills nor the biases of the Linguistic Society of America and the American Dialect Society.

Some indication of what those observers recorded (not what they thought, since they apparently theorized little or not at all about language processes) can be got from the quotations that follow. I have chosen a few representative ports, primarily for their importance in the slave trade, in West Africa and the Americas for the attestations of Pidgin English there. There are obviously certain differences in the transcriptional practices, but I believe that the basic uniformity emerges through the differing orthographies employed. The citations have been chosen as typical. This list is, of course, far from exhaustive:

SIERRA LEONE

(1791–93)
Oh! he be fine man, rich too much, he got too much woman.

(Anna Maria Falconbridge,
Two Voyages to Sierra Leone,
1794, p. 77)

God amity sen me dat peginine [pickanniny], true,
suppose he no black like me, nutting for dat, my woman
drinkee red water, and suppose peginine no for me, he
[i.e., the wife] dead.

(Ibid. p. 82)

BONNY

What be dat ditto? Can I eat 'em—or drink 'em—or wear
'em? I think he be some thief man and big rogue that
make that thing ditto.

(Hugh Crow, 1791, pp. 93–94)

No fear—it be Capt. Crow palaver!

(Hugh Crow, p. 96)

Crow! What debble man send this hard and sauce mouth
fellow to Bonny?

(Hugh Crow, p. 96)

Ya Ya, what me do to me god!—puncheon of brandy!
go away! I no want you at all!

(Hugh Crow, p. 86)

Poor boy! you can't havey king.

(Hugh Crow, p. 87)

You no play man no more, you devilly man, Crow, you
have quite spoil the king!

(Hugh Crow, p. 95)

*(African from Bonny on Crow's ship, in Montego Bay,
Jamaica)*

Massa Crow, something bite me too much, and me no can
see 'im; and me want you for give me some was mouth
and two mouth tacken.

(Hugh Crow, p. 45)

(King Peppel—or "Grandy King George"—of Bonny)

[A letter of diplomatic protest to George IV of England]
Brudder George . . . send warship look um what water

bar ab got, dat good . . . E no send warship, for
cappen no peakee me, no lokee me face. No, no, no; me
tell you, No. Suppose you come all you mout full palaver,
give e reason why e do it, me tell you, you peakee lie,
you peakee lie, you peakee d--m lie. Suppose my fader,
or my fader fader, come up from ground and peakee me
why English man do dat, I no sabby tell um why.

> (W. F. W. Owen, *Narrative of
> Voyages to Explore the Shores
> of Africa, Arabia, and Mada-
> gascar*, 1833, II:203. In Claude
> Wauthier, *The Literature and
> Thought of Modern Africa,
> A Survey*, n.d., p. 41, this same
> speech is attributed to
> "Grandy King George." Both
> Owen and Wauthier attribute
> it to the same place—Bonny—
> and approximately the same
> date—1824.)

Why you make many things stand for table one time? dat
makee me sick, appetite no come up.

> (Owen, II:205)

OLD CALABAR

(Duke Ephraim to new consul, Mr. T. J. Hutchinson, 1856)
I beg you to do something to stop white men from going
into the house of Calabar men and knocking them. You
white men have fashion to bind men to keep the peace,
so I beg you to do this, and no let palaver come up again.

> (K. O. Dike, *Trade and
> Politics in the Niger Delta*,
> p. 17)

SURINAM

(1718—Orthography is Dutch)
My belle well.
Jou wantie sie don pinkinine?
Jo wantje gaeu wakke lange mie?

> (J. D. Herlein, *Beschryvinge
> van de Volksplantinge
> Zuriname*, Leeuwarden 1718,
> pp. 121–123)

JAMAICA

(Kingston)
God bless massa! how poor massa do? Long live massa, for
'im da fight ebery voyage.

> (Hugh Crow, p. 120)

(Inland plantation)
Dey good nyamn [sic, for more usual *nyam*] for him neger,
massa! Him, Sir Charles Price, good nyamn for him
neger, massa! Him good as hims hens pickeniny, massa!

> (*Marly, or Life in Jamaica*,
> 1828, p. 52)

*(A preacher, therefore speaking rather differently from the
other slaves)*
Him Adam and him Ebe, hab lib upon an estate, and it
called Paradise. It hab be a greedy big estate, much grandy
better dan Paradise to leeward; and dere was dere, ebery
ting good for nyamn, and all de fruit on it, him Adam and
him Ebe, could nyamn but de forbidden fruit.

> (*Marly*, p. 135)

*(Speech of a slave and a comment on Marly's understanding
of it)*
"Eh, mosquitos, hab grandy nyamn on dat new buckra
[i.e., Marly himself]." Marly being ignorant of the
corrupted negro dialect, or talkee talkee language, did not
understand the expression . . .

> (*Marly*, p. 174)

24

BARBADOS

(Between 1772 and 1785—songs, with approximate musical notation)

Massa buy me he won't killa me
Oh Massa buy me he won't killa me
Oh Massa buy me he won't killa me
Oh 'for he kill me he ship me regular.
   'For I live with a bad man
oh la 'for I live with a bad man o budda-bo
   'For I live with a bad man
oh la 'for I would go to the Riverside Regular.

Anté Nanny, Open da door, Pater want da
sour-sop soup, Anté Nanny, open da door,
Pa-ter want da sour-sop soup, Run Mr. Cunningham,
run for you life, run Mr. Cunningham
run for you life. Pater da come wid a o-pen knife.

(In Granville Sharpe ms. "An
African song or chant," Hard-
wicke Court Manuscripts
[England: Gloucester Record
Office] Plate IIa. Reproduced
in Jerome S. Handler and
Charlotte J. Frisbie, "Aspects
of Slave Life in Barbados:
Music and its Cultural Con-
text," *Caribbean Studies* II,
No. 4, 1972, Plate II)

BARBADOS, GRENADA AND ANTIGUA

What for me isn't free? We have good massa, good country,
plenty to eat, and when me sick, massa's doctor physic me;
me no want free, no not at all.

(H. W. Coleridge, *Six Months
in the West Indies in 1825*)

ANTIGUA

Me no longer young, sir, and have a daughter to maintain.
(*Ibid.*)

CHARLESTON, SOUTH CAROLINA

One dollar more for 'em da; I have 'em, negra buy buckra
now! Three bit more for 'em da; I have 'em, negra buy
buckra now!

(Hugh Crow, p. 9)

(*ca. 1856*)
All berry like you, massa. What a many family you hab,
massa.

(William Ferguson, *America
by River and Rail*, 1856,
p. 129)

OUTSIDE CHARLESTON

(*ca. 1780*)
Tankè you whitè man, tankè you; putè some poyson and
givè me. Two days and me no die; the birds; ah me!
(Crèvecoeur, p. 224)

(*ca. 1923*)
Yo' see, Boss, dat deer been a punish [i.e., was being
punished] wid de miskeeter bite um, coz him bin a lib een
de swamp and das weh de skeeter lib and breed.

(Jane Screven Hayward,
Brown Jackets, pp. 53–54)

(*ca. 1949—Edisto Island*)
Ma Master show me all kind of thing. I think it been a
Friday, in July. He show me hell; he show me heaven; he
show me how to get religion. And when he get through,
he open a big Bible; and then he bless my soul. Then he
tell me—he say: "Go in peace and sin no more. Your soul
is set free." And after while I come out, and all various

thing I see. The most I see been a young mans, and a girl, and children, and my father and people—all up in a bundle.

> (Turner, *Africanisms in the Gullah Dialect*, p. 271—the transliterated and regularized version)

NORTH CAROLINA

(1775)

Kay massa . . . you just leave me, me sit here, great fish jump up into de canoe, here he be, massa, fine fish, massa; me den very grad; den me sit very still, until another great fish jump into de canoe; but me fall asleep, massa, and no wake until you come; now, massa, me know me deserve flogging, cause if great fish did jump into de canoe, he see me asleep, den he jump out again, and I no catch him; so massa, me willing now take good flogging.

> (J. F. D. Smyth, I:121)

PHILADELPHIA

(1782)

Boccarorra [a variant of buckra] make de Horse workee, make de Ox workee, make ebery thing workee; only de Hog. He, de Hog, no workee; he eat, he drink, he walk about, he go to sleep when he please, he libb like a gentleman.

> (Benjamin Franklin, "Information to Those Who Would Remove to America," in *Writings*, ed. Smythe, V:606)

(1850)

"I'm in de cheap line, massa," said the other,—"no 'nop'ly's my word."

"Cheap!—neber mind him, Sa; he's only a nigga from Baltimore, just come to Philadelphy . . . I'se born here,

Sa, and know de town like a book. Dat ere nigga not seen good society yet—knows nuffin—habn't got de polish on. —Git out nigga and clean you self."

(Alexander Mackay, *The Western World or, Travels in the United States in 1846–47*, p. 133)

HALIFAX, NOVA SCOTIA

(ca. 1791)

No Work, No Yam.

(Robin Winks, *The Blacks in Canada*, 1971, p. 84)

(1791)

No, massa, me no hear nor no mind. Me work like slave can not do worse Massa in any part of the world, therefore me determined to go with you, Massa, if you please.

(Clarkson ms., Howard University Library)

(1791)

Massa Governor no mind King, he no mind You.

(Add. MS41262B, fol. 9, British Museum. Cited in Christopher Fyfe, *History of Sierra Leone*, 1962, p. 33)

(1791—probably a traditional text associated with the Maroons, from Jamaica)

Top lilly bit; you say me must forsake my wife. Only one of them. Which that one, Jesus Christ say so? No, no, massa; Gar A'mighty good; he tell somebody he must forsake him wife and children. Somebody no wicked for forsake him wife. No, massa, dis here talk no do for me.

(Duncan Campbell, *Nova Scotia in Its Historical, Mercantile, and Industrial Relations*, 1873, p. 201)

("Old Negro proverb")

When buckra tief, he tief plantation; when nigger tief,
he tief piece of cane.

> (Ida C. Greaves, *The Negro
> in Canada*, McGill Economic
> Studies, 1930, p. 71)

(Nova Scotian Indians)

Suppose me killum?—scalpum?

> (Henry Young Payzant,
> *People: A Story of the People
> of Nova Scotia*, 1935, p. 163)

Pictou man no shootum dead goose.

> (*Ibid.*, p. 176)

Mattie, my wife? He gone long way off. He no come back.
He dead twelve moons gone.

> (*Ibid.*, p. 116)

NEW YORK CITY

(1741)

His master live in tall house Broadway.
Ben ride de fat horse.

> (Daniel P. Horsmanden, *The
> Negro Plot*, 1744, p. 128)

Backarara . . . 'Negro language, signifies white people'

> (*Ibid.*, p. 331)

the house . . . This in the Negroes dialect signifies
houses, i.e., the town.

> (*Ibid.*, p. 209)

Not only in the slave trade but in some more humane
commerce, American and British sailors were exposed to Pidgin English at sea and in port. According to Granville in
A Dictionary of Sailors' Slang (1962), the influence of Pidgin English on "those officers and men who have served in
the China trade" with the Royal Navy remained appreciable

even as late as World Wars I and II; that is, it extended well into the period when relatively standard varieties of English came into widespread use as a world lingua franca. What that influence must have been in the eighteenth and nineteenth centuries can now be guessed by evaluating the sources that happen to have reported it. The evidence suggests that the influence of Pidgin English on seagoing and migrating populations was very great indeed—which is astounding to those who have never considered the historical process.

The inventory of Pidgin English terms in British sailor slang is sizable, with a quite respectable number of words available to even a relatively unsophisticated vocabulary collector like Granville. He is fully aware of the Portuguese connections of some Pidgin English vocabulary, although he says nothing about Pidgin English having been modeled on a Portuguese Trade Pidgin model (relexification). His report on the use of *maskee,* for example, matches the fictional testimony of the practices of American sailors in *The Sand Pebbles,* a novel (1963) by Richard McKenna.

> 'It doesn't matter; it is of no account.' . . . Skeat derives the word from Portuguese *mas que* 'it doesn't matter,' 'it makes no odds,' etc.

Like many another investigator, however, Granville took some forms for Spanish that might well have come from other Romance languages, or from the Lingua Franca. A good example is *loco.* Apparently as a result of his dependence upon Spanish, he took *loco da poco* as "a fanciful elaboration of *loco,*" whereas a quite reasonable Romance derivation of that term is possible. This would not, of course, preclude fanciful or jocular use of the term by sailors; precisely that use has been made of forms from the maritime trade languages for some time. Krio, of Sierra Leone, has *lóko,* 'crazy', but no other Spanish vocabulary.

Granville was on somewhat firmer ground with *joss* and its derivatives:

The word is Pidgin-English for the Portuguese *deos* (Latin *deus*), a god, hence *joss house*, a temple or church. *Joss* means luck or good fortune.

(As we will see, many of the same words, combinations, and meanings were common in those parts of the American frontier where Chinese speakers were present.) Granville also lists the derivatives:

JOSS-HOUSE MAN.   Parson

JOSSMAN.   Measure of Plymouth rum with picture of monk on bottle.

JOSSPIECE.   Talisman or mascot of any kind. Popularly supposed to bring luck to its wearer.

CHINCHIN JOSS.   Church service ashore in China.

Although Granville does not trace *chin food*, 'gossip or meaningless boring conversation', to Pidgin English, it seems obvious that such was its origin. Some of these expressions are recorded in the attestations of Pidgin English on the American frontier, some are not. Since the records are sketchy, it is probably safe to conclude that the failure to record them is a result of the sparseness of attestations and some of these expressions were actually used there. Some probably were not, but *joss*-words were certainly in use on the Western frontier, and there very likely were others that did not find their way into Royal Navy slang. One can still see "Joss House" on a sign in midtown Manhattan advertising a tour through Chinatown.

Since Granville's work is not a historical dictionary, it would be impossible to say conclusively when any of these compounds were formed; therefore, one can only guess which ones American sailors encountered around 1784. But given the priority of the Portuguese Trade Pidgin, it seems quite likely that *joss* itself was part of the vocabulary they learned in the earliest times. Derivative compounds would

31

have followed soon. Of course, Pidgin English was not a static language; new forms were introduced and dropped at a much greater rate than the usual one for languages.

Interesting comparisons can be made between Chinese Pidgin English, including those forms of it learned by British sailors, and other contact varieties, even those that are not English-based in vocabulary. There is, for example, the compounding element *-side*, as in *China-side*:

> The China station. In Pidgin English, side = place. Cf. Top-Side, Shore-Side, etc.

Topside is familiar from "Topside Galah," the famous Pidgin English translation of Longfellow's "Excelsior." But such use of *side* also suggests Cameroonian Pidgin English *husay* 'where?' and Krio *usai* in the same meaning. (In both of these Creole languages, the second element is usually thought of as derived from *side*; some Anglicizing orthographies spell the word *whose side*.) Krio has, additionally, *us-pat*, 'whose part', or *we-pat*, 'what part'. In terms of the underlying semantic principle in word formation, *side* and *say* function a good deal like Haitian Creole *koté* (*ki koté* 'what side', that is, 'where'). Papia Kristang has an analogous formation, *turu-banda* (literally, 'all band'), 'everywhere'.

A couple of other Royal Navy slang terms, which respectively represent somewhat lesser and greater assimilation to ordinary English word-forming devices, are *makee-learn* and *decky learner*. The former, which is very normal pidgin in its word structure (compare Cameroonian Pidgin English *watch night* for *night watchman* and Owen's [see above] *was mouth* for *mouthwash*), is defined as:

> . . . Naval novice, a beginner in any branch of the service.
> 2. A Merchant Navy cadet or 'apprentice'.

The entry concludes that the equivalent term for the fishing fleets may be *decky learner*. On reflection, it is not so strange that the fishing fleet should have a derivation pattern closer to that of ordinary English: lacking direct experience in the China service, the fishermen probably got their Pidgin English forms second hand from the Royal Navy. As will be suggested later, a great deal of Pidgin vocabulary entered American English via such an indirect route, passing through different professional groups and undergoing changes in the process but still being relatively easily recognizable as Pidgin in origin.

Whatever its ultimate source, the Chinese Pidgin English term *chop chop*, 'at once, immediately, on the run', is both Chinese Pidgin English and British sailor talk. Granville identifies it only as "China-side," but many other sources (like Leland's *Pidgin English Sing-Song*) stamp it Pidgin. Granville does give a definite "Chinese pidgin" label to:

LOOK-SEE.   Check up or general look around; a cursory inspection.

This expression, which is in American English colloquial usage just about everywhere, is an interesting example of general pidgin and creole serial verb construction. Ramon F. Adams in *Western Words: A Dictionary of the American West* (1968) took it for

a cow-man's term for an inspection tour or an investigation of some sort; the word *look* is rarely used by itself.

Considerable attention will be given later (see Chapter IV) to the relationship between the vocabularies of Pidgin English and cattle ranching. *Look-stick*, 'telescope or long glass', while not a serial verb construction, looks Pidgin, even though Granville did not label it as such. It is also likely that

MERRY-MERRY.   Slightly intoxicating drink sold in Gibraltar. Ingredients dubious

and the famous *Johnny-come-lately* are Pidgin. The last, according to Adams, was one of many Pidgin expressions taken over by the American cowboy. It became an integral part of American popular culture, as did "Sorry 'bout that," which apparently comes directly from Pidgin English in Vietnam.

Equally likely, although generally unknown to Americans, is *cookem fry*, where the second syllable of the first word (as printed) is obviously the transitivizer (the suffix which marks a transitive verb in many varieties of Pidgin English), and the entire expression looks like a serial verb construction. This "odd expression"

> is a survival of those lawless times when sailors had reputations so bad that they never expected to be candidates for heaven, and were, therefore, reconciled to 'cookem fry' in Hades.

Missionaries were bringing the "solace" of Christian theology China-side quite early, and an expression for frying in Hades would fit into the sociocultural pattern of part of the China coast as well as into the linguistic patterns of Pidgin English. Additionally there is the evidence of *chin chin joss* that religious concepts expressed in Pidgin were picked up on the China Station by British sailors. The transitivizer occurs again in *Bring-'em'near*, a telescope.

Although Granville does not so identify it, *no want-chee*,[42] "I don't want it," is a Chinese Pidgin English expression which turns up again on the American frontier. Granville does provide the very useful information that the expression is "Wardroom," or officer talk (in contrast to "Lower Decks," language of the enlisted men) and that it is from China-side. But the lower decks are the locale of the various *foo* words,[43] even though Granville (like many another) is somewhat carried away by the Chinoiserie of the sound and forgets that, since very few Royal Navy personnel learned Chinese well, it is more likely to have been transmitted through Pidgin English. We are told that *"foo foo* is the Chinese for faeces and is also used as a pejorative adjective," and we might speculate (of which more later) about the influence of this usage on the U.S. armed services' (and later the whole U.S.') use of *shit* and *shitty* in a general pejorative sense. At any rate, Granville also attests the compounds *foo foo barge* ("sewage barge in the Yangtse River"), *foo foo band* ("squeegee band"), and *foo foo valve*:

> Like WIFFLO GADGET, this is any piece of mechanism to which the non-technical cannot give a name.

There are some parallels to the last in modern American, as perhaps in any slang. Some may wish to put such practices under the snobbish heading of "Poverty of Vocabulary," but they could equally be filed under "Inventiveness in the Contact Language Situation." (See Chapter IV.)

However Chinese it may be in origin, *Chai*, 'tea', a corruption of the Chinese word *tchi*, was also pidgin-transmitted. Since British sailors in particular could be expected to have their own word for tea, the myth that words are added to a lexicon because of communicative needs is once more exploded. Like most of the pidgin words current outside the language contact situation itself, such terms are retained for jocular and allusive purposes, to try to impress the outsider. The situation in the past was undoubtedly not greatly different from that described for the present by Keith Whinnom:

> The transient population of soldiers and sailors, who can scarcely differ greatly from their predecessors of previous centuries, acquire perhaps half a dozen elementary phrases but no facility in the dialect, and derive some amusement from instructing unsuspecting natives in obscenities or comically grotesque locution.[44]

On the China coast itself and with the Chinese, *yow-yow*, a Chinese sampan, may have been useful in communicating with the Chinese. In service slang, its function would be stylistic—and perhaps ego-building.

Interesting for speculation but not much more at this

point is *fly*, 'artful', which could betoken a maritime Pidgin origin for some very popular Black ethnic slang of today. The term is also listed as "rogues' " or traveling underworld figures' slang in the nineteenth century:

fly—knowing; up to him.
"The bloke was fly." The man was aware of what I wanted.[45]

Ash cat or *bunker cat*—"R. N. stoker serving a coal-burning vessel, though the term is often applied to a fireman in a merchantship"—is interesting for the same reason, since *cat* in such words as *hepcat* has been shown by David Dalby to have a reasonable origin in Wolof *hipicat*. Mixing of maritime and African vocabulary is one of the interesting facets of the contact varieties. The Black English vernacular *higo* (possibly from *here go*), 'here is', and *dago* (possibly from *there go*), 'there is', have direct parallels in the usage of Pitcairn Island English; Pitcairn Island had many sailors but few if any Africans among its settlers.[46]

Another possibly direct African contribution can be seen in the familiar term *Davy Jones's locker*. Conventional dictionaries try hard to make it come from the Welsh, but Layton's *Dictionary of Nautical Words and Terms* traces at least part of the expression to African influence. According to Layton, *Davy* is a version of *duffy* (more usually *duppy*), a well-known African term, widespread in the Caribbean today, for ghost. The phonology here is somewhat doubtful, but Layton's etymology has as much to recommend it as those of more conventional scholars. Davy Jones (the last name is thought by Layton to be a "corruption" of *Jonah*) is the evil spirit of the sea who lies in wait for seamen. European sailors, themselves prone to superstition, quite possibly picked up a term from African spirit lore and then shaped it to their own naming habits.

The reason why some creolists see striking resemblances

between the China-coast language contact situation and that of the Americas is demonstrated by the entry:

> TALKEE-TALKEE. Conference or mass meeting. A 'matter party'. Wardroom via China-side.

Taki Taki (*Talkee Talkee*) is a widely used designation in Surinam and Sierra Leone, among other places, for Pidgin English or for a language variety developed from a pidgin. Its basic meaning seems to be "just talking"; as such, it reflects the pidgin/creole speaker's diffidence about his own language ("It ain't no language—we just talkin'!"). Semantically parallel language names are seen in *Papiamentu* (*papiar*, 'to chat', with the abstract suffix *-mentu*) for the Portuguese-based Creole of Aruba-Bonaire-Curaçao; in *Papia Kristang* for its close structural relative in Malaya; and in *patois* for French Creole (and sporadically for Jamaican and other English-based creoles) in the West Indies. According to an informant from Nevis, *speak* tends to be reserved for the standard dialect, *talk* for the island creole variety. Thus on Nevis "Is he speaking?" is approximately equivalent to "Has he learned Standard English?" There is, of course, some jocular quality—and perhaps a little false modesty—involved when the ship's officers call their meeting *Talkee Talkee*; but the genetic origins of the phrase are both interesting and obvious.

There may be some doubt about whether *chinky*

> A rating who is always talking about his adventures on China-side and using Pidgin English. The lower deck's version of CHINA-BIRI.

is "true" pidgin or a Royal Navy innovation on the analogy of pidgin forms. It is in the nature of pidgins that such issues are almost unresolvable: by the time it has become possible to produce a dictionary with official approval, the pidgin has become something else. Sailors in actual life, like those in *The Sand Pebbles,* have always been fond of playing around with pidgin and pidginlike structures. Whatever the exact details of its origin, *chinky* has the enclitic vowel as in *piecee*

> *olo piecee,* China-side for OLD PIECE

and

> *piecee one,* first class; anything that has priority.

The enclitic vowel and other factors in the compounding structure leave no doubt about

> OUTSIDE WALKEE. Paddle steamer whose paddles "walk" outside the hull

or its opposite, *inside walkee.* Of course, the reader will immediately perceive the obvious superiority of the "technical" terms *outboard* and *inboard*! But the pidgin terms at least make possible the "Chinese description of a four-funnel cruiser which runs" cited by Granville:

> Large piecee war junk, four piecee puff-puff, inside walkee, no can see.

As Granville points out, *no can do* is definitely pidgin. It was the title of a song that achieved Tin-Pan Alley popularity in the 1940's, and thus is one of the most widely known pidgin phrases among Americans in general. More important for these purposes, it figures indispensably in one of the most interesting linguistic matters to emerge from Granville's data, the functional distribution of pidgin-derived words and phrases and those from other varieties. Granville makes the point most clearly:

> M.R.U. Much Regret Unable. The formal signal made by officers unable to accept . . . The informal is N.C.D. (No Can Do).

Elsewhere, other pidgin phrases are shown to be appropriate to less formal levels of communication:

> MASKEE. "It doesn't matter; it is of no account." Pidgin English used on informal occasions for the more

serious-sounding "Belay." "You can *maskee* that, Bosun, we shall not want it after all."

It becomes apparent that the pidgin or contact language form continues its life and stretches its domain in the "slang" or technical "jargon" of some particular group (like the woodsmen of the Northwest; see Chapter IV). In fact the contact languages, whether through "spontaneous" creation or as avenues of importation from sources like Chinese not otherwise likely to have provided loans into English, appear to be very likely candidates for the mechanism by which a great deal of that "slang" was created. Furthermore, the contact languages were very widespread, particularly in the simplistic geographic sense; and although they were not absolutely uniform, there is a startling degree of similarity in the varieties that existed in different places.

The same maritime contact factors that the British sailors encountered were basic to the early American experience. Unfortunately, however, we have no work for American naval slang comparable to Granville's dictionary of Royal Navy expressions. We do, however, have dictionaries for special occupational groups from which some of the same conclusions can be drawn. (See references, in later chapters, to McCulloch's *Woods Words* and to Adams's *Western Words*.) Furthermore, the China-side and Melanesian situations were approximately the same for the Royal Navy and the U.S. Navy. The testimony of fictional works like *The Sand Pebbles* is that the linguistic situations were closely comparable.

Although I know of no evidence of widespread U.S. Navy use of *foo foo*, my own experience in the Navy in World War II testifies to the almost universal use of *shit*. *Shit* is very obviously Germanic and Anglo-Saxon, so only something distributional and semantic could have been affected by pidgin influence. But Pidgin English gives the word a more generalized, less indecent function. In Cameroonian Pidgin English, *shit fo' fire* means only 'ashes'; and in Melanesian

Pidgin English *shit belong fire* has the same meaning. There are many comparable phrases involving *shit* in the various pidgins. But American sailors would have been more sensitive to the indecent connotations than the Chinese or the Melanesians, to whom it was only part of an auxiliary language.

Many words that are taboo in ordinary English are perfectly innocuous in pidgins. Another example is *ass* (here the equivalent of British *arse*), which means 'base' or 'foundation' in Pidgin English. In Melanesian Pidgin English, *arse belong house* is 'foundation of a house', *arse belong mami* is 'base of a yam', *arse belong diwai* is 'foot of a tree', and *arse belong musket* is 'gun butt'. So far as I know, no one has ever traced the origin of such expressions as "Get your ass out of here!" or "I'll whip your ass!" Lacking textual evidence, I am not yet ready to claim them for Pidgin English. But the principle of such a derivation is a workable one. Krio uses expressions like *ah go buss you wais* ("I'm going to bust your ass"), "I'll deal with you" and *heice you wais* ("hoist your ass") , "get up."

The reaction of Europeans to Pidgin English and other contact language varieties has been uniformly bad. As acute an observer as the nineteenth-century traveler Captain W. F. W. Owen could write:

> Along the West Coast of Africa, those natives who speak English are in the habit of using a number of words and phrases, often so strangely misapplied as to create amusement. To enumerate them all would fill a volume; but among the most remarkable are, "bob" for noise or threats; as "Suppose I teif [sic] dat man wife, bob come my side." — "lib" or "live" for remain, or to express locality; — as "Ship lib here two moons;" "rock lib here;" — "chop" for eating; as "Suppose go long way among Bullaman, he chop you."[47]

The most important mistake here is Owen's assumption that these "misapplied" phrases are peculiar to West Africa.

In fact they were quite widespread in the pidgins. *My side* clearly parallels *China-side*, etc., of Chinese Pidgin English. *Bob* strongly suggests *bobbery*, defined as 'every kind of noise, disorder, quarrel, disagreement, fuss, and trouble' in Charles G. Leland's *Pidgin-English Sing-Song* (1876). Apparently everywhere in eighteenth-century Maritime Pidgin English, it exists but is comparatively rare in Krio today. *Suppose* (more accurately *spose*) meant 'if' in Chinese Pidgin English, West African Pidgin English, and American Indian Pidgin English. *Tief*, 'steal', is attested even in the Black English of Canadian Negroes.[48]

But what these "strangely misapplied" phrases really show is the ability of human beings, no matter how unfavorable the situation, to come up with a solution to linguistic problems. Among such adaptations attested by Owen are the use of *two mouth tacken* (cf. p. 22), 'a stocking with two mouths', to express what Owen himself would have called "drawers" and what would be called "underwear" or "shorts" by most Americans of today.

Lexical creativity in a pidgin situation has been convincingly demonstrated by Ian Hancock;[49] for the pidginist, it is one of the more encouraging facts that emerges from what is often otherwise a history of exploitation of large population groups, separating them from their homes and native languages or complicating the situation so much that the native language is no longer considered adequate. The contact language solution is generally bad-mouthed by both the European and the "native"; but considered in perspective, it appears to be a tribute to human ingenuity.

It is probable that the unfavorable attitude on the part of Europeans (who were often imitated by educated Africans, Asians, and others) helped to limit investigation of the contact languages, which have received especially short shrift from the linguists. Even Noam Chomsky has labeled the Mediterranean Lingua Franca (Sabir) not a natural language.[50] But to the sailors and those with whom they communicated, whether in cooperation or exploitation, the lingua franca tongues seemed natural and useful. In fact, they were indispensable. For better or worse, world history since about 1400 would have been very different without them.

The sea and the frontier were the two most important aspects of the early history of the Europeans on the "new" continent. Neither has been given adequate attention in our language histories, and what they have in common has never been evaluated. The early colonists consistently underestimated the distance between the two oceans, often taking large rivers as the beginning of the Pacific. More than Chicago-based dialectologists could ever intuit, the early American colonists had a maritime orientation and mentality. And to a greater degree than was perceived, it now appears that the language of the sea became the language of the frontier.

The Maritime Pidgin English, transmitted to West Africans in the slave trade and heavily influenced by West African languages, became the English Creole of the plantations from Nova Scotia to Surinam. (See *Black English*, 1972, for the details of that process.) In the former Dutch Guiana, extreme varieties of English Creole, heavily Africanized throughout, became the language of the "bush Negro" tribes and a medium of trade with the Indians of the interior.[51] Runaway slaves transmitted their own variety of English to the Seminoles and probably to the other Indian tribes; the Plains Indians of the United States were making extensive use of Pidgin English by the end of the eighteenth century. (See *Black English*, Chapter IV, and Chapter III below.) Dutchmen in Surinam, plantation owners and their children in the American South, and frontiersmen like James Fenimore Cooper's fictional Natty Bumppo learned Plantation Creole or American Indian Pidgin English in order to deal with Black slaves or Indian tribes. Those who used Chinese immigrants as cheap labor in the gold rush immediately thereafter had to learn Pidgin English in order to deal with what was almost another supply of slave labor. The American frontier reflected the language contact processes of the sea much longer and much more exactly than has hitherto been realized.

In ports like New York and Halifax, Nova Scotia (see attestations above), pidgin as such was probably virtually unknown after about 1800, although varieties of the derived Black English continue to be spoken in those areas to the present day. Benjamin Franklin (see attestation above) revealed his knowledge of Pidgin English, and there is other evidence that it was used in Philadelphia during and slightly after his lifetime. As the port of entry for a great deal of the immigration to the United States, Philadelphia had a special need for contact languages. Either because Pidgin was no longer commonly used in his area, or because he was an academic and academics never know what is going on around them, the lexicographer Noah Webster gave no indication that he was aware of it. But the pioneers who were pushing across North America—and the Blacks and Indians whom they pushed—were, to judge from the records they left behind them, pretty generally aware of Pidgin English. Insofar as we can tell from the written testimony they have left, a considerable number of them made extensive use of it.

The linguistic reflexes of this identification of the sea and the frontier were many. *Caboodle*, which Leland and Barrere attributed to New England sailors, was believed to be a cowboy's word by Ramon F. Adams (*Western Words*). With an interesting amount of semantic change, *caboose* made the same switch from maritime to land travel.[52] A relatively early observer of American English wrote:

> In England *caboose* (Dutch *kombuis*) is a nautical term for a ship's galley or kitchen, and the "caboose-car," like much of the American terminology connected with modes of travel, has been borrowed from sea life.

43

Chapin, who came well before H. L. Mencken, was not only right about *caboose* but also put her finger on one of the most important historical facts about American English. A great deal more will be made of the sea-frontier relationship in Chapter IV. All that need be established here is that there is much that the overland reconstruction tradition cannot tell us about the early history of American English—will, in fact, inevitably get wrong. For the complete picture, we have to look to the sea.

This is, again, a direct contradiction of the received attitude. Thomas Pyles's representative history of the English language (1964) states flatly: "Since language undergoes no changes as a result of crossing an ocean, the first English-speaking colonists in America continued to speak precisely as they had done in England."[53] While it is true that a tourist flying across the Atlantic or taking a five-day boat trip will alter his language so little as to justify the verdict "no changes," an immigrant who is entering a new life, with different people, in altered social relationships, is in very different circumstances. This is particularly true if the immigrant is relatively young, but even an adult immigrant may make some changes under those drastic conditions.[54] Pyles and his colleagues may have made the trip as twentieth-century tourists, but they did not make it as eighteenth-century immigrants. None of us, of course, can have done so; but we can look at what was reported by eye- (and ear-) witnesses of those immigrants. What they reported suggests something very different from the conventional conclusions of histories of the language.

II

THE AMERICAN KOINÉ

———————◆··◆———————

THE FREQUENTLY MADE ASSERTION THAT "REGIONAL" DIALECTS
of seventeenth-century England came without change to the
North American colonies is an especially unfortunate one.[1]
All of the British immigrants to the Americas encountered a
linguistically complicated situation—although, obviously, not
the same kind of complexity faced later by non-British immigrants—but the *Mayflower* passengers, who are often chosen
as the illustrative example, provide especially obvious exceptions to the alleged principle that unmodified British English dialects came to the Americas.

Regionally, the Pilgrims may have been more homogeneous than others of the generally heterogeneous British
emigrating groups. The seat of the little congregation, which

eventually led the way across the sea to New England, was in Scrooby in Nottinghamshire. A majority of the members came from that general geographic area. Thus the Pilgrim group may at one time have actually represented a "regional" British group with its dialect. A great many complications, however, occurred before the group even set sail for America. And language contact was a major part of the complications.

What is well known to historians, but apparently forgotten by authorities on American English, is that the Pilgrim group went from England not directly to the Americas but to Holland. Leaving secretly to escape religious persecution, they came to Amsterdam in 1607 and 1608. Dissatisfied with Amsterdam, they moved on to Leyden in 1609. Although their early descriptions of the latter city are glowingly enthusiastic, they soon found reason to feel that they should leave. The specific reasons are rather interesting for language history:

> They were breaking under the great labor and hard fare;
> *they feared to lose their language.* [emphasis added][2]

The Pilgrims were also apparently of the opinion that in the Dutch situation they had no opportunity to educate their children.

The fear of losing their language may have been a real one. Several writers have commented on the linguistic assimilation the Pilgrims' language underwent, in a comparatively short time, in Holland:

> It is curious to notice how these English people became absorbed in the Dutch, so that not only their names have acquired a Dutch form but even their signatures have this Dutch form.[3]

Assimilation to Dutch ways also increased the associations with the sea that all American immigrants have had to one degree or another. One historian describes the situation in the following terms:

Their children were marrying off among the Dutch, and were seeking their fortunes in the four quarters of the globe, wherever Dutch ships sailed. They were making no converts. Their sect was too obscure to attract notice, and it was rapidly losing its identity.[4]

Thus when the *Mayflower*

went on alone, bearing one hundred and two passengers, two-thirds of the whole, picked out as worthy and willing to undertake the voyage,[5]

it carried passengers who did not represent the "regional" dialects of England at all—much less in pure form.

What happened to the Puritans, linguistically, in Amsterdam and Leyden could hardly have involved the learning of Maritime Pidgin English. For those who went to sea, the story may have been different, although the documents are too scanty to permit any certainty about the situation during that period. What went on, on land, between the English and the Dutch—so that the former "feared to lose their language"—was more nearly *hybridization* than *creolization* (see pp. 253–254). But even before Plymouth Rock, the Pilgrims were veterans of the complex world of language contact.

The limited records we have from the Pilgrim Fathers reflect neither much Dutch influence nor appreciable English "regional" dialect survival. According to Sydney G. Fisher:

The diaries and letters of colonial native Jerseymen, the pamphlets of the time, and John Woolman's *Journal* all show a good average education and an excellent use of the English language.[6]

Excellent use of the English language is the kind of phrase that recurs repeatedly in the records of observations of the speech of North American colonists, including the Pilgrim Fathers. In this case "excellent" cannot mean "like a native," since every observer knew that all of them were native speakers of English. It may be well to examine how a language variety that attracts the adjective "excellent" developed—particularly among people who were not among the elite of England and who may not have had the best of educational opportunities.

This will include many groups besides the Pilgrims. For all their symbolic value to American history, the Pilgrims were neither an especially large nor especially significant group, as Andrews points out. And even in their own supposed haven from the wicked outside world, they were not alone for long. Nearby—too near for the Pilgrims—Thomas Morton soon moved his infamous group. Morton, who named himself "Lord of Misrule"—perhaps in parody of the properly behaved and ascetic Pilgrims—and who is famous from Nathaniel Hawthorne's "Maypole of Merry Mount," was an annoyance to the Pilgrims, who felt that he introduced an irreligious element into the new land. But Morton and his followers may have been more typical than the Pilgrims of what really came to America.

That part of the new "American" population that came directly from England—and as our population is constituted today, it is a definite minority—was in itself diverse and heterogeneous. The members of it came to what became the United States for a great variety of reasons (seldom those recognized in the history textbooks of the public schools and often those not fully acknowledged by the colonists themselves). What they had in common was that they were rarely —almost never, except for a few leaders like William Penn the Younger—members of the British upper class, that many of them fled from—or thought they were fleeing from—religious or political persecution, and that in the main they were seeking economic opportunity—an aim that could less reverently be called the desire to make a fast buck. As William Eddis wrote on June 8, 1770:

> The colonists are composed of adventurers not only from every district of Great Britain and Ireland but from almost every other European government.[7]

48

The American Koiné

For many of them, particularly for the New Englanders, the maritime trade remained, for a long time, the principal economic element in which they could operate. They were thus never beyond the maritime influences on language detailed in the previous chapter.

There is also the very important but often forgotten factor that the early colonists had strong associations with the West Indies. To some degree, the relationship of an individual continental colony to the islands may have been stronger than its relationship to another colony. Bernard Bailyn reminds us:

> The colonization of the American mainland had been part of the same movement of European expansion that led to the peopling of the West Indies, and New England grew up, as it were, in the company of these island dependencies. The Pilgrims at one point had considered settling on the Caribbean Coast of South America.[8]

Nor were the early New Englanders guiltless in the slave trade for which the West Indies and the Southern states are remembered:

> And it was in that year [1643] that the first triangular slave voyage in New England history was made by one of the vessels trading in the Canaries, for she returned via Barbados where she bought tobacco "in exchange for Africoes, which she carried from the Isle of Maio." This voyage introduced New England to the trade in Negroes; but more important was the fact that its success stressed to the merchants the rich possibilities of commerce with the West Indies.[9]

In the West Indies and elsewhere, the New Englanders would have been exposed to the Pidgin and Creole English of the slave trade.

But for the British-derived colonists, considered somewhat artificially (as they regularly are in history books) as a self-contained unit apart from immigrants from other countries and the "aboriginal" Indians, the major language contact development was something that could have happened with equal naturalness in a nonmaritime environment: it was the leveling of differences between the many different British dialects the early groups brought with them. This is a quite natural process in the migration of groups that speak the same language. The resultant language variety is called a *koiné*.[10]

Obviously, the koiné did not develop the day the first English colonist set foot on the continent of North America; on the other hand, its beginnings probably go back to the time before they boarded ship. From the available evidence (some of which is presented below), it seems probable that the full koiné stage was reached in the middle of the eighteenth century. Dialect leveling tendencies were apparent from the first period of the American immigration, however.

A great deal of effort has been expended to prove that the early British colonists, particularly those in Massachusetts, brought with them the "regional" forms of England.[11] In fact, this has been the basis of the dialect history of American English.[12] It has been widely asserted that the great majority of American immigrants came from the southeast of England, that—perhaps because of their sheer bulk of numbers—they dominated the speakers of other "regional" dialects, and that the kind of dialect diversity they brought from England formed the basis of subsequent dialect diversity in American English.[13] It has even been asserted that the Black English Vernacular is attributable to an amalgam of dialect features from areas of England like East Anglia.[14] Kurath has asserted that virtually all the "regional" dialects of British English made the trip to North America, and that all of them are reflected in American English.[15]

The demographic data upon which such suppositions are based are, however, far from conclusive. A work often cited by those of this persuasion, John Fiske's *The Beginnings of New England* (1889) provides a confident statement:

While every one of the forty counties of England was represented in the great Puritan exodus, the East Anglian
counties contributed to it far more than all the rest. Perhaps it would not be out of the way to say that two-thirds
of the American people who can trace their ancestry to
New England might follow it back to the East Anglian
shires of the mother country.[16]

Fiske's conclusions provided the background for early work
like Allen Walker Read's "British Recognition of American
Speech in the Eighteenth Century" (1933). More recent
studies have not been so certain of this distribution.

Anders Orbeck,[17] while remaining relatively orthodox
insofar as emigration, immigration, and dialect features go,
was somewhat less sure of the dominance of "Eastern
Anglian counties":

If he [Fiske] meant to include in his "Eastern Anglian
counties" Essex, Middlesex, and London, as well as Norfolk, Suffolk, Cambridgeshire, Northamptonshire, Bed-
fordshire, Hertfordshire, it appears that his statement of
the origins is more than borne out, for in the above distribution slightly over 71.52 percent *of those who can be
traced* [emphasis added] are represented as coming from
these counties. If Essex, Middlesex, and London, however,
are not included in the term, the number that came from
"the Eastern Anglian counties" was 47.44 percent.[18]

The clause "who can be traced" is important here, since
only a relatively insignificant portion of the original emigrant group can be traced with any confidence to their
"homes" in England. Orbeck concluded:

On the whole the above tabulation shows a slightly more
scattered distribution than Fiske's statement indicates.
The center of the exodus was certainly Suffolk, and omitting London the two adjoining counties, Norfolk to the
north and Essex to the south, came next.[19]

Every county of England was in fact represented in the "exodus."[20]

Despite the uncertainty of the demographic data, Orbeck continued with what would have been expected in the reconstructive tradition:

> Linguistically the tabulation means that we are to look for the roots of eastern Massachusetts speech in the eastern dialects of England.[21]

But Orbeck did not find the expected, even for the limited area of three seventeenth-century towns in Massachusetts:

> Altogether it does seem strange that the records, written by men from various parts of England, should reflect a form of speech so uniform in character and so near the standard speech of England.[22]

And he frames a rather hesitant conclusion:

> On the other hand early New England speech may reflect the east midland and, to a lesser extent, the southern and southeastern dialects, the main features of which had in the early modern period blended to form the basis of standard London speech.[23]

Such basically inconclusive results, not only timidly stated by the researcher but based upon a sampling procedure that would not inspire confidence in the most optimistic statistician, hardly give strong support to the assumptions of the reconstructive tradition, particularly when one remembers that the researcher was predisposed to find British "regional" origins for American dialect forms. In fact, Orbeck was forced into a provisional consideration that was positively heretical for the dialectology of his time and somewhat later:

> Nor is it impossible to think that some of the divergencies enumerated above may reflect not regional but class dialects, some features of which may have passed into regional dialects not too remote from London.[24]

Orbeck's findings do not, certainly, justify Kurath's 1965 statement:

Spellings gathered from town records and diaries by
Orbeck, Simpson, and Gibson [none of these is identified
by any kind of bibliographical reference] such as *libity*
for *liberty, patchis* for *purchase,* and *ort* for *ought* leave
no doubt but that as early as 1700 some New Englanders
did not pronounce an /r/ after vowels.[25]

Although Orbeck himself records no forms "without r," he
does record some cases where

[r] is confused with [l][26]

If the first three of these examples are taken overseriously,
one could conclude that the speech of the earlier Puritans
had been influenced by some foreign language, like Chinese;
one or another of the American Indian languages; or some
West African language. The [r] ~ [l] interchange will even
fit into the Sabir tradition! For objectivity, then, it would be
well to point out that Orbeck also records *adbitration* for
arbitration.

Orbeck's findings suggest a course of action that was not
adopted for quite some time:

The evidence on [British] dialectal attributions is admittedly slender and except for one single point extremely
doubtful in character. We must of course exclude such
features as had already developed in standard British English of the period, even though they were of dialectal
origin to begin with and *have since disappeared from
standard pronunciation.* [emphasis added][27]

Although the "one single point"—the Kentish, southern, and
southwestern past participle form without -*n*—has not survived in any significant way in American English, and
although nothing else could be advanced with any kind of
confidence by even a precommitted researcher, one can
assume that evidence provided by Orbeck and his two sha-
dowy colleagues Simpson and Gibson, who are never identified, indicated that British dialects—perhaps even "regional"
dialects—were to some small degree represented in Massa-

chusetts speech around 1700. This would mean that the almost complete leveling of British dialectal forms took place later.

Although the emigrant groups from England came chiefly from relatively low social strata, they did not transplant the English class/caste relationships. Integral groups (the lord of a manor, say, and his peasants) did not migrate together. The old social order was broken up. Although those who seek to leave a certain social group and way of life characteristically take with them more than they think in subconscious behavior patterns, social conditions in England were not reconstituted in any precise way in the thirteen colonies. Except for professions (one's status in which might be preserved) and other special relationships like membership in the underworld, the social dialects of England had as little direct reflection in North America as the "regional" dialects.

These are matters of basic importance in understanding the history of American English. In the conventional formulations, geographic and social factors are always stated as the most important in dialect distribution, whether it is considered historically (diachronically) or synchronically (at one point in time). Geographic factors have traditionally been overemphasized, although the imbalance is beginning to be corrected now.[28] When geographic distributions in the United States and in England have been compared and conclusions about migration patterns drawn,[29] it has all too often been the case that the regional dialect distributions of about 1900 in England (approximately the date of Wright's *English Dialect Dictionary*) have been taken for the ca. 1600 dialect distributions that would have affected the colonies directly—assuming that regional distributions in the mother country affect those distributions in a colony. Modern studies suggest that this is not the case.[30]

Professional and religious affiliations were, as a matter of fact, much more likely to have been maintained and to have continued to exert an influence on colonial behavior patterns, including language. Since religious freedom was often the slogan that united a group of immigrants, and since formerly separated and persecuted groups came together in new geographic areas where "religious tolerance" (for themselves, if often not for others) could be practiced, the linguistic influence from religious groups could have been of paramount importance. The most obvious example is the Quakers:

> They gave offense [in England] by refusing to remove their hats in public and by applying to all alike the words "thee" and "thou," a form of address hitherto used only to servants and inferiors.[31]

A more general example was recorded by the Scottish physician Alexander Hamilton on August 17, 1744:

> This humor [i.e., trait] prevails, even among the lower class of people here [Connecticut]. They will talk so pointedly about justification, adoption, regeneration, free grace, reprobation, original sin, and a thousand other such chimerical knick knacks, as if they had done nothing but studied divinity all their life-time . . . to talk this dialect in our parts would be like Greek, Hebrew, or Arabick.[32]

But there is no such evidence for the continuity of "regional" dialects; and on the basis of the general principles of language in migration, we would expect the leveling of differences that is indeed recorded by some of the early observers of American English.

William Eddis, who had naïvely expected the contrary from such a heterogeneously derived group, wrote on June 8, 1770:

> The language of the immediate descendants of such a promiscuous ancestry is perfectly uniform, and unadulterated; nor has it borrowed any provincial, or national accent, from its British or foreign parentage.[33]

Eddis found another characteristic of American English striking enough to be worthy of note:

This uniformity of language prevails not only on the coast, where Europeans form a considerable mass of the people, but likewise in the interior parts, where the population has made but slow advances; and where opportunities seldom occur to derive any great advantages from an intercourse with intelligent strangers.[34]

Like many other naïve observers, Eddis had some strange ideas about language. He apparently believed that it had to be implanted by "intelligent" people in "unintelligent" ones. (In like manner, many research projects in the inner cities in the 1960's went awry because they assumed that children —usually conceived of as being "unintelligent"—got their language from allegedly intelligent parents and teachers or not at all.)

Seven years after Eddis, the Reverend Jonathan Boucher wrote:

It is still more extraordinary that, in North America, there prevails not only, I believe, the purest pronunciation of the English tongue that is anywhere to be met with, but a perfect uniformity.[35]

In the same year, Nicholas Creswell wrote:

They [the inhabitants of the American colonies] in general speak better English than the English do. No Country or colonial dialect is to be distinguished here, except it be the New Englanders, who have a sort of whining cadence that I cannot describe.[36]

Because we know that certain other population groups (like the West African slaves and the North American Indians) were speaking greatly divergent varieties of English, such statements may at first seem puzzling.[37] But it soon becomes clear that Boucher, Creswell, Eddis, and the many others who made similar statements were reporting on the only Americans about whom they knew anything—the white descendants of Englishmen and those few other whites who had completed the process of assimilation without difficulty. The more complicated general picture begins to emerge if we consider the observations of a few more wide-ranging commentators.

The Reverend James Adams was a linguistically sophisticated man for his time. His *Pronunciation of the English Language Vindicated from Anomaly and Caprice* (1799) embodies a kind of perception about the relationship between spelling and the spoken word that was unknown even among professional linguists until a few years ago.[38] Adams recognized not only the koiné of the British-derived immigrants but also the Creole of the less voluntary "immigrant" from West Africa:

> The Anglo-Americans speak English with great classical purity. Dialect in general is there less prevalent, except among the poor slaves.[39]

Others, perhaps not so advanced linguistically as Adams, saw the same things:

> It is a curious fact, that there is perhaps no one portion of the British empire, in which two or three millions of persons are to be found, who speak their mother-tongue with greater purity, or a truer pronunciation, than *the white inhabitants* [emphasis added] of the United States.[40]

Not only did this commentator show some awareness of differences in the "colored" population, but he went on to offer an explanation for the "curious" uniformity among the whites:

> This was attributed by a penetrating observer [identified by Read as perhaps John Witherspoon whose weekly papers called "The Druid" had appeared in Philadelphia in 1781] to the number of British subjects assembled in America from various quarters, who, in consequence of their intercourse and intermarriages, soon dropped the peculiarities of their several provincial idioms, retaining only what was fundamental and common to them all; a

process which the frequency or rather the universality of school-learning in North America, must naturally have assisted.[41]

Like many others, this "penetrating observer" attributed to parents and to teachers what children (see pp. 59–62) were largely responsible for; but this is so universal a fault that we could hardly have expected anything else from him.[42] Even modern linguists are much too inclined to look to the home and the schoolroom rather than the playground for language influences.

These early reporters, whatever their limitations as sociolinguists, were not limited in their geographic experience of the colonies. They characteristically tried to get the overall picture—perhaps because many of them hoped to write a book about the upstart nation-in-the-making when they got back to England. John Harriot, a military man who came to America in 1793, asserted that American English was

> better spoken by the whole mass of people, from Georgia to Quebec, (an extent of country more than 1200 miles,) than by the bulk of people in the different counties of England.[43]

As will be noted, the inclusion of Georgia in koiné territory agrees with my overall timetable (pp. 67–70), in accordance with which "Southern dialect" was not yet formed.

The variations *from* (NB: not *in*) this American koiné that were being noted were not geographic but social—more specifically ethnic. Many, like Adams and the anonymous London editor, commented overtly on the "dialect" (Plantation Creole or West African Pidgin English, by my interpretation) of the West African-derived slaves. Others like John Davis, C. W. Janson, and J. F. D. Smyth reported relatively long stretches of the speech of Black slaves.[44] A quite large number of others quoted American Indians who were very obviously using Pidgin English. The Reverend Jonathan Boucher also saw some influence from European languages in "some scanty remains of the croaking idioms of the Dutch, still observable near New York."

But aside from the slaves, whom the caste rules prohibited from using the koiné even if they ever had an opportunity to learn it,[45] and some still unassimilated white ethnic groups,[46] the speakers of English in the North American colonies had achieved the kind of unity that astonished European visitors.

The use of phrases like "good English" and "English of great classical purity" by eighteenth-century observers has tended to confuse the issue for language historians. If the standards of the twentieth-century classroom are projected onto the earlier century and the very different situation, "good English" will be interpreted as involving the "proper" choice in such schoolmarm shibboleths as "ain't/aren't/isn't" and "The game was called due to rain" versus "The game was called because of rain."[47] Somewhat more advanced schoolmarms, who think in terms of developing their reluctant students into literary figures, may think in terms of the literary dialect—or in terms of some kind of special colonial talent in literary production. Actually, both these possibilities were rendered impossible by the circumstances. As is well known, the American colonists had little access to books and little opportunity to master the kind of literary dialect purveyed by the London coffeehouses and magazines of the time. While there may have been some cases, like medieval Iceland, of a kind of inherent talent for literary creation in the entire population, the poor colonial literature that has reached us does not attest to any such productive miracle in eighteenth-century America. "Good" obviously means something quite different in this context and must be interpreted in a different frame of reference.

What the statements quoted above do show is that "good" meant "without recognizable, stereotypable social or geographic features."[48] For the immigrants to North America who had enjoyed the advantages of such liberty as was provided in the new environment, access to the koiné dialect required just one generation.[49] Although the American colonists, like the British visitors, had chauvinistically—as adults—chosen to credit the accomplishment to grownups and even to schoolteachers, it had been the children who had actually brought about the situation.

How can uneducated and inexperienced children accomplish in a few years what the most highly trained pedagogues cannot accomplish in decades? Well, mainly by aiming at practicable results rather than the high-flown impossibilities of schoolteachers. For a subsidiary explanation, we can point out that children work on language in an out-of-awareness situation, at play, rather than in the schoolroom, where obvious attention to language is developing self-consciousness. The process has been known for some time, and frequently commented upon:

> The explanation [for linguistic assimilation in the United States] is of course the public schools, where the American children americanize the immigrant children in a rough and ready fashion, making life miserable for them if they ever use a foreign word.[50]

In the early days, what children did was to "make life miserable" for any other child who used not just a word but even a pronunciation or syntactic feature that could be observed to be peculiar, individual (in terms of the group norm), or unusual. Whatever "regional" or other dialects their parents may have retained when they came to the Americas, the children learned the koiné for the best of linguistic reasons: if they did not, they would have to bear the ridicule of their peers.

That was not a peculiarity of the colonial situation or of the early United States or of the melting pot. Given an equivalent mixture of dialects, the koiné-izing process will take place anywhere—as long as there are not insuperable social rules (like caste/class barriers) which forbid its working. The process has been explained, with special reference to French dialects, by the great Indo-Europeanist Meillet:

> The fact that French is spoken at the present time in Paris by a majority of provincials and of foreigners is, I believe, of great importance. At first sight, the effects are not appreciable, but the fundamental result is that "Parisian" is disappearing, drowned in a sort of Koiné (common speech), just as Attic formerly disappeared drowned in the Greek Koiné. The idiomatic character of the "Parisian" is being progressively effaced.[51]

In fact, the koiné-forming process may have taken place a very large number of times in human language history. Although seldom discussed, it deserves a much more important place in dialect history than it has ever been accorded.

The American colonies were not alone in this process insofar as the British migrations were concerned. We find conclusive evidence of the same process in Australia. As is well known, the British who emigrated to Australia came from many parts of Britain. The preponderance of convicts among the early settlers is familiar and no doubt exaggerated; responsible historians have pointed out that the "convicts" were often people guilty of no greater crime than being poor and in debt. But the Australian immigrants, like the American, were not upper class and came from all parts of the mother country. The conditions for a koiné were perfect; the additional parallel to the North American situation in the use of Pidgin English has already been referred to (see Chapter I).

There are reports about the language of the early population of the continent "down under" that parallel those of the thirteen North American colonies. In *Shall I Try Australia?* (1892), G. L. James wrote that the English of Australians was

> free from any distinguishing accent or provincialisms to a marvellous extent.[52]

And there are other such statements quoted in J. R. L.-B. Bernard's "On the Uniformity of Australian English," (*Orbis*, 1969).[53]

Obviously, the Australian koiné was not the same as that utilized in the American colonies. The dialect mix was somewhat different, as was the relationship to the maritime varieties; but the most important factor must have been the different group of "aboriginal" and other languages that were in contact with Australian English, mostly through the medium of Pidgin English. Also, Australia had no parallel to the great numbers of immigrants who came to the United States from other European countries.

When dialect differences developed in Australia—as they inevitably would, given the complex linguistic situation— they reflected a very interesting pattern of distribution. Bernard's article, cited above, describes the lack of "regional" dialects in Australia. G. W. Turner comments:

> The homogeneity of Australian English is remarkable . . .
> Even if we include New Zealand, differences are hardly more marked than we find with the eastern United States.[54]

Turner's explanation is:

> The nomadic life of the rural workers helps to explain the uniformity of Australian speech and idiom.[55]

This may have been true in Australia; but as we shall see later, the most "nomadic" group of Americans was deeply involved in the change from uniformity to diversity.[56] Bernard also indicates that the variants do not have social distribution, in the usual sense of that term. It seems, however, that he may have had a narrow definition of *social distribution* restricted to something like "correlated with class/caste stratification," overlooking equally social factors of age grade, sex, profession, religion, etc.

Very possibly, if it had not been for the many immigrating European ethnic groups, the Spanish, French and other colonizing groups, and certain of language contact factors to be discussed in the following chapters, American English would have attained a geographic uniformity of dialect distribution about like that of Australia. As it was, however, there were a great many social, economic, and political differences, some of which—like the changing attitudes toward slavery—eventually correlated with region.

A later immigrating British group came to the Appalachian Mountains in the eighteenth century—considerably later than the main group that has been discussed here. They and their offshoots who later migrated to the Ozarks did not participate in the same koiné formation as the main immigrant body. Today, their speech is still felt to be old-fashioned, and the folk belief that they speak "Elizabethan English" must be constantly denounced by linguists. Nevertheless, they surely participated in a dialect leveling process of their own. Technically, they might be said to have produced the second American koiné.

It would be interesting and instructive to know something about the American koiné, but there are barriers to easy knowledge. The eighteenth-century British approvers of American English were not nearly so specific as the nineteenth-century disapprovers. The device of internal reconstruction—a kind of very learned, very complicated guesswork—has been rejected for the purposes of this study, and for a very basic reason: internal reconstruction has never allowed for contact varieties like pidgins and koinés, which historical documentation shows to have been of basic importance in the history of English in the United States.

After the period of British-visitor approval of American English was over, commentators began pointing (not always with favor) to characteristics of American English like the combination of a verb with a preposition (*build up, look out, see to, think about*). This construction was not unknown, as language historians have always recognized, even in the Old English period (approximately 700 to 1100

A.D.); but it became more common in British English in the early eighteenth century than ever before. Shortly thereafter, however, it lost favor in British English; relatively few examples are to be found today. In American English, on the other hand, the construction is much more widespread than it ever was in earlier English. British philologists consider expressions like *lose out* to be Americanisms, and the British-slanted *Oxford English Dictionary* does not list *cotton to, brew up, fall for, start up, write out, hurry up, build up, burn up,* and *burn down.* By the negative evidence of absence from British dictionaries, two-preposition verbal phrases (*meet up with, marry up with, visit with, lose out on, look down on, go down on, drop in on*) seem to be American innovations.

We cannot, however, draw such conclusions from this kind of evidence. Knowing what is more prevalent in modern American English than in present British English does not equal knowing how it came to be that way, especially if there are no records of the transmission. That such structures were almost as frequent in earlier British English as they are in modern American English is suggestive but still not conclusive information. To take an obviously absurd possibility, Americans did not in some mystic way reach back into the British past (say the thirteenth and fourteenth centuries) in order to acquire linguistic structures that were otherwise not transmitted to them by any process whatsoever.

It may be possible to explain this apparent mystery by analogy to the development of a segment of the American English vocabulary. Early documents are in striking agreement in blaming innovations, which Englishmen often regarded as "corruptions," on the Americans. These accusations, interestingly enough, were essentially nineteenth-century phenomena. In most cases, the complaining Englishmen cited word usages that they said no Englishman had ever heard before he listened to the Americans. The Americans, it was concluded all too hastily, must therefore have made up either the stigmatized words or the "new" meanings which had been attached to them. A few of these words were actual American innovations. But the great majority of them have turned out to be old Britishisms, either obsolete in the British Isles or restricted to nonstandard dialects, which the literary men who made the complaints did not happen to know.

These words, then, were in use in England at some time in the past. Later, they turned up as Americanisms, which the Americans "naïvely" took to be good English. These words must have made up at least a part of the vocabulary of the koiné. From general linguistic theory, we can say that the vocabulary of the colonists, like that of any group, was very large; most of it would have been identical, or virtually identical, to the British dialects—the main other varieties of English in existence at the time. But naïve listeners to language are virtually deaf to similarities and marvelously adept at perceiving differences. Englishmen who reported on the speech of Americans would, therefore, have singled out for comment those words that made up part of the distinctive vocabulary of the koiné.

Some of the condemned "Americanisms" that turn out to be British in origin have completely disappeared from the language—except, of course, in earlier literature. Among the words for which David Hume criticized Benjamin Franklin in the latter part of the eighteenth century, *pejorate* fits into this category, whereas *colonize* and *unshakeable* are so familiar today that we cannot imagine how anyone could object to them. They have apparently been reabsorbed into British usage and the stigma removed from them—which is one of the major relationships between British and American English cited by those who disbelieve Mencken's thesis about a separate "American Language."

Pejorate is, of course, related to *pejorative*, and the linguist is forever talking about *pejoration* (the opposite of *amelioration*) in historical semantics. Almost all of the distinctive koiné words have cognates or historically related forms in present-day English vocabulary. They are neither exotic nor sensational terms, but they seem to be of prime importance for the history of the koiné.

The words of this type that can be isolated are a heterogeneous group—some as staid as *pejorate*, others as racy as *bamboozle*. Some that are slang today probably were not in the eighteenth century. But historically most of them seem to have one common trait: they were not widely used in the American multilingual contact variety, Pidgin English. One possible exception is *swap*, which may actually have been transmitted through the pidgin and not the koiné. (See below, p. 125.)

Here is a partial list of such words:

bamboozle
banter
belittle
boatable ('navigable')
budge
calculate ('suppose')
carry on ('raise a pother')
chaperon
cleared
clever (one meaning of)
coax
collide
creek (one meaning of)
derange (verb)
enterprise (verb)
expect ('think, suppose')
extinguishment ('extinction')
fall (time of year)
feaze (verb)
fellow countrymen
   ('countrymen')

fib
fop
fun
gap
guess ('suppose, opine')
illy
influential
immigration
loan
lynch
memorialize
notify ('inform')
portage
progress (verb)
reckon ('suppose, opine')
row ('a disturbance')
spur
square ('a small city
   park')
statehouse
stingy

suppose	touchy
swap	upland
swimmingly	wobble
talented	

A look at the dates of occurrence, in England and in America, for several of these in the *Oxford English Dictionary* provides some interesting insights into the vocabulary of the colonies and the early United States. Of *square*, 'a small city park' [NB: NOT *square*, 'what you can't do to the circle', or *square* 'unhip'!], Mencken says it is

> not an Americanism. The DAE [*Dictionary of American English*] traces it to 1698 in Philadelphia, but the NED [or OED] finds an English example eleven years older.[57]

Bamboozle, which looks so American that it was automatically attacked by many commentators, "was under fire before [Samuel] Johnson attacked it [in his dictionary]" and was used by Colley Cibber (1702) and attacked by Jonathan Swift (1710). *Budge* was

> old in English, and was in good usage until the seventeenth century, but for some reason the purists of the eighteenth century took a dislike to it.[58]

The word was listed as slang in F. Grose's *Classical Dictionary of the Vulgar Tongue* (1785).

Analogous statements can be made about all of the words listed. In most cases, however, the first recorded American usage is somewhat later than 1698; the dictionary-listed forms tend to cluster between 1720 and 1730. It may, then, be a fair working hypothesis to say that the koiné was being formed slightly before 1700, that it was in its heyday around 1730 (dictionaries, which depend on written usage, always reflect the situation of a few years earlier), and that its partial decline began around 1780, when other influences from the complex multilingual situation in the United States began to make themselves felt so strongly they could no longer be ignored.

But one must remember that the "decline" of the koiné was a relative matter. The results of the koiné-forming influences are still felt in the prestige accorded to a relatively unmarked American dialect, and even in the insistence upon it in most aspects of the electronic media (except for comedians and sportscasters), in publishing, and in the schools.

If we can trust travelers' reports and the evidence left by the American speakers, the "pure" koiné was achieved fairly early in the eighteenth century and began to "fade" in the latter part of the century. It never completely disappeared. Efforts to maintain it—which are often mistaken, even by those making them, for something else, like preserving "good" English or encouraging literary creativity—have continued, with a certain amount of success, to the present time. These efforts are discussed below (pp. 74–76). What concerns us here are the factors that threatened it.

Paradoxically, purism is one of the greatest threats to the leveled dialect. Those who looked to outside models—in this case, British English—constantly sought to remold the koiné on some other pattern, which in effect meant changing it into something else. These included the many American schoolteachers who terrified generations of schoolchildren with the "rule" that their natural pronunciations of words like *secretary, cemetery* and *dictionary* should be replaced by "secret'ry," "cemet'ry," and "diction'ry" as well as those few who kept trying to impose British vowels in *path* and *bath* ("pahth" and "bahth"). They did not succeed in changing the pronunciations, but they did convince many an American that "correct" English was some mystery into which he had not been initiated.

Every college department of English or of linguistics has probably received at least one call from a local radio station or media agency frantically asking for advice on a "technical" question of grammar like: "Is it really correct to say 'you are'? Wouldn't it be better to say 'you is' when you mean only one person?" The inquirer has been thinking too much about grammar, just as many a stutterer thinks too much about what he's going to say or how well he's going to say it. Inquirers like these and the people who take those newspaper-advertised courses on "how to improve one's English" exert a minor influence upon language that is the opposite of the leveling process.

Almost from the beginning of the use of English in America there were Anglophiles who sought approval and "correction" of American usage from England. British influence was always stronger on the eastern seaboard; and New York, for reasons to be explained below (pp. 188–190), was never a real locus of the koiné or of the post-koiné standard. Other examples of direct Anglophilic influence may perhaps be found in the adoption of the British "r-less" pronunciations of words like *card, yard, car,* and *far,* in certain cities.[59]

But Anglophiles and usage-worriers operate at the within-awareness level of language where not much happens anyway. The more serious competitors with the koiné were the other language varieties which abounded in North America. And the agents of the challenge to the leveled dialect were the same ones who had been originally responsible for it —the children. The obvious speakers of foreign languages, pidgins and creoles and "accented" ("hybridized," in the sense discussed below, pp. 194 to 195) varieties were the non-British and nonassimilated minority groups who were frequently employed as household servants and children's nurses in British-derived families. Like Europeans in Africa, South America, and Asia today, the First Families of Massachusetts and Virginia could not resist the temptation of cheap baby-sitters. A result was that

In this strong basket, fashioned by an Indian mother, many a white child has been swung and sung to sleep.[60]

It is not known how many colonial children grew up speaking the Indian languages; but from observations of French children in the Cameroon and gringos in Puerto Rico, we can be quite sure that more colonists grew up bilingual from childhood than ever became so from conscious study as adults.

In the American South and in the West Indies, being cared for by a Creole-speaking "Mammy" meant that the slaveowners' children learned English Creole. More important, "Mammy" probably had children who were brought along to play with "Young Massa or Mistress" while Mammy did the work. There was also the institution of "play children" chosen from the slave population on the big plantations. (Primarily it was a way of getting some return out of the slave children before they were big enough to work profitably in the fields, but it offered an unexpected lagniappe linguistically.) This situation is discussed in some detail in *Black English* (Chapter V).

But the strongest and most effective threat to the koiné came in the myriad language contact situations on the frontier. (Because of the nature of the written records, most of the discussion in Chapter IV deals with the adults in those contact situations. It should be remembered, however, that their children were in almost all the same situations, and that the children were really more effective agents of linguistic change.) Hunters, miners, trappers, and scouts, who went out beyond the "civilized" area and dealt with people who were by and large not native speakers of English, were no longer in a dialect-leveling or dialect-maintaining situation. And this very different type of contact situation had the greatest influence on the fading of the koiné so far as the common man was concerned. (Linguists who may have read this far will please read on before jumping to the conclusion that I have committed myself to a "substratum" explanation!) With the proliferation of those conditions, the koiné came to be more and more relegated to the media, the pulpit, and the schools.

If eighteenth-century English travelers marveled at the "astonishing uniformity" and "great classical purity" of the Americans' English, the nineteenth-century traveler was full of no such praise.[61] Rather, he tended to be like Thomas Hamilton, who wrote:

> Though the schoolmaster has long exercised his vocation in these states, the fruit of his labours is but little apparent in the language of his pupils. The amount of bad grammar in circulation is very great; that of barbarisms enormous. Of course, I do not now speak of the operative class, whose massacre of their mother tongue, however inhuman, could excite no astonishment; but I allude to the great body of lawyers and traders; the men who crowd the exchanges and the hotels, who are to be heard speaking in the courts, and are selected by their fellow-officials to fill high and responsible offices.[62]

A host of other writers like Charles Dickens (*American Notes* and the American scenes in *Martin Chuzzlewit*) joined in the condemnation. John Witherspoon, a transplanted Briton who was president of Princeton and author of "The Druid," a column in the *Pennsylvania Journal and Weekly Advertiser* (Philadelphia), sounded the alarm as early as 1781, although many of his criticisms of current American usage were pedantic and some of them may have been individual "performance errors." The romance between American speakers and British observers was over by the late eighteenth century. The time at which British observers switched to calling American English "bad" rather than "good" can be taken as at least a rough indication of when the mixing process made dialects other than the koiné the most common varieties of ordinary speech.

The Americans themselves regarded the frontier as the special locus of "bad" English. We have statements like that of Ethan Allen Hitchcock of the "prominent defects [in language] among our border people, West and South."[63] These were the areas in which the pidgin contact languages were in use. Hitchcock himself related incidents in which Blacks and Indians used Pidgin or Creole English. He also recorded the case of a Mr. Foreman, a Cherokee, who was engaged in translating the Bible into English.[64] This gentleman is not further discussed, but his "pure English, . . . free from border defects," must have been one of the rare successes among the generally inefficient attempts to teach the Indians English. (See Chapter III, pp. 106 to 109.)

Like Hitchcock, Albert D. Richardson, author of *Beyond the Mississippi* (1865), heard "bad" English in the less thickly populated areas. He wrote:

> In Kansas [about 1858] one heard the slang and provincialisms of every sector of the country, beside some indigenous to the soil.[65]

A more finicky dialectologist than Richardson would say that since the slang and provincialisms "of every sector" were heard in Kansas, they were not really peculiar to those sectors; rather, they "belonged" to speech communities and not to regions. But the thrust of Richardson's observation is clear enough. His book is also a good source for Pidgin and Creole English use in the American West.

John G. Bourke (*On the Frontier with Crook*, 1892) was explicit about the English of Arizona when that state was characteristically frontier:

> While the language of conversation [at a dance] was entirely Spanish, the figures were called off in English, or what passed for English in those days in Arizona.[66]

To these reports we can add the well-known fictional evidence of writers like Bret Harte and Mark Twain. There is wonderful evidence of the latter's mastery in a short story like "Buck Fanshaw's Funeral."

Although no one seems to have thought of putting them all together before, comments from all sections of the frontier tend to agree in this particular. In 1866 Colonel R. B. Marcy wrote of the Southwest

> The people inhabiting the rural districts of the Southwestern states have . . . adopted many words and phrases which are not found in Webster's Dictionary or sanctioned by any of our grammarians. They have also taken the liberty of changing the pronunciation of many words in such a manner, and applying them in such novel ways, that it is almost impossible for one not familiar with these peculiarities to comprehend their meaning in ordinary conversation.[67]

Marcy, like other amateur observers, was better at recording his impressions than he was at detailing what made up "these peculiarities." In this context, he gives only a few pronunciations:

. . . they call	bear	bar
	door	do
	chair	char
	stair	star
	crop	crap

Marcy also quotes a number of the frontier residents to whom he talked. One of them, Black Beaver (a Delaware Indian interpreter who had moved from the Northwest), spoke American Indian Pidgin English. One Negro woman (p. 377) spoke a partly decreolized version of Plantation Creole. But the frontier whites had, according to Marcy's evidence, a distinctly nonstandard dialect of their own.[68]

During the same period, similar reports were coming from other parts. World traveler Sir Richard Francis Burton was astonished at what he heard in Salt Lake City:

> Every word was apparently English, but so perverted, misused, and mangled, that the home reader would hardly have distinguished it from high Dutch: e.g., "Im intire

made as a meat axe; now du don't, I tell ye; say *you*, shut up in a winkin, or I'll be chawed."[69]

The schools and their allied agencies struggled valiantly to maintain the koiné against even such odds as these and against the unrecognized handicap of Anglophilism. In retrospect, given the nature of the enemies they were struggling against, it is amazing that the forces of linguistic "respectability" succeeded even as well as they did.

By the end of the eighteenth century, statements about the diversity of American English were becoming commonplace. But recognition of diversity was not approval—quite the opposite, in fact. Attempts to eliminate variation and restore uniformity, whether or not motivated by eighteenth-century grammatical theory, tended to center around the schools, the church, and the early media. Of these, only the schools have been given any real attention, since they were the early seat of the purism the twentieth-century linguists have consistently attacked.

The early schoolteacher, whether male or female, was sanctimonious in his/her mastery of "good" English and scornful of the pupils' "ignorant" variation. (This is, as everybody now knows, a very poor foundation upon which to build successful language teaching.) And the schoolteacher frequently confused the task of maintaining uniformity or, even better, of teaching the students a dialect lingua franca with that of expunging "bad" English. All too often, the "correct" variety toward which the teacher aspired was British English—not any variety mastered by the teacher—sometimes even "Oxford" English, for which there were no real models around. Not really cognizant of British pronunciation, the teacher all too often simply insisted that pupils "pronounce all the letters"—a failing of pedants that, on the evidence of the pedant Holofernes in Shakespeare's *Love's Labour's Lost*, must go back a very long way.

Frequently, the rules of the school grammars were based

upon Latinizing or pseudological considerations ("Two negatives make a positive"). "Rational grammar" has a respectable linguistic status,[70] but hardly in the common schoolteacher's meaning of the term.

Nonetheless, schoolteachers have exerted a positive force on the language. The desire to achieve unrealistic and unachievable models was a drive toward "universal intelligibility." In its better manifestations, this drive approached the very sensible ambition of having a dialect taught to all speakers that would be usable in all situations.

Even in the twentieth century, those supreme repositories of purism, Freshman English handbooks, have aimed at an English that is:

> Reputable
> National
> Current

The first requisite probably represents a desire to avoid those "shocking" four-letter words. The second militates to some degree against the development or use of localisms—and has thereby earned the undying enmity of the American Dialect Society. The third is an injunction against using the older varieties of English—Old, Middle, Elizabethan, etc. (although the same pedantry has insisted that students should study what they are not allowed to use).

But the major factor in the maintenance of the "common" dialect has been the internalized attitudes of American speakers. Even the dialect geographers have been forced to give sporadic recognition to these attitudes. Dialect geographer E. Bagby Atwood acknowledged:

> Gillieron's method of merely asking an informant to translate a term into his dialect would have little value in the United States, since no one wants to admit that he speaks a dialect.[71]

As early as the eighteenth century, there was a kind of generalized feeling that American English was "its own thing" and that there was one relatively uniform variety. These attitudes have been reflected—not created by—teachers and textbook writers, including Webster. Even the most egregious speakers of nonstandard dialect believed and still believe, in a kind of linguistic heart of hearts, that "real" American English is good and that dialects are bad.

When the very different needs of the frontier promoted diversity rather than uniformity in American English over the entire geographic extent of the nation, the uniform dialect was not completely forgotten. Schoolteachers taught the frontier children; and speakers of American Standard English came from the East to lecture and entertain them and their parents in series like the Lyceum[72] and the Chautauqua.[73] Soon widely circulated books and magazines presented written models of the uniform dialect. By the time radio was invented, it was a commonplace that radio announcers must speak "good" English and only comedians could use dialect. (After the famous test case of Dizzy Dean in St. Louis, sportscasters were given essentially the same dispensation as comedians.) By the time of network television, these norms had been so thoroughly established and accepted that linguists now speak with confidence of "Network Standard."[74]

The American koiné is hardly a "dead" language. It has managed to adjust to the times remarkably well and to adapt itself to new situations and demands. If the schools will only remove their kiss-of-death labeling of it as "good" English and utilize it for what it is, the uniform dialect has as bright a future as any other speech variety of mankind.

III
IMMIGRANTS
AND MIGRANTS-
WILLING AND UNWILLING

WHEN THE VERY COMMONPLACE PHRASE "A NATION OF immigrants" is used about the United States, it most frequently refers to non-British immigrants. It is a salient fact of the nation's history that, after the "true-born" Englishmen of the eighteenth century and the Scotch-Irish of the early nineteenth, large numbers of Germans came in the 1840's and 1850's; many Scandinavians in the 1850's and after, reaching a peak in the 1880's; and large numbers of other groups like Jews, Italians, and Poles somewhat later.[1] It is all too often forgotten, however, that West African slaves began to arrive en masse almost as soon as the Puritans, and that the American Indians, who were already here, were forced to move around in order to accommodate the land

77

hunger of the European groups. Each of these groups had
its home language—in some cases, two languages or more—
and together they introduced a very different type of complexity from that represented by the mingling and ultimate
leveling of British dialects.

New York City was always one of the most linguistically
complex parts of the colonies. Dutch was, of course, the
official language up to 1664, when the stronger British
"traded" Surinam to Holland for New York; and it remained
the language of many speakers for a long time afterward.
The linguistic complexity of Holland itself was reflected in
the use of Flemish and Walloon in the American colony.
Palatinate Germans early settled along the Hudson. The
British—including Irish, Scots, and Welsh—moved in even
before the "trade" was made. Jewish traders were present
from early times and even had a Hebrew school. Italians and
Portuguese were also involved in the early commerce of the
port of New York. All of these competed with Swedish set-
tlements in Delaware, and there were Danes in New York
itself. Even if we leave out—as it has become traditional to
do—the American Indians and the Black slaves who were
numerous on Manhattan Island until the late eighteenth
century, we still find a picture of extreme linguistic complexity in New York City and in other Atlantic ports from
the very beginning.

The most simplistic means of evaluating the influence
of such language groups on American English is called the
substratum principle.[2] In effect, it means direct influence,
through interference, on a new language, which a group of
native speakers of another language initiates.[3] Interference
is easily observable when a speaker of Spanish, which does
not have a phonemic contrast between /b/ and /v/, con-
fuses English *bowels* and *vowels*. Or a Spanish-speaking
person might be confused by the English word *hot*, since it
covers both the Spanish words *caliente* and *picante*. (Other
uses of *hot* as meaning 'sexually excited', 'musically stimulat-

ing', or 'right in fashion' are best left out of the discussion for the time being.) According to the simplest version of the substratum theory, a Spanish speaker might be expected to choose the English word *piquant* as a translation of the Spanish *picante* and to use it as though it were an everyday word in cookery. It is easy to show that this kind of direct influence of one language on another is quite limited in scope, and the kind of absolute proof often demanded in historical linguistics is extremely difficult to establish for substratum relationships.

But the relationships of even two languages in contact are not so simple as all that. Even an unsophisticated Spanish speaker will soon realize that choosing Latinate English words reflects his lack of familiarity with the new tongue, and he will try studiously to avoid the Latinate vocabulary altogether. He may therefore describe a person as having a "hot" personality in order not to use the Latinate *piquant*.[4] If he comes to realize that the Romance languages use *actual* in the sense of 'at the present time' whereas English uses it to mean 'real' or 'existing', he may avoid the use of that word altogether. This particular process, which might be called "reverse carry-over," is part of a group of processes that require a much more complicated picture of what goes on in language contact than the substratum theory.

In a country dominated by the ideology of the melting pot, like the early United States, sounding "native" carried a high prestige value, and second-generation immigrants made every effort to sound different from their parents. No real incentive beyond a little insistence within the family circle was provided to retain the mother tongue.

A group trying to be *unlike* its parents may *overstress* the differences between their language and English. It is a commonplace that interference from German leads to overuse of *already* in an attempt to render the German *schon*, which has no direct one-word equivalent in English. But if children deliberately exclude *already* from their vocabulary as a reaction against their parents, then the "influence" of German is still being felt in the English of the second-generation immigrants. Furthermore, many a second-generation child was so eager to avoid the stigma of "bad" English that he held rigidly to the precepts of the school and utilized an English devoid of slang and colloquialisms. He might be much more likely to "talk like a book" than the children of generations of English speakers. And these more subtle processes are more lasting than the simple interference patterns of substratum relationships.[5]

Investigators of American English, whether advocating the substratum or any other theory of language change, have accepted the obvious fact that the immigrants brought a great deal of new vocabulary to American English. Mencken's 1919 edition gave ten pages to "Loan-Words and Non-English Influences," but he kept expanding the treatment until Supplement I (the last to deal with the matter) devoted thirty-one pages to the topic "The First Loan-Words," along with long sections later on "Loan Words and Non-English Influences" and "Foreign Influences Today." Mencken, who lacked even the rudimentary linguistic training available in the universities of his own day, was at ease with no phase of language except lexicon. All that he was really equipped to do to prove that "the American language" was different from English was to show that its vocabulary was different. He therefore presented a vast amount of data on the influence of immigrants' languages and other foreign languages on the lexicon of American English. Those who came after him were, in a shallow sense, more sophisticated linguistically; they assumed that Mencken had been factually right, but theoretically wrong. They further assumed that he had exhausted the evidence (which was concerned almost exclusively with vocabulary). Aside from the inevitable lip service to the migration of British "regional" dialects, they often concerned themselves almost exclusively with putting Mencken's data into what they conceived as a more professional framework. But his academic limitations aside, Mencken had sounder and deeper insights than most of those who followed him knew, and his initial insights are worth a great deal more than the value now generally assigned to them. We still must pay a great deal of attention to immigrants and migrants in order to understand the history of American English, although the vocabulary they introduced is not the only matter we must look at.

The classical immigrant paradigm is:

First Generation—	"old-country" language and heavily accented English
Second Generation—	bilingual, with some preference for English, especially outside the home
Third Generation—	essentially monolingual in English, with perhaps some ability to speak the old-country language, reluctantly, when visited by grandparents, etc.

Many observers have considered that this assimilatory process is now complete, and have rejected the idea of foreign-language influence on American English almost *in toto*. From this point of view, the features of American English have to come from British dialects—or British "folk speech"— since there is no other possible source for them.[6] Supporters of this position have not even been aware of the existence of pidgin and creole varieties. And if they have known something about the English of New York City Jews whose first language is Yiddish, or of Pennsylvania Germans, they have found it convenient to suppress that knowledge.

On the other hand, a sociologist of language like Joshua A. Fishman, bringing the perspective of another discipline to the well-worn study of American English, can easily point up the absurdity of ignoring those immigrant groups.[7] As Fishman points out, hardly sixty million of the present American population of two hundred million or so can trace their ancestry to England with anything like confidence. In view of that relationship, it would be amazing if even the most proficient paleographer of language could draw meaningful connections between British dialects and the English that almost all the two hundred million of us speak.

There were, in fact, enough exceptions to the simplistic immigrant assimilation paradigm to warrant a full-fledged second paradigm. Where large groups of Pennsylvania Germans banded together to the almost complete exclusion of other groups, traces of old-country language persisted in their English long past the three-generation period.[8] And where —as in the case of Jewish immigrants—an ethnic group and a religion have coincided, "foreign words" have often been maintained against all outside influences.[9] There are enough such examples in American history to suggest that they cannot be handled as merely an exception to the general type; they deserve to be treated as a type of their own.

The traditional "substratum" treatment does not lend itself to such reconsideration. For those to whom this was the only possible exception to the assimilation pattern, ordinary statements like the following seemed significant and even conclusive:

> In perhaps one fiftieth of the United States there are linguistic substrata. These are formed by the French in parts of Northern New England and Louisiana, the Spanish of the Southwest, the small German colonies of Pennsylvania, and the Negroes in some districts of the Southeast.[10]

A statement like this is obviously inaccurate in that it allows for Negro speech differences only in the Southeast; but it was far ahead of the dialectology of its time, which allowed no Negro differences (except for the case of Gullah). It is also strange that Spanish-speaking Mexicans were ignored, but

Chicano Power was not to develop until many years later. As might be expected, the author saw no need to take the native Americans into account.

Italians are not even mentioned in such a statement, although any visitor to the cities of the eastern seaboard can still see plenty of evidence of their existence, and even of their language. Standard sources like the *Dictionary of Americanisms* acknowledge "Americanisms of Italian origin" only in such items as *spaghetti, macaroni, antipasto, ravioli, minestrone, pizza, baloney* (from Bologna), *Mafia,* and *lasagna*; and there are reservations as to whether two or three of these are bona-fide Americanisms—that is, as to whether they entered the language in this country or in England. It would appear that the Italians had as little influence as the Irish, from whom we supposedly get (according to the hesitant suggestions of a few etymologists) a few words like *speakeasy,* which may have been current in Erin before they came to the United States, until it becomes necessary to invoke Irish invariant *be* in order to forestall the creolist interpretation of that feature of Black English. See below, pp. 90–94.

But the influence of the Irish, like that of the Italians, may have been a more subtle matter. William Labov has done a masterful job of showing how the latter group has influenced the spread of some pronunciation features that we now think of as being characteristic of New York City. Italian, he points out, has no [æ], the sound that most of us (outside of New York) produce in *cat,* and first-generation Italian-Americans tend to use their native Italian low vowel [a] very roughly equivalent to the first vowel in *father*) for the class of English "short *a*" words. But the second-generation Italian speakers reverse that tendency; they produce *cat* with a "higher" vowel, almost like that of *let.* As Labov points out, this is more nearly a reflection of the Yiddish interference pattern on English. But for second-generation Italians, the native-speaker models for English were largely Jewish-Americans, in whose English there were still some traces of Yiddish interference. Reaching "for native status by removing themselves as far as possible from the low-prestige pattern of their parents," second-generation Italians imitated and even exaggerated the originally Jewish tendency.[11] The upshot is that today in New York City the "raised" pronunciations of the vowel of *cat* are more marked in the speech of Italians, even though direct Italian interference would tend to result in a "lowered" articulation.

This looks like another case of reverse carry-over. Although not so crude a contact relationship as a "substratum" influence, it is nonetheless part of a development that could not have taken place had there not been foreign-language groups in the United States. The development is no less a consequence of the presence of Yiddish and Italian in New York City because the speakers of today do not happen to carry over the exact vowel patterns of their parents' language.

Aside from the more perceptive researchers like Labov, who are able to examine indirect as well as direct influences, the Yiddish contribution to American English has been given short shrift. Thomas Pyles, in *Words and Ways in American English* (1952), calls the language "basically German . . . with a large number of words from Hebrew and Slavic" and cites as "its principal contributions to the American vocabulary" (in fact the only ones widely known outside New York City):

> *dokus (tochus)*
> *kibitzer*
> *mazuma*
> *schmo*
> *schmaltz* (and presumably *schmaltzy*)
> *schnozzle*
> *phooey*

to which could surely be added *schlemiel, shmuck, borscht, gefilte fish,* etc.

Those of us who listened to the radio in the early days

heard and were puzzled by gags that revolved around the use of phrases like *Who's Yehudi?* and *What's a schlemiel?* And at least one radio comedian liked to include as a running gag, the statement, "Today I yam a man." We, never having heard of a bar mitzvah, assumed that the pronunciation (with initial palatalization of *am*) was what everyone found so funny. As Lilian Feinsilver's excellent book, *The Taste of Yiddish*, makes clear, the growth of electronic entertainment media and of various media of communication is bringing an ever-increasing familiarity with Yiddish-tinged English to the entire nation. This is partly explainable by the fact that New York City, which contains about two million Jews, is the most important center of such communications and entertainment.

When we who listened to the radio in the hinterlands grew a little more urbane, we learned "Mink, schmink—so long as it keeps you warm!" and "Oedipus, Schmedipus—so long as he loves his mother!" We began to perceive, even in some cases to utilize, phrases with a specifically Yiddish tinge like "What else?" "Dun't esk!" and "Why not?" (specifically to questions like "Why did you do X?").

The last expression, as Feinsilver points out, is very similar to a Pennsylvania German-English idiomatic pattern. So are expressions like *(I don't have) what to eat, foggel,* 'a light fog', inverted word order in some sentences ("Throw Mama from the Train a Kiss"), *-ay-ay-ay-ay-ay* (except that Jewish speakers have more tendency to stress the third of the series than the Germans), and *already* in the final position. In the long run, these common expressions may reflect the importance of German in the formation of both Yiddish and Pennsylvania German. (The latter is often called Pennsylvania Dutch, from a kind of Americanization of *Deutsch*, German for 'German'.)

There are many German communities in the United States, and Germanisms can be heard in places like Sanger and New Braunfels, Texas. But the best-known and probably the most important such group linguistically is the one that has come to be known as the Pennsylvania Dutch.

Settling primarily in central Ohio and Lancaster County, Pennsylvania, beginning around 1720, the members of the "Anabaptist" protestant group who came from the Alemannic-dialect-speaking area of Germany tended to remain together. They were soon observed to be speaking a variety of German which

> with the exception of certain Alemannic peculiarities in the morphology and vocabulary, and numerous evidences of English influence in the syntax and vocabulary, resembles most closely the dialects spoken in the eastern half of the Rhenish Palatinate.[12]

For subgroups like the Amish, who isolated themselves from outsiders, English was a language to be used only with outsiders—and it remains so today. Less extreme sects like the Mennonites have assimilated to a much greater degree.

Today, in perhaps the closest approximation that exists in American English to a simple substratum relationship, the Pennsylvania Dutch speak a heavily German-influenced English, although many of them know no German.[13] Some of their patterns, like the identification or confusion of *let* and *leave*, both of which are *lassen* in German, are well known:

> Leave him have it.
>
> The man wanted to kiss the girl,
> but she hadn't left him yet.
>
> Since you are rather large in the hips,
> I shall have to leave out the seat.

Like other German-derived groups, the Pennsylvania Dutch also use *make* in senses that other American-English-speaking groups do not find idiomatic:

> Make the window shut.
> It make down (rain) soon.
> The bell don't make. Bump.

The verb form in a conditional clause, long a bugaboo for American schoolchildren of all ethnic groups, has a special twist in Pennsylvania Dutch:

> If she would be here.
> You better wouldn't do that.
> If he would be here, you wouldn't say that.

Anyone with some experience of Pennsylvania German English who is asked to give examples of the dialect will immediately cite *spritzen the lawn* and *outen the light* and some use of *all* to mean 'finished', as in the Broadway comedy title *Papa is All*. Even the old saws like:

> Throw your father down the stairs his hat.
> Throw the cow over the fence some hay.

have a kind of representative validity, like most stereotypes. Tourist publications in the Lancaster, Pennsylvania, area make a lot of the *ferhoodled* ('crazy') English. They are, of course, more interested in collections of oddities than in seriously collected data, but there is a certain accuracy to the forms they record.

My favorite Pennsylvania Germanism came not from any of these sources nor from a published article,[14] but from a bidialectal informant who grew up near Reading. Reporting on the linguists' predictions, over a period of some decades, that the dialect would "soon" be dead, she commented, "I vunder vat iss meaning to a lingvist soon."

There is some indication that Pennsylvania German may have a livelier linguistic history than has been dreamed of in conventional treatments. As a variety used in bilingual, if not mutilingual, contact situations, it participated in a great many kinds of language activities that demanded a lingua franca. John H. Beadle, a nineteenth-century writer, reported on a "Hoosier dialect" which he called

> the result of union between the rude translations of 'Pennsylvania Dutch', the Negroisms of Kentucky and Virginia, and certain phrases native to the Ohio Valley.[15]

Some of Beadle's cited forms do look like Plantation Creole (and are thus "Negroisms" in some sense); it would take considerable research to determine whether his more general statement is true, but many such things were going on on the border (see Chapter IV). Very few other writers have linked Pennsylvania-German-influenced English and Plantation Creole, and on the surface there is little evidence of a connection between the two. But the use of *ain't* by the Pennsylvania Germans (*It's a nice day, ain't?*) is strikingly like the use of *enti* in Gullah (*You mus' be t'ink dem duh hoe, enty?*).[16] Translation of these expressions into ordinary English being almost impossible, one is virtually forced to explain them in terms of German *Nicht wahr?*, Spanish *¿No es verdad?*, or French *N'est-ce pas?*

The historical records of Pennsylvania German have apparently not been looked into at all, but they are there for the examining. The English traveler William Ferguson, who produced *America by River and Rail* (1856), quoted "a Dutchwoman" (i.e., German):

> You must go dat road, straight, one little way, den you see
> stable directly—dat road, straight, house directly.[17]

Like these groups, others of the more willing immigrants to the United States remained essentially unassimilated. The Acadians ("Cajuns") of Nova Scotia, whose struggle to get to Louisiana is celebrated in Longfellow's *Evangeline*, have maintained either their own variety of French or a heavily accented English—or both. Their peculiar pronunciation may have influenced some of the place names of Louisiana and eastern Texas, like Mexia (locally pronounced *muh-HAY-uh*). The Mexicans of the Southwest, partly because of color and partly because of religion and other cultural factors, have tended to remain highly "visible," with full assimilation for only a comparative few. A Texas Mexican boy who attempts to speak unaccented English may be the target of the sarcastic comment "Tryin' to be a big man!" There is now some proud insistence upon a valid "Chicano" language.[18] Puerto Ricans in the Eastern cities, for perhaps the same reasons, tend to retain a heavy Spanish influence. Sometimes the picture is complicated by the sharing of ghetto areas, schools, and basketball teams with Black English speakers. Many of the Puerto Ricans who grew up on the continent and have now returned to the island use a good deal of the grammar of Black English. In the case of *Where you go?* and a few other such structures, it is not always clear whether Spanish interference or Black English is involved.

The internal reconstructive tradition in linguistics has always insisted that a much heavier proportion of British "regional" dialect was retained in the speech of American Blacks than in any other dialect of American English. This is, on the face of it, absurd. It says, in effect, that the population group whose ancestors had the least history of residence in the British Isles must be considered linguistically the "most British" of all the population groups in the United States (and, as it happens, of the West Indies).

The reason for this absurdity is, of course, the necessity of resisting any notion of influence from outside the Proto-Germanic → Old English → Middle English → Modern English reconstructive tradition. Linguists have felt it especially necessary to reject the possibility of any kind of influence from outside the Indo-European group of languages— and to avoid the shadow of a possibility of any influence from African languages. Since the creolist tradition obviously incorporates a great deal of African influence, the reconstructive tradition desperately needed to deny the spread of Creoles in the continental United States, even at the cost of ex post facto historical formulations.

The explanations of the mechanisms by which British "regionalisms" could have been transmitted to West Africans who had never been in or near those regions are extremely vague. The transmission is simply assumed to have taken place, even though it is well known that the Black field-hand group was segregated and treated almost like an untouchable caste by whites and Black house servants alike.[19] In such a sociolinguistic situation, developments are much more likely to be internal in the isolated group, and this is precisely what observers of the plantation system reported—a language variety that, although English-based in some sense, was peculiar to the Black field hands and very different from anything spoken by other groups, even on the same plantation.

In spite of the fact that dialect shift was very rapid on the part of immigrant groups like the Irish, the reluctance to see Creolisms in Black English vernacular usage has led to the currently popular fantasy that the durative *be* (*He be running*, contrasting with *He running*), widely recognized as a distinctive structure of the Black English vernacular, is derived from Irish immigrants.[20] This is in the face of the fact that the rather large Irish population in the United States has no trace of it. A rather typical statement is that of Labov:

> *Be*₂ provides no strong argument for a Creole origin; the closest analogy is with Irish *be*, stemming from the Celtic "consuetudinal" or habitual copula.[21]

For supporters of this position, much is made of the trivial historical evidence that some Irishmen acted as overseers on the large plantations. This implies that the large mass of slaves took their linguistic practices whole hog from the one overseer, with no transfer from either their own native language habits or a contact variety. Such an occurrence is unknown anywhere else in a language contact situation, but those who want strongly enough to disbelieve in African influence can persuade themselves that this is what happened.

The durative *be* has played an important enough role in the discussions of the Black English vernacular to deserve very special consideration. It does seem that an uninflected *be*, which is not common to other English dialects, is common in Anglo-Irish. The structure seems to be:

It do be raining.

This is, however, about as far as the match with the Black English vernacular goes. Irish dialect does not have the form:

It be raining.

which is the more normal form for the Black English vernacular, the form with auxiliary *do* being only a relatively rare emphatic. Furthermore, Black English forms the negative:

It don't be raining.
(Do it be raining? No, it don't.)

and the negative question:

Don't it be raining?

neither of which is paralleled in Anglo-Irish. Neither, for that matter, is the contrast with zero copula:

It raining / It be raining.

And there is no parallel in Anglo-Irish to the Black English system by which *it raining* is negated as *it ain't raining* (the negative question being *Ain't it raining?*). The total grammatical system (in which negating and question-forming operations are the overt evidence which separates out the underlying categories), not just the use of "uninflected *be*," support the creolist designation of Black English as a special Afro-American dialect. As usual, Anglophilic reasoning has led to a dismal disregard for system, the one thing to which linguistics is supposed to pay most attention.

The creolist derivation of the Black English *be* from Creole *de* (as in Cameroonian *Him wife de humbug him*, 'His wife is/was giving him trouble') is not immediate and simple, although both *de* and a kind of durative *be* are found in Gullah, the English Creole of the Georgia-South Carolina Sea Islands. English Creole in something like its "original" form must have had a set of related structures:

1) Subject *de* Verb   (John de go)
2) Subject ø Adjective   (John sick)

3) Subject *de* Adjective   (John de sick)
4) Subject *be* Noun   (John be a man)

in which (4) does not have, necessarily, any of the durative function of Black English *be*; that is generally reserved for the *de* of (1) and (3).

The primary factor in change from Plantation Creole toward ordinary English structures was the desire of the slaves and freedmen to acquire the prestigious forms spoken by those more fortunate. In this process, *de* clearly stands out as the Africanism.[22] In the linguistic assimilation process, it would be the most obvious target for elimination—perhaps in a fairly self-conscious sense. Under the stress of *"Don't say de!"* the speaker would find himself with a set of permitted structures like these:

1) Subject X Verb   (John X go)
2) Subject ø Adjective   (John sick)
3) Subject X Adjective
4) Subject *be* Noun   (John be a man)

Since one cannot articulate an X, the symbol for an unknown, there was obvious pressure to find something to replace the eliminated *de*.

If the items listed above fall into a natural linguistic set, then it is likely that the X would be replaced by another member of the same set. Since ø, however much it may appeal to the linguistic analyst, is hardly the kind of thing that the ordinary speaker can knowingly make into a substitute, *be* would be the logical realization of the "unknown." *Be* was already in a different distribution from ø; the change would bring it into a direct meaningful contrast. The set would now consist of the following:

1) Subject *be* Verb   (John be go)
2) Subject ø Adjective   (John sick)
3) Subject *be* Adjective   (John be sick)
4) Subject *be* Noun   (John be a man)

This is just about the situation recorded around 1790 in the literary documents. The character Cuff (from Cuffee, the West African day name for a male born on Friday) in *Modern Chivalry* by Hugh Henry Brackenridge (1798) says, "I be cash [catch] crabs." Soon thereafter, perhaps about 1830, adding *-ing* to the *be Verb* becomes obligatory.[23] The modern set is

1) Subject *be* Verb *plus* -ing   (He be going)
2) Subject ∅ Adjective   (He sick)
3) Subject *be* Adjective   (He be sick)
4) Subject ∅ Noun   (He a man)

Be has disappeared from (4), probably because of its association with the durative meaning.

In Gullah, where *de* has remained to the present day, there is a partial parallel. Optionally, a Gullah speaker may say either:

Subject *de* Verb

or

Subject *de* Verb *plus* -ing

In Turner's *Africanisms in the Gullah Dialect* (1949) we find an occasional example like:

sʌmpm de kʌmIn

for which the meaning is either 'something is coming' or 'something was coming'. According to the evidence of Ambrose Gonzales, who uses the spelling *duh* for *de*, the African-derived auxiliary verb is extendable into the *Subject be Noun* frame: "Me duh Buckruh, you duh nigguh!"[24]

Insofar as the alleged borrowing from Irish overseers goes, the really inexplicable matter would be how the slaves happened to borrow *be₂* and nothing else from their Irish overseers. Why, for example, did they not also borrow Irish *used be*? Why is there nothing like *The falling sickness is on him* for 'He has the falling sickness'? Still less is there any Irish vocabulary like *begorrah*! Survivals from African languages, while relatively few in the obvious, dictionary-entry sense, are clearly marked in the attestations.

In this regard, it is a specious procedure to criticize the accuracy of the attestations, although, of course, they must have been far from perfect. The whites (especially the British and the continental European visitors and immigrants) who kept the records would have been closer in their contacts with the Irish overseers than with the slaves. The tendency of such observers, had there been such Anglo-Irishisms to observe, would have been to overstate them—not to understate them. Yet these observers record exactly zero Anglo-Irishisms. The obvious conclusion is that, except for the spurious case of the durative *be*, there were no Anglo-Irishisms in the West Africa-derived slave community.

In any case, the history of the Black English vernacular is such as to render the presence or nonpresence of Irish drivers and overseers on the Southern plantations essentially irrelevant. Slavery in the United States, which was at least as prevalent numerically in the Northern colonies as in the Southern until about the middle of the eighteenth century, was essentially a minor adjunct of Caribbean slavery. Continental North American trade was also, in the early centuries, minor compared to that of the Caribbean; and the continental colonies were unimportant in British economics in comparison to the West Indies:

> Statistics in the records of the board of trade indicate that in a given year (1700) the Barbados were thirteen and Jamaica nine times more valuable to England than New York.[25]

It is well known that slaves often came to the colonies through West Indian staging areas, where they sometimes learned a variety of English—the pidgin of which examples are given in Chapter I (pp. 21–29). Some of them seem to have learned the contact language even before they left the "factories" of West Africa, and others on the ships on the way over. This Pidgin English and its Creole descendant (and later, decreolized varieties) were learned by slaves and by those who had close dealings with them, like the Indians, from Nova Scotia to Surinam.[26]

The demographic movement of slaves to the Northern colonies has been well described, although these important studies have apparently not been read by some of the historians of American English, who have been inclined to think of slavery as a uniquely Southern institution and of the language of slavery as therefore Southern. Lorenzo Greene's *The Negro in Colonial New England,* Robin Winks's *The Blacks in Canada,* and Roy Ottly and William J. Weatherby's *The Negro in New York* provide excellent details of that demographic distribution. Winks's book especially shows how commonplace movement between Jamaica and Nova Scotia was.

New York City figures prominently in the early slave trade, although most of the slave ships probably sailed out of ports in Massachusetts. I. N. Phelps Stoke's *The Iconography of Manhattan Island* reports

> The negro quarter of the slaves of the West India Co. is also laid down on the Manhattan surveys. Its location apparently was in the East River shore, just North of the Saw Kill, in about the present 75th Street.[27]

And Flick's *History of the State of New York* (1933) states that

> New York, at the end of the seventeenth century, had a larger percentage of Negroes in its population than did Virginia.[28]

Leonard's *History of the City of New York* (1910) reports: "Slavery, the worst blot upon American history was never worse in its aspects than it was in the city of New York at that time [the end of the seventeenth century]." Leonard is supported by Ferenc M. Szass: "New York had regulations barely less strict than those of South Carolina."[29]

There are some records of the speech of slaves in the New York City area. Perhaps the most interesting (at least in nonfictional writings) is that of Justice Daniel P. Horsmanden, who in 1744 wrote *The Negro Plot* to justify his own not-unbiased view of the causes of that probably exaggerated uprising. Of the language of Jack, one of the ringleaders in the alleged conspiracy, Horsmanden wrote:

> his dialect was so perfectly negro and unintelligible, it was thought it would be impossible to make anything of him without the help of an interpreter.[30]

In this case, interpreters were available in the persons of two young (white) men who had known Jack long enough and well enough to have learned his dialect. Among other things, Horsmanden's materials reveal that this ancestor of the present Black English vernacular was never any kind of linguistic aberration or corruption but was learnable by anyone who had adequate exposure to it.

Justice Horsmanden himself was apparently able to understand some of Jack's speech—which may mean that Jack had some knowledge of a relatively decreolized variety of English. The judge quoted the prisoner: "His master live in tall house Broadway. Ben ride de fat [i.e., white] horse."[31] Horsmanden also recorded the word *backarara*, 'white man', a variant of *buckra* or *backra*, a word very characteristic of West Indian varieties of English and of Gullah. He further documented the use of day names (Cuffee, Cudjo, etc.)[32] in New York, and commented several times on "the negroes' dialect," giving a few other illustrative phrases.[33]

Elsewhere in the Northern colonies, observers noted Black speech. Benjamin Hobart in *A History of Abingdon, Mass.* quoted a Cuff (short for Cuffee, 'born on Friday', for a male), "By and by you die, and go to the bad place and after a time Cuff die, and go and knock at the good gate."[34] And George Sheldon's *Negro Slavery in Old Deerfield* quotes another eighteenth-century Massachusetts slave: "Couldn't stop 'em no how massa."[35] Added to the fictional representation of creolelike Negro speech in the Northern colonies,[36] and to the evidence from Nova Scotia,[37] this amounts to a rather impressive amount of evidence that the early stages of Black English vernacular were associated with slavery and not with any particular region.

When slavery lost its economic appeal to the Northern colonies, they became strongly abolitionist in sentiment, as had Great Britain before them—and for the same reason. But the states that had abolished slavery were not necessarily strong on tolerance, as Alexis de Tocqueville early noted:

> The prejudice of race appears to be stronger in the states which have abolished slavery than in those where it still exists, and nowhere is it so important as in those states where servitude never has been known.[38]

Although de Tocqueville might have been hard pressed to name those states "where servitude never has been known," the general truth of his basic observation is attested by other observers. Segregation—a potentially great factor in maintaining language differences—often remained strongly in force in the "free" states.

With the heavy concentrations of slaves in the Southern states (associated, originally, with the predominance of agriculture in those states) and with the greater opportunities for assimilation that obtained in the North, Black English became, to a great degree, a Southern dialect. It seems to have very strongly influenced the speech of Southern whites, particularly those of the plantation-owning class.[39] But some indications of varieties of Black English spoken well into the nineteenth century remain in the Northern states.[40] In fact, only those who worked with the preconceived assurance that American English dialects were basically and intrinsically geographic could advance the theory that Black English had died out in places like Harlem before the migrations immediately after World Wars I and II introduced a less decreolized variety into the Northern cities.

For Afro-American anthropology and Black cultural studies, the status of Black English vernacular (including its early history) is of the utmost importance. It has even been suggested that the symbolic system of English prevented any significant African transmissions in such areas as religion and folklore:

> Apart from such isolated cases . . . the African impress upon the English language was negligible. Everywhere English became the accepted method of communication and English folk beliefs and superstitions were given an enormous advantage over African forms.[41]

The above statement is quoted by Norman Whitten in his 1962 article "Contemporary Patterns of Malign Occultism Among Negroes in North Carolina" (*Journal of American Folklore*, 1962) as a key argument to prove that the belief patterns of Negroes derive basically from England.

If it is true that a language system exerts such a strong influence on a belief system and, further, that the English spoken by Blacks in the United States has always been essentially a form of British-derived English, then it would follow that American Blacks' folklore and beliefs are essentially European. But both of Whitten's premises (the latter of which is borrowed from Puckett) are highly suspect—and, indeed, probably false. Therefore, students of pluralism in American culture can continue to rely on the theoretical work of the great Afro-American anthropologist Melville J. Herskovits (*The Myth of the Negro Past*, 1942) and on such practical work as that of LeRoi Jones (*Blues People*), Marshall Stearns (*The Story of Jazz*), and Alan Lomax (see Bibliography), all of which provide extensive evidence of African influence in areas where Whitten and Dorson (see Bibliography) deny the possibility of such influence.

The West Africans who were brought to the Americas

retained traces of their original tongues through the medium of a lingua franca that developed among slaves and slave traders. A similar situation existed among the Chinese brought in as exploited labor in the mid-nineteenth century, and the use of Chinese Pidgin English in the gold rush and thereafter is well attested. In marked contrast, Pennsylvania Germans, Chicanos, Cajuns, Jews, and certain other groups which had a great deal of integral cohesiveness from the beginning, have maintained their ethnic languages and/or dialects as a function of their group solidarity. The West Africans, on the other hand, had a bewildering diversity of languages and cultures, although some common currents can be found in them.[42] The obtuseness of the Europeans, who saw only the skin color and heard only a strange speech, kept them from realizing how diverse the Africans were. Yet tribal animosities persisted, in some cases, into the period of slavery in the New World.[43]

For the Blacks, the complexity of the language contact situation demanded the use of Pidgin English and the retention of Creole for a long period. The "visibility" of black skins plus the color-caste system, which accompanied and extended far beyond slavery, further impeded the chances for assimilation (including linguistic assimilation) for all but a relatively small portion of the descendants of West Africans. Thus, these involuntary "immigrants" were the furthest from the simplistic language assimilation paradigm. Their only real "competitors" in this unprofitable contest would be the American Indians, an almost equally "visible" group.

Slave labor was a major requirement of the Europeans who came to the Americas in the colonial period. As everyone knows, West Africans were the primary victims of that exploitation. But before the Africans were brought, the Europeans attempted—usually with only marginal success—to enslave American Indians, either to work in mines or to till the soil.

Long before the appearance of the Europeans, the Indians had worked out solutions to their own language contact problems, which stemmed from the fact that there were many different North American Indian languages belonging, it appears now, to language families that are only distantly related, if at all. There was, however, a basic difference in the solutions found by the coastal Indians and the plains Indians.

The coastal Indians seem to have evolved at least one lingua franca of their own.[44] J. Dyneley Prince found evidence, in a manuscript he judged to be from the late seventeenth century, for

> a Trader's Jargon, used between the Delaware River whites and the Indians, almost grammarless and based chiefly on English construction, like the Chinook and Eskimo traders' idioms of the North.[45]

Prince was a talented researcher with wide-ranging interests, but his linguistics were old-fashioned even in 1912. No one should have described a language variety as "grammarless" unless he meant that the words and other forms occurred in purely random order. And Prince is far from proving that the "jargon's" grammar came from English. (As far as that goes, he seems to be wrong about Chinook jargon, also.) But he presents interesting data like the occurrence of *kabay*, 'horse', from Spanish or Portuguese; *hodi*, 'farewell' (compared to the English *howdy* by Prince himself); *pone*, 'bread'; English *me* for the first-person singular subject pronoun; *paia*, 'fire', from English by regular phonological development (Prince compares Chinook jargon *piah*, 'fire'); and *brandywyne*, 'rum'. The Algonquian words *squaw*, 'wife', and *papouse* (*sic*, for *papoose*), 'a suckling child', suggest the beginnings of a pattern, which would later become quite general.

Apparently, the Indian "jargon" Prince discovered had been mixed with some Europeanisms by the seventeenth century. But it is in the main Indian. It, with other evidence, suggests that a natural solution to the language contact problems posed by the polyglot nature of the Eastern tribes had been reached before the Europeans arrived.

The plains Indians, on the other hand, utilized the well-known sign language. There are, however, considerable numbers of testimonies that it was "a sealed book to the coastal and mountain tribes [but] understood by all the Indians of the plains."[46] This means of communication continued to be used until the late nineteenth century. Bourke observed how some Crows communicated with the other Indian tribes:

> Squatting upon the ground, with fingers and hands deftly moving, they communicated through the "sign language" . . . things which would astonish persons ignorant of the scope and power of this silent vehicle for the interchange of thought.[47]

It is very likely that the coming of outside groups like the Europeans and the African slaves fostered the gradual relinquishing of sign language in favor of a spoken version of a contact variety—Pidgin English. Later, the Indians found Pidgin English useful in contact with the Chinese who came in around the time of the gold rush and who, like the Blacks, were more willing to relate to the Indians as peers than were the Europeans. There was also the problem of coping with Spanish and French as well as English, especially in the South and West. The American Indians found themselves in the European Lingua Franca tradition, once removed.

Although the earlier attestations of American Indian Pidgin English antedate those of any other Pidgin English variety,[48] it is significant that they regularly turn up about ten years after the introduction of West African slaves into the area of the Indians.[49] The Africans had even earlier experience with the Europeans and the language contact problems they introduced. In *Black English* (1972), I argued that Pidgin English was transmitted from the Africans to the Indians, and further investigations have strengthened that belief. Europeans, who by and large were never masters of the Indian language "jargons," may have assisted the process because they were better able to deal with Pidgin English. The mixing of the plains Indians with the coastal Indians, who had been forced to migrate, produced a stand-off in which neither the sign language of the former nor the Indian "jargon" of the latter could dominate, and Pidgin English was a kind of compromise. Furthermore, the Black slaves, who had to use Pidgin (Creole) English in their own group and who carried it with them when they escaped to the "wild" Indians or worked beside the "tame" ones on plantations[50] were an important force in extending Pidgin English still further.

Certain linguistic features common to West African and American Indian Pidgin varieties of English virtually preclude independent origin. Among these are the use of preverbal auxiliary *been* (*Him been go*), the *-um* postverbal transitivizer (*Heap big chief drinkum fire water*), the use of *spose* (generally assumed to be a "corrupt" pronunciation of *suppose*) in the meaning 'if', and *bimeby* (often spelled *by and by*) as a future-time adverbial. The West African Pidgin English word *grandy*, as a general intensifier, was replaced by *heap* in American Indian Pidgin English. Before human nouns, it becomes *heap big.*[51] Otherwise, West African Pidgin English and American Indian Pidgin English share the general characteristics of Pidgin English everywhere, including the overrated simplification that makes *goes* into *go*.

Although sign language generally gave way to Pidgin English, it did not disappear completely. Many Indians developed a proficiency in both. Black Beaver, whose fluency in sign language is attested in the same source (see below), was quoted in Pidgin English by Colonel R. B. Marcy:

"Bob Jones [a rich Chickasaw] he say, s'pose find um copper mine, give um four hundred dollars."

"I s'pect maybe so I not go, Captain."

"Delaware law, s'pose show um 'Merican mine, kill um."[52]

In addition to the auxiliary language, each Indian had, of course, full competence in his native language.

Although frontiersmen and other observers did not know what to *call* American Indian Pidgin English, they recorded many examples of it. Famed Indian painter Catlin recalled:

"You white man, where you come from?"

"How white man come to England? How you face come to get white, ha?"

"Among white people, no body ever take your wife— take your children—take your mother, cut off nose —cut eyes out—burn to death."

"No!" "Then *you* no cut off nose—*you* no cut out eyes— *you* no burn to death—very good."[53]

Another of its recorders, Thomas Woodward, who quoted a rather long passage in Pidgin English from an Indian (*Woodward's Reminiscences of the Creek or Muscogee Indians*, 1859) knew no name for the variety either. But he felt compelled to meet the objections of those who might doubt his accuracy:

Now the above is an Indian speech, and no doubt will appear silly to some who have not been accustomed to these people. Should it, however, fall under the eye of those who were along at the time, they will recognize John's speech, and call to mind our old friends. (p. 70)

The many attestations of this Indian variety are full of such familiar expressions as "Ugh!" [Uxʔ], "How!" and

"Heap." Many of us learned long ago to regard these as fabrications of the movies. It begins to appear, however, that some movies utilized reasonably good historical background material. Reports of all three words, and many other such familiar "Indian" expressions, are commonplace in the historical literature. They go back at least as far as Jean-Bernard Bossu's travels in 1751–62:

> The [Indian] audience replied with shouts of "How! How!" which means, "True! True!"[54]

In more recent times, there is testimony from Jay Silverheels, a Mohawk Indian who just happens to have played Tonto, the Lone Ranger's unfortunately named sidekick. Silverheels, founder of an Indian actors' workshop and a student of the language and culture of his own people, has defended the character of Tonto, who among other things spoke American Indian Pidgin English.[55]

Statements about use of sign language are much easier to find than statements about the use of Pidgin English, probably because most of the reporters thought the Indians who spoke Pidgin were simply using "bad" English. An occasional coincidence tells us more than the observers realized. For example, more than one source reported about the Indian named Black Beaver and his communicative abilities:

> Black Beaver's ability to hold communication with different tribes whom the exploring party met was not due to any knowledge of the oral language of those tribes, but to use of the sign language, which is universally understood by all the Indians of the plains, but which is a sealed book to the Coast and Mountain tribes.[56]

But the same sources also quoted Black Beaver, described as "a Delaware living the last years of his life on the Washita" who "had long experience in the Northwest":

> "Captain, I no tell him that Indian no fool and he know that not true, for I see heap and know that one big lie, for

104

I live with white man long time and no see thing like that."[57]

As a matter of fact, the source of the last two quotations, historian E. C. Campbell, is a kind of textbook case. He defends sign language as "more than an elaboration of gestures ordinarily used by every person"[58] and stigmatizes Pidgin English as an example of the Indians' inability to correlate the pronouns used by the white man with the subject:

> My sister, he say.
> Bob Dunlap, she mighty good man.[59]

English gradually came to replace Spanish as the primary language for governing and dealing with the Indians as Anglo-Americans took the leading roles in planning campaigns against the "wild" Indians (the Navajos and the Apaches, for example) and in planning for the future of the "civilized" ones (like the Pueblos). Under the influence of Indian scouts like Kit Carson and military men like Colonel William Donovan, even the making of treaties came to be in English. Of course, a treaty was an official document which might be sent back to Washington and which would be in the most formal, schoollike English of which its framers were capable. Such informal records as we have tend to show, on the other hand, that Pidgin English was the variety in which Anglo-Indian interactions most often took place.

Formal government sponsorship of the use of English among the Indians of the Southwest began around 1870. Before that, American policy with regard to the area had been limited to consolidating the U.S. military position. It had been necessary not only to cope with the Indians (and their refusal to see the pattern of "Manifest Destiny") but also to plant bulwarks against possible Confederate power in the West. Not insignificantly, some of the first attempts at responsible administration of the area—favorable to the Indians in a way, despite obvious paternalism—came under

President Grant, who had been a part of the army most concerned with preventing the Confederate spread.

In the days before cultural relativism had begun to penetrate even the most advanced academic circles, the primary concerns were, of course, converting the Indians to Christianity and "educating" them—that is, bringing the white man's type of schooling to them. Missionaries were also teachers, and few if any of them emulated John Eliot and Roger Williams, who in an earlier century had tried to bring Christianity to the Indians in the Indians' native languages.

With the prevailing ideas about good English, it is a safe bet that the missionary-teachers did not utilize—or probably even tolerate—American Indian Pidgin English, in the schoolrooms or out. Thus the foundations (linguistic and otherwise) were laid for the current situation, in which the Bureau of Indian Affairs "helps" the Indians by providing for them what the white men want them to have. It would not, of course, have occurred to them that anything but their universal insistence upon the English language was feasible, advisable, or morally tolerable.

How much attention the Anglo-American teachers gave to the language background of their Indian students is in an absolute sense unknowable; but the records we have make us believe that it could seldom have been very great. In *Western Wilds,* John Beadle gives an account of the activities of the Reverend W. S. Robertson at a mission where the teachers of the Creeks (Uchee, Natchee, Alabama) were selected and paid by the Presbyterian Board of Home Missions. For Beadle's benefit, two Uchee boys were set to conversing in their native language while Beadle sat and played the virtuoso phonologist by watching their lips:

> It [the Uchee language] is entirely devoid of labials; for five minutes they touched the lips together but once. It also rarely requires the dentals; and thus to a Uchee it is almost impossible to distinguish between *b* and *p, d* and *t,* or *a* and *e.* This inability produces most ludicrous results

in spelling. Pronouncing the words to be spelled orally, the teacher can not possibly determine in the quick sound whether the spelling is correct or not—that is, with Uchee beginners. But, when they come to write it on the slate, bat becomes *p-e-t*, hat *h-e-d*, bad *b-e-t*, etc.[60]

Elsewhere, we are told of teachers who had to teach Indian children, not one of whom knew a word of English —obviously an impossible handicap for the poor teacher! Implicit in these reports is the notion that English is the normal language of instruction, and that those who cannot manage English in a native-speaker fashion are deficient in some way.

By some weird stroke of genius, someone thought of boarding schools for Indians. According to Spicer,[61] the first was Hampton Institute in Virginia where, mixing with Negroes, the Indians were able to continue their historical association with Plantation Creole. By 1881 Hampton had Pimas, Papagos, and Apaches from the Southwest, as well as more easterly tribes. Carlisle Institute, founded in 1879 by General Pratt, had some two hundred students from the Southwest (Apaches, Navajos, and Pueblos) by 1885. Nearer to home in the Southwest, boarding schools were established at Albuquerque in 1884, at Tucson in 1888, at Santa Fe and Fort Mojave in 1890, at Phoenix in 1891, and near Riverside, California, in 1892. Obviously these tribally mixed boarding schools were happy hunting grounds for Pidgin English; and some unwary educators and educationists still report how it is "springing up" in tribally mixed boarding schools today. Spicer reports, with a naïveté surprising for one of his otherwise apparent sophistication:

> A sort of boarding school dialect of English developed, recognizable as a "foreign" version of English, but still perfectly intelligible to non-Indians.[62]

Whether it was at all times perfectly intelligible to those who had not learned Pidgin English is still a moot point.

According to Spicer, the great majority of all Indians who attended the white man's schools from 1878 until 1900 were in those boarding schools with their mixed-language environment. And although Spicer doesn't say this, such environments are perfect for the spread and perpetuation of the contact variety, Pidgin English. The situation did not come to an end with the turn of the century. In 1917 there were 6,949 young Indians at a linguistically impressionable age, from New Mexico, Arizona, Utah, and Nevada in the boarding schools. Spicer guesses that within fifty years of the inauguration of the church-dominated school program at least one-tenth of the Arizona and New Mexico Indians had been enrolled for greater or lesser periods.

For the other nine-tenths, there were different kinds of contact situations with nearly the same results. John C. Cremony's *Life Among the Apaches* (1868) quotes a typical Indian conversation:

> You good man. You stay here long time and never hurt Apache. You want the 'yellow iron'; I know where plenty is. Suppose [if] you go with me, I show you, but tell no one else. Mangas your friend, he want to do you good. You like 'yellow iron'—good! Me no want 'yellow iron.' Him no good for me—can no eat, can no drink, can no keepee out cold. Come, I show you.[63]

The partial assimilation, economic and linguistic, which was to cost the Indian dearly in years to come is, of course, obvious in such a quotation.

The Bureau of Indian Affairs was blissfully unaware of the linguistic realities and convinced that all those Indians were receiving the "civilizing" influence of (Standard) English and were being taken away from their "vernaculars." Spicer quotes a rule of the commissioner in 1887:

> Instruction of Indians in the vernacular is not only of no use to them but is detrimental to the cause of education and civilization and will not be permitted in any Indian school over which the government has any control . . . It

is believed that if any Indian vernacular is allowed to be taught by missionaries in schools on Indian reservations it will prejudice the pupil as well as his parents against the English language . . . This language which is good enough for a white man or a black man [irony!] ought to be good enough for the red man. It is also believed that teaching an Indian youth in his own barbarous dialect is a positive detriment to him. The impracticability, if not impossibility of civilizing Indians of this country in any other tongue but our own would seem obvious. (p. 301)

In more recent times, especially the 1970's, bilingual education programs have brought some sophistication to that narrow linguistic view. But they, like the Bureau of Indian Affairs in an earlier century, have grossly failed to realize what variety there is within the "one language" English.

Beyond the relative naïveté of the reports a typical sociolinguistic distribution begins to become apparent. Among the "bilinguals" to whom Spicer refers so optimistically, most were users, in descending order of competence, of:

The Indian language (the "vernacular")
Pidgin English
Standard English (the language of the schools)

That part of their linguistic behavior that was most on public view was probably carried out through the medium of Standard English, often by unofficially designated spokesmen who were more proficient than the average in Standard English. That is what Spicer apparently means when he says:

They interpreted what was going on to their relatives and friends in the Indian communities as they heard or read about it in English.[64]

Since there was nothing written in Pidgin English, "English" here must mean Standard English—as almost always in the works of educators.

There was, however, an occasional writer like the Cherokee poet, philosopher, and farmer War Bow, who wrote:

WAR BOW HEAP FARM
by War Bow, Blanket Indian
Colony, Oklahoma

War Bow think he goin' to farm;
Like country life, got plenty of charm;
He goin' to raise it, plenty of corn
Will heap much plow in early morn.[65]

War Bow, who was obviously educated and knew Standard as well as Pidgin English, addressed the accompanying letter to "Honorable Commissioner, Indian Affairs, Cato Sells."

Pidgin English and literacy were not, it is obvious, mutually exclusive. Bourke reports how an Apache proudly showed off his literacy by writing:

MY WIFE HIM NAME KOWTENNAY'S WIFE
ONE YEAR HAB TREE HUNNERD SIXTY-FIBE DAY.[66]

With the considerable aid of the Pidgin, English progressed more rapidly among Southwestern Indians than Spanish had. According to Spicer, the knowledge of English was much more extensive after seventy-five years of contact, even among the Sonoran tribes, than knowledge of Spanish had been after two hundred years of exposure. (What is missing from such a statement, obviously, and what has never been investigated in conventional treatment, is an evaluation of what role contact varieties—perhaps of languages other than Spanish—may have played in the earlier situation.) The school could, in a sense, claim some of the credit for the spread of English; but, to a degree hardly realized by anyone, the language contact of the dormitories was a more effective agent than the contact of the classroom. Spicer estimates that the learning of Spanish ("except for the acquisition of a few Spanish words by Navajos in a largely hostile situation in Northern Arizona") had ended by 1850.

Other Indians in other parts of the nation, specifically the Northwest, found another solution to the language contact problem in a variety known as Chinook Jargon. Like other contact varieties, Chinook Jargon picked up words from many sources. One of its better known derivatives, *Siwash*, may come ultimately from the French *sauvage*. It mixed with the Pidgin English which moved west and north, so that one cannot always be sure whether an early text from the area is Pidgin English or translated Chinook Jargon (although, on the other hand, it probably made no practical difference of the kind that an actual speaker would pay any attention to). At any rate, one is forever being mistaken for another by the commentators on and visitors to the area. Besides *Siwash*, general American English picked up *skookum* from Chinook Jargon.

But there was more to it than that in the earlier period, since Chinook Jargon was a very important language in the Pacific Northwest. Like the other languages of its general type, it was especially accessible to those who were immigrating or migrating, whether of their own volition or not.

As more recent historical studies have shown, many who came in as "voluntary" immigrants existed in the United States under conditions little better than slavery. Among these, the Chinese obviously had much in common with the other "colored" American populations, the Blacks and the Indians. Not officially classified as slaves at any time, they were exploited and mistreated to a degree that left them little enjoyment of their "freedom." They had, however, independence of spirit enough to demand their rights, as in the following Pidgin English assertion from Nee and Nee, *Longtime Californ'*:

> Eight hours a day good for white man, all the same good
> for Chinaman. *(p. 41)*

Although the travel of the Chinese was more nearly willing migration than that of the Blacks or Indians, they were frequently taken advantage of by unscrupulous contractors and shipped to places where they had no desire to go. Although their greatest concentrations were on the West Coast, they had penetrated to most parts of the United States by the third quarter of the nineteenth century.

The story of the post–gold rush Chinese in the American West has been told before. (For something on the language, see *Black English*, Chapter IV.) Reports, emphasized far beyond their importance, have been made of translations into Chinese Pidgin English of Longfellow's *Excelsior* ("Topside, Galah!") and "My Name is Norval."[67] But Chinese Pidgin English was generally characteristic of more degrading pursuits than poetry.

Among other things, Chinese women were, before legal restrictions were placed on their importation, frequently exploited as prostitutes. Herbert Asbury's *The Barbary Coast* (1933) describes the prostitution scene in San Francisco around 1869. He quotes Chinese prostitutes:

> "China girl nice! You come inside please."
> "Your father, he just go out."[68]

Asbury explains the second strange approach in terms of Chinese custom by which it was a great honor for a young man to have intercourse with the same girl as his father. But his most interesting quotation, to me, is:

> "Two bittee lookee, flo bittee feelee, six bittee dooe!"[69]

This matches almost exactly a brothel token in my collection from the China Doll in Dodge City, a gift from William A. Stewart (who got it at an antique shop) :

> 10¢ Lookie
> 25¢ Feelie
> 50¢ Dooie

The "contact" patterns of ethnic groups on the frontier and in the West were obviously multifarious, but the vehicle of contact was usually Pidgin English.

Whether because they had no opportunity to learn the

koiné-derived American Standard English or because the sociolinguistic rules of their community or ethnic group forbade it, there are still many groups in the United States that retain markedly "nonstandard" varieties of English. Some of these can be directly related to the "old-country" language their ancestors brought over. More often, the more complex and less direct factors in language contact are responsible. But to leave them out of the history of American English is to leave out most of the people who speak it.

IV
FRONTIER
SPEECHWAYS

———————————◆•◆—————————————

THE "TRUE-BORN AMERICAN" IMMIGRANT WHO CAME TO THE frontier found it not empty linguistically but teeming with life. The language situation was not, however, designed for his convenience; at first, he did not dominate it. Gradually, he won control, as the European had done on the west coast of Africa a century or two before. But in the beginning there were many times when the British-derived white migrant to the West had to adjust to a language contact situation not of his own making and not made for him. This extreme linguistic situation left its mark on the speech of the American frontiersman and to some degree of all subsequent Americans.

In many ways, the multilingual situation and other social

factors of the frontier resembled what the frontiersman's British ancestor had run into at sea in the situation described in Chapter I. The movement characteristic of the new American society and the relationships of the frontier brought speakers of American English back into contact with the language problems of the European maritime expansion.[1]

The sea is, of course, as Archer B. Hulbert put it in *Frontiers, The Genius of American Nationality,* "the oldest frontier known to man." And the movement over vast, thinly populated areas, the strangeness of the relatively few people with whom the travelers came into contact, the daring (and sometimes quasi-criminal) element that made up the exploring groups, the necessity for accumulating and carrying along provisions for the entire trip, the emergencies encountered when additional supplies became necessary—all were conditions common to travel across both the oceans and the prairies.

Even some of the terminology was the same. In a strikingly significant metaphor, the large wagons with canvas hoods used by the settlers entering the West were called *prairie schooners. Caboose,* the Dutch maritime borrowing for 'cook's cabin or galley',[2] was first used for the cook wagon, then for a stationary cook house, and finally for the car on the train that contained the provisions and the facilities for cooking them. The rangeland name for the food carrier was the well-known *chuck wagon,* which seems suspiciously like the British Navy's *chuck barge,* the bread bin or cask in which the ship's biscuits are kept. Layton's dictionary also identifies *chuck* as "lower deck and civilian slang for 'bread'." The familiar Westernism, *cache,* 'a hiding place', is recorded first in the *Voyages of Sir Francis Drake* (1595): "The inhabitants hid their treasure in casshes."[3]

Frontier thinking died hard in the United States, vide the New Frontier slogan of President John F. Kennedy. Mencken, whose perceptions tend to become more and more impressive in retrospect, saw the importance of the concept:

The old American Frontier, of course, had vanished by the end of the nineteenth century, but it is not to be forgotten that, to the immigrants who poured in after 1850, even the slums of the great Eastern cities presented what were reasonably describable as frontier conditions, and that there were still cultural, if not geographic, frontiers at Hollywood and Miami, not to mention Oklahoma, Nevada, and Mississippi.[4]

The frontier was the defining characteristic of the United States during all the period specified by Mencken, and it is to the frontier that we must look for the significant developments in language history.[5]

Linguistically, the American population never became the kind of sedentary, long-settled group that is described in most of the works on language history.[6] In order to understand the development of American English, we cannot limit ourselves to the British-derived Americans, as though they were alone and worked out their own language development with only minor influences from elsewhere.

Conventional histories, in their concern with the claims and counterclaims of the European nations to the "new" continent, find it all too easy to overlook the fact that two of the most prominent groups with which the "white" Europeans came into contact were the American Indians and the West Africa-derived slaves. They concentrate on the taking of the Louisiana territory from the French and the Texas territory from the Spanish (or Mexicans), overlooking the fact that the Europeans were all usurpers of lands from the Indians and that all of them utilized the involuntary services of Blacks.[7]

These overlooked relationships had their equally overlooked linguistic consequences. The Blacks especially were important participants in the language contact situation that grew out of the European expansion and utilized the lingua franca of the maritime trade; they themselves added a great deal to the lingua franca tradition.[8] Indoctrinated into that hard-knocks school of translation, they were able to act as interpreters for the whites on many parts of the frontier.[9]

Sometimes the slave interpreters knew the native language of the Indian group that had to be dealt with. Often they did not, and it was necessary to conduct negotiations through an intermediate language. In parts of the Southwest, what is often called "bad" Spanish in the documents served that lingua-franca function. Brevet Brigadier General James F. Rusling, whose *Across America; or, the Great West and the Pacific Coast* (1875) records many such incidents, tells how, in an attempt to converse with some Indians, "our driver, Worth, came to our rescue, with some mongrel Spanish he had picked up, when soldiering formerly down in Arizona."[10] But many of the Americans who crossed the plains simply had to learn to cope with diverse Indian groups themselves, without the luxury of an interpreter. Gustav Dresel's *Houston Journal* (1838) relates such an incident:

> The old man understood some words of English and Spanish, and I was acquainted with some telling Indian expressions, so that with the assistance of the sign language I could make myself understood without any interpreter.[11]

An example of the speech of the Alabama Indian concerned is given:

> "No, gshaw, papeshillo; plata, plata, shocke ma fina!"
> ("That is nothing, man; silver, silver is fine, good the sterling.")[12]

Frequently, the Indians' knowledge of Pidgin (usually called "broken") English helped out. In 1849 traveler Grant Foreman reported the case of a Kickapoo who acted as interpreter because he "could speak a little broken English." The quoted phrase is conventional in such reports, but the attestation given indicates the ability of the interpreter to speak more than "a little":

> Me friends; maybe so well we all find a grave today, all go one way; Comanche may be so fight, and may be so

friendly; we must no run not be fraid. Sometime I fight Camanch [*sic*] wid only tree or four; but we sixteen, and hab plenty guns. We heap! we no run!

My boy may be so better man than me; he no scare; may be so me little scare in here. We must no let Camanch see us fraid.[13]

Impressively often, in the Southwest especially, the Pidgin English seems to be mixed with Spanish. In the late nineteenth century, John G. Bourke wrote that "The Apache scouts, however, insisted that we were to find a 'heap' of Indians 'poco tiempo' (very soon)."[14] In his *Across America* Brigadier General Rusling provides some relatively late examples, like that of an Indian identified only as Charley:

Me been playin' cards till now! Charley gamble a heap! *Mucho! O mui mucho!* Lost all. Coat, hat, shirt all gone. Me beggar now; got nothing.

Rusling further reports the conclusion of an Indian pow-wow held in Pidgin English:

This was followed by a general expression of "Bueno! Bueno!" by the rest of the Indians, and so the powwow ended.

Rusling had still another encounter, this time with an Indian who addressed Rusling's group:

"Ugh! White man."
To which we, in true Arizona dialect, responded
"How! Buenos días, Señor."
His dignified and elegant answer was
"Heap good! 'Bacco? Matches?"

This interview concluded with a favorable statement from the Indian, "Pimos! Americanos! Much friends! Mui mucho."

The language mixing evidenced by the Indians may not, however, have been anything so simple as a mere Spanish admixture. Prince's cited *kabay*[15] and other evidence seems to indicate that the American Indian lingua franca tradition crossed fairly early with the Romance lingua franca tradition of the European maritime trade. Some otherwise seemingly innocent evidence attests to this kind of relationship. Historian Josiah Gregg, writing in 1844, reports on the Indian use of the word *capitan*, noting:

> Most of the prairie Indians seem to have learned this Spanish word, by which, when talking with the whites, all their Chiefs are designated.[16]

But it is an open question whether this *capitan* (or *kabay*) really comes from Spanish. Similar words were learned by other populations, as is the case, for example, with the Black slaves of Haiti, where through Eurocentrism a very similar form is often assigned to "French" origin. Douglas Taylor, the great authority on Caribbean Creole languages, has written in a very important article:

> And had the slaves arrived in the French islands speaking nothing but their native African languages, it is most unlikely that the Frenchmen there should have taught them words like *capitou* (cf. Ptg. *capitão*) 'chieftain, leader'.[17]

The anthropologist Richard Price reports that the undoubtedly related *kabiteni*, 'village headman', is used in Saramaccan, the English Creole of the deep bush in Surinam which has about as much Portuguese vocabulary as English.[18]

Such explicit statements as are to be found in travel accounts, like this one from 1846, predictably refer to the Romance element in the mixture as Spanish:

> We were visited by a half-breed Delaware Indian named Charley Tirrell, who spoke very fair English, although strangely mixed with Spanish and Indian idioms.[19]

The statements that occur in fiction provide considerable additional evidence. Dion Boucicault's *The Octoroon; or, Life in Louisiana* features an important Indian character named Wahnotee with whom the whites have difficulty in communicating. In Act I one of them reports explicitly: "He don't understand; he speaks a mash-up of Indian and Mexican." The same character addresses Wahnotee: "Wahnotee Patira na sepau assa wagiran." The second word certainly seems Spanish (a version of *partirá*, 'he will leave') and the last three words seem believably "Indian," at least for dramatic purposes; but *na*, which certainly means 'to' in this context, is more nearly Portuguese Creole, from which it has spread to some of the other Creole languages.

Elsewhere, Wahnotee utilizes—and those who speak to him utilize—a great deal of French vocabulary. Threatened with a gun, he begs another character, "No tue Wahnotee," where *tue* is obviously a version of a French word meaning 'kill'; but the grammar is not French at all. He also objects to a weapon on the grounds that "No, carabine tue." Still another character informs Wahnotee that "Closky tue Paul," reporting an incident in which one Jacob M'Closky had killed Wahnotee's friend named Paul. Wahnotee at one point uses the word *fire-water* to describe rum. He even uses sign language to some extent.

Evidence like the speech of the fictional character Wahnotee cannot be overlooked, for it bears upon one overwhelmingly important factor, not entirely absent from other areas but not focused in them the way it was in the Southwest— the contact and conflict with Spanish and its speakers:

> As the English frontier moved westward, the Anglo-Spanish borders overlapped in a succession of areas, and one by one a series of conflicts resulted—in the Caribbean, in Georgia, in Florida, in Louisiana, in Texas, in New Mexico, in California.[20]

And the evidence of Louisiana Indians, as fictionally typified by Wahnotee, recalls the necessity of accounting for French and for American Indian languages in the total picture. The usual assumption has been that ad hoc strategies were worked out in each of these encounters; but in view of what is known about the language contact process in general, it is worthwhile to examine whatever continuities may have existed between the Southwest and other areas.

Pidgin English had spread to the Southwest by the time of the Anglo-Spanish conflicts in Texas. Gustav Dresel's *Houston Journal* (quoted above, p. 118) quotes a Coushatta Indian: "You good man, you papeshillo [glossed in a footnote as 'man'], you Dutchman." Even from this evidence, it is reasonably certain that more languages than Spanish and English entered into the competition of languages in the Southwest.

Three stages are discernible in the Spanish-English contact in Texas and the Southwest. During the first there was a contact with several languages, including French and Indian languages, in addition to Spanish. The second was the bilingual period in which some Texans learned the cattle-ranching trade in Spanish from Mexicans. In the third, the current situation, "Anglo" Texans are aloof from any Spanish influence.

Shortly after the Louisiana Purchase (1803), citizens of the United States began moving beyond that newly won territory into areas owned by Mexico. Between 1809 and 1818, the Mexican government seems actually to have encouraged such migration. It did, however, attempt to lower the preponderance of "Americans" by encouraging the immigration of groups like the Germans.[21] Mexican officials seem to have believed that many of the immigrants were at odds with their state or federal government. The troubles that came upon the Mexican government soon afterward—the loss of territory and the quick political changes by which Texas became a part of the United States—are too well known to need retelling here. But there are apparent contradictions in the language contact history which still need to be resolved.

The entrepreneur Moses Austin, who led his followers into Texas in the early years of the nineteenth century, intended a fully orthodox migration. He recognized the need for his followers to know Spanish. He sent one son to Mexico to study; and his more famous son, Stephen F. Austin, frequently corresponded in a highly unidiomatic Spanish which was in effect a word-for-word translation from English. Although census data are not available, it is unlikely that the masses of Americans who came in with Stephen F. Austin were more proficient in standard Spanish than their leader. Texas was not the first stop in their migration, so these pioneers of the first stage of language contact were the ones most likely to have used a lingua franca. Since they passed through Louisiana, we might even consider whether it was anything like the "mishmash" used by Wahnotee.

Many of them did make an earnest attempt to assimilate to the language and culture of Mexico. Stephen F. Austin ultimately agreed—no doubt more to avoid pressure than from conviction—that all his followers would become Catholics and attend mass.[22] They were accused of being insincere Catholics and subsequently defended by one Padre Sosa on the grounds that their Spanish was too defective to enable them to become really good Catholics (since they did not understand the language used at religious services) and that they were too busy working to have any opportunity to learn "good" Spanish.[23] For a time, at any rate, the situation now current in Texas, New Mexico, and Arizona was reversed; English-speaking people lived in large numbers in an area where the official language was Spanish. What they actually used makes up an interesting part of the history.

As late as 1842–44, Texan "Anglos" were still reported as swearing in "bad Spanish" at the depredations of Mexican soldiers. But many kinds of language can be called "bad Spanish"; the term used to be applied regularly to Papiamentu, the Portuguese-based Creole of Aruba, Bonaire, and Curaçao. Ever since the seventeenth century, according to reports from travelers like Philadelphian slave dealer Jonathan Dickinson,[24] English-speaking Americans had used something like Spanish in their contacts with Indians as well as with native speakers of the Iberian language. Dickinson records the word *totus*, which may be just a nonnative speaker's way of recording a nonnative-speaking Indian's pronunciation of *todos*, 'all'. But Dickinson also recorded an Indian's saying *Nickaleer, no comerradoe*, 'Englishmen were not his friends', an utterance that uses words from a kind of general Romance lexicon but not specifically from Spanish. In fact, it seems more nearly in the lingua franca tradition, which has some intimate historical connection with the development of Creoles (Portuguese-, English-, French-, and Spanish-based) in the Americas and elsewhere.[25]

In the border area between Louisiana and Texas, painter George Catlin observed, around the year 1850:

> And then a "talk" was held, in which we were aided by a Spaniard we luckily had with us, who could converse with one of the Camanches [Comanches] who spoke some Spanish.[26]

The term "some Spanish" is, of course, as ambiguous as "a little English" in many travelers' descriptions of contact situations (in some of which it clearly means Pidgin English). But even at that time Spanish and Spaniards were to some extent the go-betweens where Anglo-Americans and Indians were concerned. In other cases, it is hard to tell from the records whether the words used by the Indians represented Spanish or English: the Indian squaws who were asking for "sooker" in Kansas in 1858 (as quoted in Richardson in *Beyond the Mississippi*) could as easily have been seeking *azúcar* as *sugar*. From the point of view of the Indian, the point was to communicate with the European; a word that was not *either* Spanish or English but *both* would be ideal. The word, as an approximation of *sucre*, might even have communicated to a Frenchman.

Occasionally, recorded Spanish utterances have some of the characteristics of Pidgin languages—for example, the zero copula (omission of a verb, especially the verb *to be*, in a linking function, as in *They free* for *They are free*). That particular structure is foreign to known dialects of Spanish. J. Ross Browne, in *A Tour through Arizona, or Adventures in the Apache Country* (1864), recorded, "No tira! Yo amigo!" As even high-school students of Spanish must know, *soy amigo* is a much more likely form than *yo amigo* in non-contact Spanish. Failure of subject-verb concord, as in Rusling's *Tu no vale nada* (ordinary Spanish *Tu no vales nada*, 'You aren't worth anything') and failures of adjective-noun agreement like *bueno noche* (for *buenas noches*, 'good night') may be just failures to learn Spanish. Rusling reports that he was studying Spanish from a phrase book at the time. But the Creoles dispense with verb endings, and Spanish-influenced Papiamentu uses phrases like *vaca gordo* (ordinary Spanish *vaca gorda*, 'fat cow').

Further north, in Nebraska, a traveler from the East, Mollie Dorsey, reported around 1860:

> They [Indian women] immediately surrounded me and began their gibberish of "Wano Squaw," "Wano White squaw" (good squaw).[27]

Historian Josiah Gregg found a Comanche, closer to the South, who "informed us that some of his party had a few mulas para *swap*" (mules to trade).[28] Considering that *mulas* and *mules* may not have been easily differentiated by an English speaker listening to the Spanish/English of an Indian, filtered as it were through Indian language phonology, the dividing line between the two European languages becomes unclear indeed. There is, furthermore, considerable evidence that *swap*, although a reasonably old British word, had become a special contact-language form by this time in American English.[29]

With the other evidence of a contact variety of Spanish, evidence like that of two eighteenth-century advertisements for runaway slaves begins to seem significant:

> One Indian boy . . . speaks French, English, and Spanish
> but all bad. (*Boston Gazette*, May 14–21, 1739)
> Spanish Indian lad . . . speaks indifferent good English.
> (*Boston News-Leader*, May 9, 1715)[30]

Admittedly, the term "bad" may be applied to a language for a number of reasons. Naïve observers use it for all pidgins and creoles.[31] It often means "accented" speech (i.e., with interference from the native language of the speaker). But it is also applied to the contact varieties, including the Creole languages, which are now spoken primarily by the descendants of West African slaves. Given the intimate associations of those former slaves and the American Indians, and the probable contact language influence of the latter on the former,[32] there is reason to be wary of the expedient of dismissing these reports as reflecting nothing more than interference patterns.

A reexamination of the Western and cattle-ranching vocabulary that has been attributed to borrowing from Spanish, considered as a means of resolving this problem, yields some interesting results. The English forms turn out not to be explainable in terms of English phonological interference on Spanish. This raises the interesting question as to whether all the Texas cattle-ranching vocabulary, which spread to other parts of the range country and even as far north as Montana, can be traced to Spanish with the requisite degree of etymological accuracy.

Besides the familiar *savvy* (see Chapter I), there are several rather basic Western lexical items that can be attributed to Romance language sources, although not to Spanish.[33] It would be hard to imagine a more elementary cowboy word than *lasso*. According to lexicographer Ramon F. Adams, "though the Mexicans introduced this name to the cow range, the word comes from Portuguese *laço*, meaning snare."[34] A few dictionaries record Spanish *lazo* as the source, citing its "American" pronunciation with medial /s/;

but for reasons to be considered below, this explanation is less satisfactory. The Portuguese derivation suggests that possibly both Mexicans and "Anglos" were using a special language in the contact situation.

There is an earlier recorded pronunciation of lasso with /uw/ (the vowel of *Luke*) rather than /ow/ (the vowel of *boat*) in the second syllable. The pronunciation is not entirely obsolete; it provided a rhyme in the song "Sioux City Sue" that was popular in 1947. This would place earlier *lassoo* in a group of words that have /uw/ in ordinary American English but /o/ (a "quick" vowel, not as long as the vowel of *road* but otherwise similar) in the nearest Spanish cognate. Where there is an unequivocal Spanish origin, English has /ow/ (the vowel of *load*) /rówdiyow/ or /rowdéyow/ from Spanish /roðéo/. Portuguese, on the other hand, has a final, lip-rounded glide which makes it a more likely source for what is realized as /uw/ in English borrowing.[35] In the same way, *buckaroo* was, until quite recently, regularly traced to Spanish *vaquero*, 'cowboy'. In 1960, however, Julian Mason pointed out that there were semantic features of *buckaroo* and spellings in the earliest attestations that pointed rather to the Gullah (reinterpreted in my *Black English* as Plantation Creole) word *buckra*.[36] Again, the /uw/ final vowel of the English makes it quite unlikely that the word has an uncomplicated derivation from Spanish. There is a pejorative suffix -*roo* in use in some contact varieties, which probably reinforced the Creole source.[37]

Both *vamoose* and *mosey* are supposedly from the Spanish *vamos*, 'we go' or 'let's go'. There are, however, some complications. The cowboy in the Western who says, "Vamoose, hombre, savvy?" may be applying the 'let's go' interpretation of Spanish, but his *vamoose* can't mean 'we go'. An expression like *I'm going to vamoose out of here*, furthermore, doesn't fit either Spanish sense. There is, again, trouble with accounting for the English pronunciation if the words are derived

127

from Spanish. *Vamos* in Spanish is accented on the first syllable; *vamoose*, in English, is accented on the second.[38] In the terms of a popular joke, the English etymologists are acCENTing the wrong sylLABle.

Mosey has an acceptable vowel pronunciation for that framework of derivation, but again the stress is wrong. If Spanish had vaMOS, instead of VAmos, then we could account for the derivation of English /mowz/ (as in the name of Mose, the old man who was dead).[39] But then the final syllable remains unexplained. Etymologists do not accept such loose procedures when they are deriving, say, hypothetical Proto-Germanic from hypothetical Proto-Indo-European. There is no reason why sloppiness should suddenly come to be tolerated in tracing the Southwestern English vocabulary.

Like the forms cited by Jonathan Dickinson and others, *vamoose, mosey, lassoo,* and their entire class suggest Romance—but not Spanish—origin. So do *galoot*[40] and (*kit and*) *caboodle*.[41] The same is true of *calaboose,* supposedly from Spanish *calabozo.* The Spanish etymology is from the *Dictionary of Americanisms,* which had its first entry in 1792. The *Oxford English Dictionary,* which had no citation earlier than 1837, traces the word to "Negro French (of Louisiana) and Spanish"; but the OED's first citation is from the works of Thomas Chandler Halliburton (whose pen name was Sam Slick), a Nova Scotian who set his stories in a fictional town (Slickville) in Connecticut. The OED obviously embodies knowledge not available to or utilized by the DA; but neither the Spanish nor the "Negro French" (presumably, French Creole) derivation can be accepted without reservation. It seems much more likely to have been Lingua Franca.

Here again, travelers' records provide information either obscured in or missing from the dictionaries. (It is very hard, when reviewing the evidence, to resist the conclusion that dictionaries are the result of selectivity that attempts to make

Southwestern words seem to come from Spanish.) Sir Richard Burton, passing through Louisiana, observed, "At every few miles was a drinking "calaboose."[42] And his footnote explained:

> The Spanish is Calabazo, the French Calabouse. In the Hispano-American countries it is used as a "common jail" or a "dog hole," and as usual is converted into a verb.

In *Omoo*, Melville gives an account of his incarceration in a *Calabooza* (*Calabooza Beretanee*, 'British jail') on Tahiti. Margaret Mead provides a twentieth-century attestation of *calaboose* in use on tiny Manus, just north of New Guinea.[43] Inasmuch as the word has been also reported for Cameroonian Pidgin English, *calaboose* appears to be international and originally maritime, rather than characteristic of any narrowly geographic locale like Louisiana. And neither French nor Spanish but the maritime Lingua Franca seems a likely source for it.[44]

French Creole, as part of the language contact situation created by the French in the Americas, was certainly a factor in Louisiana when Moses Austin and his colonists came there in the early nineteenth century.[45] French Creole words like *lagniappe* (the first entry in the *Dictionary of Americanisms* credits the word to "Creole Negroes," although the dictionary itself calls no special attention to the source)[46] are still regarded as somehow diagnostic of the area; they have obviously been passed on from the Blacks to the whites, as have many other usages in the South. The followers of Moses Austin probably learned at least some of what may have been at the time either a French-based Creole or an international Romance Lingua Franca. This would have served to communicate with Spanish- and French-speaking people and with Indians—perhaps even with Germans and other European groups who had been exposed to the same maritime tradition. The Spanish, who still called Texas the "New Philippines," may have helped all those who struggled with polyglot communication along by using a Romance-based contact vernacular with which they were familiar.[47]

Whatever the details, the cowboy lingo was a more international one than has so far been recognized. *Waddy*, one of the favorite Western words to designate the cowboy himself, has a striking cognate in Australia. Coming from Pidgin English, the Australian *waddy* meant first 'an aboriginal war club', then 'to strike, beat, or kill with a war club' (OED).[48] Among American cowboys, the word took on the meaning not 'kill' but 'strike', in the special sense involved in the phrase *punching cows*—keeping cows moving, going where the cowboy wants them to go, perhaps through a bit of prodding. *Cowpoke* is an alternate designation for the same occupation. Ramon Adams, compiler of *Western Words*, traces the word (wrongly, I think) to the English *wad* or *wadding*; but he also cites *donkey puncher*, 'the engineer or operator of a *donkey* [a machine used in logging]', and *dough puncher*, 'a cowboy's and logger's name for the cook'. *Waddy* itself could also be used in the compounds *cow waddie*[49] and *trail waddie*.[50]

But probably not even *waddy* has the international associations of *palaver*. Coming from the Portuguese *palavra*, 'word', the form was used in the Pidgin English of West Africa in the sense of 'a meeting', 'a discussion', or even 'a dispute, or a disturbance'.[51] In that meaning, and in the form *plaba* (influenced by West African phonological patterns), it became part of Jamaican English, although Cassidy and LePage miss the point rather spectacularly in their *Dictionary of Jamaican English*.[52] In 1863 Sir Richard Burton reported a Sierra Leonian speaker of Krio who said, "What he mean, dis palaver?"[53] Francis Grose wrote in his *Classical Dictionary of the Vulgar Tongue*, in 1785:

> Palaver—used by Portuguese travelers of parleys with natives in West Africa, and brought thence by English sailors.

By the nineteenth century, at any rate, Southern observers regarded expressions like *to sorta palaver on,* 'to go on talking', as typical Negroisms. In the Western United States the word is, of course, familiar from writings like Mark Twain's "Buck Fanshaw's Funeral."

The second stage of English-Spanish contact in Texas and the Southwest was a less international affair. It involved more conventional bilingual contact on a local scale and therefore has been better handled by conventional approaches. It took place farther west than the first stage. Stephen Austin's followers tended to stay in East Texas to practice cotton and corn agriculture of a type which they had learned in the American East. But some more intrepid "Anglo" Texans moved out west and learned the cattle-ranching trade from Mexicans.

In that relationship, an even more extreme example of a diglossic situation, with Spanish as the public and English as the private language, prevailed.[54] As apprentices to the Mexicans in the ranching business, the "Anglos" learned reasonably technical vocabulary like *herrar,* 'to brand'; *arrastre,* 'an iron raking implement'; *coliar,* 'to tail down [a cow]'; and *cargador,* 'mule packer'. The well-known Spanish accretions to the Southwestern English vocabulary, listed in many sources, became part of that vocabulary: ranching terms, names of animals, foods, plants, places, etc.[55] Some of these words are phonetically rather unlike the Spanish source (*wrangler* from *caballarengo; dally* from *dar vuelta,* 'turn'; *cavvieyard* from *caballada,* 'string of horses') and are conventionally explained in terms of the "bad" Spanish pronunciation of the *gringos*. But most evidence indicates that a great part of the cattle-raising Texas population, unlike the farmers of the eastern part of the state, were for a time genuinely bilingual. Such phonological changes as they produced in Spanish were by and large the simple ones of *dobe* from *adobe* and *hoosegow* from *juzgado*.

The third stage of the contact relationship between English and Spanish in the Southwest began sometime after the defeat of Mexico in the mid-nineteenth century and led to the situation that exists today. As linguist Janet B. Sawyer has shown in an excellent study, "Aloofness from Spanish Influence in Texas English" (1959), "Anglo" citizens of Texas are now so aloof from Spanish and the "Latins" who speak it that all language influence must go in the other direction. (Mexicans who live in the area say *el chalke*, 'chalk'; *el trocke*, 'truck', etc.) In the past few decades, perhaps only one word, *Chicano*, has been a new borrowing from Spanish into English. Many of the old ones (*resaca*, 'drainage ditch', *enchilada, chili con carne, frijoles, tamale*) have been thoroughly—to some, horribly—Anglicized in pronunciation. The town of St. Patrick, which became San Patricio sometime after 1823, is now [sæn pætrI ŠIow], and Refugio has become in the pronunciation of those actually from the town and its environs [rIfyurIow]—as though the *g* of the Spanish word had become an *r*.[56] Those Texas Latins who are more bilingual often use these "Anglo" pronunciations of the old Spanish terms in their English conversations.

Many of the same processes were going on in New Mexico and Arizona. Arizona, especially, attracted the attention of nineteenth-century commentators on language. Bourke's *On the Border with Crook* reported:

> Tucson was as foreign a town as if it were in Hayti instead of within our own boundaries. The language, dress, funeral processions, religious ceremonies, feasts, dances, games, joys, perils, griefs, and tribulations of its population were something not to be looked for in the region East of the Mississippi River.[57]

Bourke's actual quotations of the language do not seem quite so foreign, but they are picturesque enough:

> "I tell you Cap," said my old friend Charlie Hopkins, "them railroads is playin' hell with th' country 'n' a feller's got to hustle hisself now in Tucson to get a meal of frijoles or

enchiladas; this yere new-fangled grub doan' suit me 'n' I reckon I'll pack my grip 'n' light out fur Sonora."[58]

Somewhat more convincing is his report of a square dance where the conversation was in Spanish but the calls were given in a kind of approximate English:

"Ally man let 'n' shassay;"
"Bal'nce to yer podners 'n' all han's roun'"
"Dozy dozy—chaat 'n' swing"[59]

Of the last sentences, *shassay* is from French *chasser*, 'to chase'; it is still used, in a meaning more like 'travel' than 'chase', in square-dance calls and in the speech of Snuffy Smith in the comic strips. *Ally* is obviously also French— *aller*, 'to go' or *allez*, ' (you) go'. The phrase *man let* seems meaningless to me; but in a square-dance context, 'to the left' would not be an impossible interpretation. In that case, it might come from *nan*, 'in' (French Creole, related to Portuguese Creole *na*), and *let* for English *left*, perhaps a simplification of the consonant cluster *-ft* by a foreign speaker. *Dozy dozy* probably means 'two by two'. It can be derived either from French *deux et deux* or from Spanish *dos y dos*—or, in the mad world of this kind of language contact, from both. Later square-dance callers took the second "two" for English *dough* and embellished

Dosie dough and a little more dough
Chicken's in the bread pan peckin' out dough.

Although it is by no means certain that the words and phrases cited by Bourke originated in the Southwest, it is clear that the cowboys from Texas and the Southwest had a far-reaching influence on American English. They carried their "intriguing, half-Spanish lingo"[60] as far north as Montana. And Ramon Adams, in his *Western Words*, has acknowledged their profound influence:

When the Texan rode over the long trails north, he carried his customs and his manner of working all the way to the Canadian line . . . Montana, Wyoming, and other northern and central states adopted much of his Spanish-influenced language. In exchange, the northern cowman gave the Texan that which he had appropriated from the northern Indian and the French-Canadian, words strange to the man from the Rio Grande.

Among the cowman's words traceable to French is *hiver-anno*:

A trapper's name for someone who had passed several winters in the Indian country. From the French *hiver*, meaning winter, and *année* meaning year. Also called *hiverant*.

When the migrating Americans got close enough to the Pacific Northwest to pick up French words in their cowboy slang, they were getting close to still another special variety, Chinook Jargon. Since the Jargon got mixed up with Pidgin English,[61] it occupied, in a structural sense, the slot Spanish had filled in the Southwest. The use of Chinook Jargon also drew a lot of attention from observers:

Oregon is the place to hear the 'Chinook' in all its glory; it has played the English language 'square out' in that land of rain, fir-trees, 'cloockmans' and canus.[62]

Some observers, like J. Ross Browne in 1854, were imprecise enough linguistically but still pretty good indicators of what was going on:

The prevailing languages spoken are the Clallam, Chinook, and the Skookum-Chuck, or Strong Water with a mixture of broken English.[63]

Today, it is usually said that *skookum* and *Siwash* (from French *sauvage*) are the only two generally known words from the jargon—and even these are largely limited to the Northwest. (My graduate students in dialectology in New York City almost unanimously professed complete unfamiliarity with them.) But a great many other words from Chinook Jargon are still used by the loggers of the Northwest. In 1958, Dean Walter F. McCulloch of the Oregon State College School of Forestry recorded in *Woods Words* a large number of logger words he traced "from Indian." Most of them turn out to be actually from Chinook Jargon. Examples are:

cultus—no good
potlacher—a generous man [from the Indian custom of competitive gift-giving]
Skookum block—actually a trade name [based on *skookum*, 'strong, tough, big, good'], but used especially to mean a big heavy main line block.
Skookum chuck—fast, dangerous or tricky waters, as falls, narrows or tide rips.

But not all the loggers' terms "from Indian" seem to have originated in Chinook or in other Indian languages of the Northwest. McCulloch points out that *wanigan*, for example, is related to

Indian word wangun in Maine, meaning bait. Hence *wanigan* became the bait boat or the eats boat.

He also identifies the word as "A float camp along the southeastern Alaska coast."

Something about the process of transmission can be learned from the work of E. N. Dick, who reported the use of *wanigan*, 'the camp commissary', around Pierre, North Dakota.[64] If the word did originate in the Maine area, as seems altogether likely, then Dick must have caught it about halfway along in its trek from the East Coast to the Pacific Northwest. And as far as we can tell, it was carried by loggers.

The language of Northwestern loggers has some terms which came from Pidgin English. We find a familiar friend in McCulloch's dictionary:

Savvy—know-how; the difference between the old-timer and the greenhorn.

We also find

No-see-um—an almost invisible fly found in the north woods, has a terrific bite.

which is obviously Pidgin, right down to the transitivizer. The *Dictionary of Americanisms*, whose editors apparently never heard of Pidgin English, nevertheless concedes:

No-see-um, in Indian speech or in imitation of this a minute biting fly or midge of the family Chironomidae, a punkie, *colloq.*

Any Pidginism may, of course, be called "colloq."; and any Pidginism will astonish historians of the language who pay more attention to the reconstructive tradition than to colloquial activity. The DA's first citation for *no-see-um* is from Thoreau's *Maine Woods*; it appears that this word, like *wanigan*, made its way across the northern United States, from east to west, perhaps carried along by loggers.

Although loggers use some of the same terms as those characteristic of the cowboy "lingo," there were, not unexpectedly, some semantic changes in the process of transmission. *Wrangler*, in the lumber camps, denotes not the herder of horses but "a teamster on a log skidding job." *Wigwam*, known along the entire frontier, becomes figurative for the loggers: "two or more trees lodged together when falling timber." And it figures in new compounds:

Wigwam maker—a faller who has got himself into a jack-pot with several cut trees wedged together.

Our old friend *vamoose* remains, however, "get out, make yourself scarce."

Free compounding of the Indian-derived terms shows how natural they became in the loggers' language. McCulloch reports:

> *Siwash logger*—along the coast, a man who got his logs by beach combing, not by logging.

and:

> *Siwash tree*—a tree left standing to change the direction of a line in yarding.

He further reports *squaw man,* in a meaning almost identical to that in which it was used throughout the frontier areas:

> A logger on the reservation, usually by dark of night.

McCulloch's definition is probably merely franker than those nineteenth-century explanations of a squaw man as one who had "married" an Indian woman. The term was commonplace enough in American English and stayed around long enough to serve as the title of Samuel Goldwyn's first feature-length movie. Elsewhere *squaw* entered into other compounds; Adams, in *Western Words,* lists *squaw ax,* 'an awkward ax', and *squaw side* (of a horse) as well as the self-explanatory *trap a squaw.*

With all the frontiersmen's preoccupation with squaws, there were bound to be some papooses around. The word *papoose* got as far southeast as the Florida Seminoles, where one Mr. Willson[65] took it for a Seminole attempt to pronounce English *baby.* And it entered into some Western compounds, according to Adams:

> papoose basket
> papoose board
> papoose coat

In earlier times, when there were Chinese working in the logging camps, Chinese Pidgin English was one of the contact media.[66] The loggers would obviously have found that language very useful in communicating with the "yellow" men who performed menial tasks for very low wages. It is, then, not surprising that we find in McCulloch's dictionary not only:

> *China boy*—a Chinese logger, at one time quite common in B. C. camps. One boss China boy would contract to put out logs, and did all the bargaining for the whole crew.

and:

> *Q*—a Chinese logger; from the long queue worn by China boys, when they first came to the Northwest. There were many Chinese fillers and buckers in B.C. logging camps.

but also:

> *Cookee*—second cook; or kitchen helper
> *Chokem*—cheese

the last two having all the earmarks of Pidgin English.[67]

In Supplement I of *The American Language*, Mencken pointed out that a number of terms from Chinook Jargon were still "familiar locally" in the Northwest:

klootchman	'a woman'
wawa	'talk'
muckamuck	'food'
tenas	'small'
hyas	'big'
chechako	'a stranger'
keekwilly	'house'
kla-how-ya	'How are you?'

Mencken also recorded attempts to derive *hooch* from Chinook Jargon, "but without much success." Both Mencken and the OED believe that the word came from Alaskan *hoochino* or *hoocheno*, for which a Jargon cognate or even transmission would be far from impossible. Mencken also felt that the derivation of *hike* from Chinook Jargon *hyak*, 'hurry', was unlikely because the word "did not come into common American use until after Chinook influence had died out." But McCulloch's work seems to prove that Chinook Jargon influence has still not "died out" among the Northwestern loggers; and it is highly probable that such a word would spread from a professional group to "common American use." The OED ventures nothing about the origin of *hike* except "dialectal and U.S."

By the folk-etymological principle that tries to make words from the contact varieties into funny-sounding English, *high muckamuck* (a semi-Chinook Jargon phrase which should mean 'big meal') has come to mean 'high-ranking person', with perhaps just a tinge of the meaning 'incompetent big shot'. (*Muck* is obviously taken as a euphemism for a more obscene four-letter word, as in Pogo's description of a diplomatic figure as a "big international chicken plucker.") This is the process that made 'a fence sitter (that is, with his mug on one side and his wump on the other)' out of the Algonquian word *mugwump*, which originally meant an important official.

These have not been the kinds of things the sterner lexicographers have concerned themselves with in their more serious moments, in part because they have known almost nothing about the pidgin and contact languages. Those varieties have nevertheless had a strong influence on the playful and informal styles of American English.

There is some complication involved in *cumshaw*, 'a handout', which Dean McCulloch declares is "from Indian." Other dictionaries, especially the OED, consider it derived from a Chinese word meaning 'to be grateful'. In Chinese ports and obviously in Chinese Pidgin English, it came to mean 'a present or gratuity or baksheesh'. Englishmen in China are recorded as using it as early as 1839. By the time of World War II, it had become a general part of U.S. service slang, meaning what the officers got out of U.S. military service that the enlisted men couldn't (like the services of enlisted men to wash their cars and mow their lawns). It is, of course, possible that discharged soldiers or sailors took jobs in the logging camps and brought the word along. But McCulloch's feeling for loggers' language is impressive; and his "from Indian" generally designates a word that has been around a long time.

Cumshaw might even be the lumberman's equivalent of the cowboy's *waddy*—an international word that became characteristic of an occupational group in a fairly restricted area. There are others of this type. In *Western Words,* Adams mentions *cowcumber*, a cowboy's form for what most of us call *cucumber*. Krio of Sierra Leone, which (according to Canadian creolist Ian F. Hancock's dissertation) has a great deal of nautical vocabulary, has a form of the word that must derive from a nautical *cowcumber* according to regular phonological patterns. It seems quite obvious that the language varieties associated with movement, whether at sea or on the plains, left their imprint on several forms of American English. Important as it was in the Northwest, Chinook Jargon had some significant companions.

Americans in various occupational groups and in several places came to know Chinese Pidgin English after the gold rush immigration began in 1849. Rusling, for example, found that in Portland, Oregon, "John Chinaman turned up again." Rusling was amazed at the behavioral Americanization of the Chinese, despite their lack of linguistic assimilation:

> They engaged in all household duties, ran errands, worked as traders, performed all kinds of manual labor, and yet as a rule their only dialect was a sort of chow-chow of "Pigeon English."[68]

Richardson, like many other commentators and observers, described the Chinese variety of English:

> Their chief deity is called "Josh;" In a violent quarrel between a Chinaman and a Jew, the former wrathfully said, "Oh, yesee; I knowee you—you killee Melican man's Josh."[69]

The astonishing assimilative powers of the Chinese in American ways apparently included even anti-Semitism, and all in Pidgin English.

Americans learned the condiment *chow-chow* from pidgin-speaking Chinese. In the Northwest, loggers and other occupational groups dealt with the special contact speech called Chinook Jargon and picked up some of its vocabulary. All in all, there can hardly have been a single American group that remained uninfluenced by one or another of the institutionalized strategies for dealing with multilingual contacts.

In this particular domain,[70] they have the same kind of importance Yiddish has had in the language of broadcasting, movie-making, and advertising. (See Chapter III and *A Taste of Yiddish*.) Languages like Chinook Jargon and Pidgin English have been given less than their due, perhaps because they do not fit into the popular picture of British "regional" dialects coming to the North American continent and then migrating westward, creating the geographic distribution of American English as they went. On the polyglot frontier, there were many groups like the Indians and the originally West African slaves who contributed a great deal to the language of the frontier—even to the English of the frontier.

Obviously, it makes a great deal of difference whether we look at Maine and Oregon with the preconception that they *must* be different in dialect because they are geographically separated. It is easy, then, to reason backward from that conclusion and to assume that the early historical factors in the formation of their dialects must have centered around geographic separation. If we look at population groups, on the other hand, we find in each of them loggers and Indians with the need to communicate with one another. An obvious source of difference is the separate Indian language groups to be found in each.

In the words of those who regard states or regions as separate entities, we find a lot of attention given to words like *spider*, 'frying pan'. McDavid calls it a characteristic of the "Charleston dialect."[71] But a notation beside that entry says "also Northern." "Northern," applied to the United States, could mean many things; but in this context it almost certainly refers to the northern part of the East Coast. The works of the dialect geographers tell us little about the West Coast, but the historical commentators have not been so sparing. Adams reports that *spider* is "in logging, a small metal tool." McCulloch also lists it as a thick iron frying pan for use over an open fire. Mencken called it, in Supplement II, a "characteristic New Englandism." Albert Marckwardt, in *American English*, placed it "in the North and in the Southern tidewater area." Another dialect geographer of the old school, E. Bagby Atwood, added to the confusion:

> *Spider*, which is fairly well known in the North and parts of the Coastal South, is nothing more than a remnant in Texas.[72]

The layman who tries to follow these geographic designations on his map may be getting dizzy by now. Unfortunately, he is all too likely to credit the professors of dialectology with a profundity that extends beyond his untutored comprehension. There is, however, another possible explanation: confusion is inherent in the attempt to segment American dialects geographically. There is no reason to believe that the meaning 'frying pan' necessarily preceded that of 'a small metal tool', or that *spider* in either meaning was a regional word before it was a part of loggers' vocabulary. In the *Dictionary of Nautical Words and Terms* (1955), C. W. T. Layton attests the use of "*Spider*. Iron band around a mast to take lower end of futlock rigging." And he points out the use of the compounds *spider band* and *spider hoop*. Although historical information is not provided, the use in compounds would make it appear that *spider* is no newcomer to the nautical vocabulary. The nautical use may well have preceded the usage 'small metal tool', and 'frying pan' could easily be the last of the semantic developments. If that is the case, then *spider* is merely one more of many nautical terms that found their way into the vernaculars of special groups of speakers of American English.

Another term characteristic of a special occupational group is *Long Tom*, familiar from Western fiction and elsewhere as a term for a rifle and to sports fans as Satchel Paige's name for his *really* fast ball. In the mining camps, however, it was, according to Adams's *Western Words*, "a type of trough used for washing gold-bearing dirt." Archer B. Hulbert, who defined the term as meaning "an artificial wooden sluice for washing 'pay dirt,' " also commented how

> the lingo of the mines is fascinating to newcomers when they hear it, and mere boys on the trail talk airily about "long toms" . . .[73]

The term came to mean 'rifle' among buffalo hunters. The rifle metaphor was obviously dominant in the use of the expression by the man who may have been the greatest pitcher baseball ever knew. In an earlier century, the distribution of the word was west-wide; differences in use (frequency or precise meaning assigned) correlated with occupational groups.

The historical issue in the cases of these terms is obviously not the etymology of *long*, *Tom*, and *spider* (arachnid). It is rather how they came to be applied to mining tools or to a rifle or to a pitch in baseball. We know more about American English when we know how Satchel Paige came to use the name *Little Tom* for his pitch which was merely blindingly fast than we do if we know only that *long* comes ultimately from Proto-Germanic (hypothetical, at that) **lango* and that *Tom* is an abbreviation of a name that comes ultimately from Hebrew. That is, in the process of knowing how these terms were used we come to understand something about the use of language by living human beings and not by some etymological fossils of linguistic paleontology.

The traditions we now have will not even explain how we got the name by which the rest of the world calls us and by which some of us call ourselves, *Yankee*. But an understanding of the early frontier and its processes may prove that this particular etymology is no such bugaboo after all.

It has been suggested—and rejected—that *Yankee* is the result of "an Indian attempt to pronounce English." The rejection has been categorical: "There is no evidence that they [the Indians] ever attempted to use the word *English*."[74] In spite of this authoritarian statement, there is considerable documentary evidence of the Indians' use of the word *English*—in addition to the a priori reasonableness of the assumption that the East Coast Indians would have needed some word to designate the men who came from afar and changed their way of life. In 1682, at a treaty-signing with William Penn, near present-day Philadelphia, a Delaware chief with the historic name of Tammany is reported as saying:

> If Yengeesman come, he pass and do no harm to Indian.
> If Yengees man sleep in path, the Indian pass and do him
> no harm. Indian say, "He's Yengees; he loves sleep."[75]

Insofar as the "mispronunciation" of the first syllable (*Yeng-* from *Eng-*) goes, similar phonological developments (palatalization of the initial vowel) are far from unknown in pidgin varieties of English. In Chinese Pidgin English we find

Ink-eli   'English'
Ying-kwo   'English Nation'
Yin-ke-li   'English'[76]

The first listed use of *Yankee* in the dictionaries is from 1758, but the form accredited to Tammany is clearly earlier.

Thomas Pyles, who declared that the Indians never attempted to use the word *English*, also reports—and rejects —the theory that *Yankee* comes from an Indian "mispronunciation" of *anglais*.[77] Leaving aside the folklore about "mispronunciation," we can see that there is an appropriateness about this theory. In the multilingual situation, in which Indians of different tribes had to communicate with Frenchmen as well as Englishmen, one form that would serve as a "mispronunciation" of both a French word and an English word would be sensationally effective. It is, furthermore, quite reasonable that the Indians would have needed to communicate about Englishmen or Anglo-Americans (although not necessarily to distinguish between the two) when talking with Frenchmen. If the first syllable of the word before it experienced French influence was already *Yeng-*, then the lowering of the vowel (/I/ or /e/ to /æ/) might be explained from the first vowel of French *anglais*. From the point of view of the Indians, the need was to talk to the Europeans, not to use French or English, whether "good" or "bad."[78]

Finally, the *-ee* of the last syllable of *Yankee* can be paralleled by other pidgin examples in terms for national origin or ethnic-group membership, like *Chinee* from *Chinese* (as in Bret Harte's "Heathen Chinee") and *Portagee* from *Portuguese*.

Much more came from the American Indians, obviously, than the place names and the few words like *persimmon*, *opossum*, and *pone* that are usually attributed to them. The blue-nosed etymologist would certainly deny them *medicine*, yet their use of the term clearly influenced frontier whites. The Indians themselves probably got it first from the French, according to attestations like that of painter George Catlin:

> These Indian doctors were called by the Frenchmen, who were the first traders on the frontiers, "*Medecins*," the French word for physicians, and by a subsequent frontier population "Medicine Men . . . "[79]

The meaning of *medicine* to the Indians, however, was quite different from that which whites gave it. To the Indians, it involved concepts more religious and philosophical than that of mere remedy and treatment.[80] Catlin, among others, points out how *medicine man* led to *medicine drums, medicine rattles, medicine dances, medicine books, medicine fire,* and other terms that do not derive semantically from either the French or the English meaning of the source word. The frontier whites picked up the Indian usage; Adams's *Western Words* lists *no medicine* as meaning 'no information', and other such uses by frontiersmen are familiar from the frontier literature.

Many figurative expressions, like "fire-water," have long been familiar from fictional and movie Indian talk; but they are also well attested from genuine historical sources. One of the first was Jean-Bernard Bossu's *Travels in the Interior of North America, 1751–62*, which lists:

prayer chief	missionary
cloth that soaks	paper
flat wood	table
fire-water	brandy
fire warriors	Spanish warriors with guns
the great lake	the sea
big canoes	ships[81]

There are comparable reports from later times, in this case 1871:

> Infantry soldiers are called by the Indians "heap walk men." Indians call Major Powell's boats "water ponies." Long trains of cars are called by the Indians "heap wagon, no hoss" . . . The Indians call the telegraph the "whispering spirit."[82]

And from still later:

> When the white man introduced new objects, words had to be coined to describe them to those who had never

seen them. The first railway train became at once a "fire wagon."[83]

It is one of the commonplaces of the linguistic treatment of the frontier that tall talk and figurative language abounded there. Convincing sources for the process have been difficult to find, although imitation of such obvious European patterns as the style of euphuism in Renaissance England have been claimed. Yet such figurative language is especially characteristic of lexical innovation within pidgins and creoles.[84] Could it be that the frontiersmen took a hint from Indian talk? They might have used it seriously—as they apparently did in communicating with the Indians. They may have used it playfully or facetiously among themselves, even to the point of caricaturing the Indians. But the Indians' figurative uses may have been what started the whole thing.

Orthodox commentators have differed greatly among themselves as to the origin of frontier tall talk, although no one has denied that it existed. Marckwardt explains it as coming, conveniently enough for one of his orientation, from the "Elizabethan tendency toward hyperbole."[85] But the almost equally orthodox linguist Charlton Laird has seen the obvious flaw in that approach:

> Both time and place give me trouble . . . If Mike Fink, Davy Crockett, and their fellow half-alligators were whoppin' out the transported speech of Shakespeare's "rude mechanicals," somebody must have been talking in like manner for more than two hundred years. Where were these people and why did nobody notice their outrageous diction and comment on it?[86]

The one group that a frontiersman of the mid-nineteenth century was almost certain to encounter and to talk with was the Indians. After his native language, the one speech variety with which he was most likely to be familiar was Pidgin English, through which the Indians' figurative usages were transmitted. If he were a native speaker of some other language than English—say, of French—then he might mix some of that with his pidgin. Indeed, one Frenchman in 1844 is reported as uttering the following colorful statement:

> "Foutre de varment! he butt me down!" exclaimed the exasperated Frenchman. "Sacré! me plenty scart; but me kill him for all."[87]

Both Pidgin English and foreigner talk are identified, in the popular imagination and in the weak formulations of the schoolteachers, with malapropism—with the formation of "incorrect" words like *splendiferous, absquatulate,* and *snollygoster. Snollygoster* is a kind of symbol of the whole frontier tall-talk process. It is regularly treated in works in American usage, a great deal being made of the fact that President Truman once used it in a public speech. None of these works call attention to the fact that the first use recorded in the *Dictionary of Americanisms* is from Dan Emmett's "Black Brigade" (1862) "We am de snollygosters and lubs Jim Ribber oysters." Emmett, who is most famous as the composer of words and music for "Dixie," was the mid-nineteenth century's best-known writer in Negro dialect —Black English. No frontiersman himself, he typified the American linguistic reliance on the innovative processes of minority groups. Among other accomplishments, they made frontier communication what it was.

The users of these words flaunted their scorn of civilization; they identified themselves with the poor but not humble outcasts of the border areas; they indulged in what the anthropologist calls "dramatic low-status assertion." And they got their cues on how to do so from practiced and expert low-status persons, members of the "minority" groups, which abounded on the frontiers.

There is no two-hundred-year time gap in the observation of Pidgin English or of the metaphorical innovations of the frontier. Frontier observers were reporting both from shortly after the time Shakespeare wrote about his "rude mechanicals" until the early years of the twentieth century.

Innovations were commonplace on the frontier. Some of them, perhaps because they are now obsolete or restricted in distribution, seem exotic to us; others have become part of our everyday vocabulary. In his 1871 *Transcontinental Tourist Guide*, Crofutt called them "Western Travel Talk":

"Hash houses"—roadside restaurants.
Waiters are called "hash slingers."

Telegraph operators are called "lightning shovers."
On the plains bacon is called "sowbelly."

Teamsters on the plains call a meal a "grub pile." Old settlers on the Plains call Emigrants "Pilgrims"; . . . Ox drivers, "bull whackers"; mule drivers, "mule skinners"; Utah Whisky, "Valley Tan." To be out of money is "in the Cap"; "on the bed rock," etc.

Some of these terms, like *hash house, hash slingers,* and *bull whackers,* have become everyday words in at least some American dialects. Others were transitory and even nonce forms. All involve frontier metaphorical innovation, like another phrase reported by a later commentator:

"Go two looks and a go by"—meaning that he should breast the horizon twice, pass the first turn-off, and take the second.[88]

Black frontiersmen participated in all parts of this kind of linguistic innovation, bringing their fancy talk with them. From Alton, Illinois, painter Catlin reported the speech of a Black servant:

"My good massa, Massa Wharton, in dese house, just dead ob de libber compliment."[89]

Compliment here is obviously a kind of malapropism for *complaint,* such relationships being abundant in the contacts of Black English and more ordinary English. Richardson's *Beyond the Mississippi* (1875) records a servant woman who had been trying to prospect for gold and who answers her master's queries about the rocks she carries with, "Speciments, mass'r, speciments." Tape recordings made in Samaná in the Dominican Republic, where the descendants of freed slaves have maintained a dialect of Black English since 1824, contain a form *paragolized* for *paralyzed*. It isn't a "performance error," either; the speaker repeats it three times.

As one of the prominent groups on the frontier whose English had not undergone koiné leveling, and as one that mixed notably with other minority groups, the Blacks were extremely important in the total situation. In the Southern states, which were more or less their point of origin, observers had long reported the high-flown fancy talk in which they indulged on special occasions. The observer might be a Yankee critic of the Southern system like Joseph Holt Ingram, who recorded:

> "Mighty *obligated* wid it [a sermon], master, de *'clusive 'flections* werry distructive to de *ignorum*.[90]

But the reporter might also be a defender of the Southern tradition, like Robert Molloy, who included in his *Charleston, A Gracious Heritage* a section entitled "How They Do Talk" which quoted a Gullah speaker:

> "He tell me a lot o' who-kill-John" means, for instance, that, in the Gilbertian sense, the speaker was employing corroborative detail to lend verisimilitude to an otherwise bald and unconvincing (and probably quite untrue) narrative.[91]

Or a fictional example could be cited:

> Gentlemuns, fur de purpose uv *'vestigatin'* de *'finity 'twixt* sugar an' salt, I takes dis case under *'visement* tell turmorrow evenin'; meanwhile, de court would thank you fur any *'thority* yer can show on de pints at issue.[92]

In 1888 a would-be grammarian of Black English reported:

> The humorous and proverbial character of many of these expressions shows a distinct feature of the Negro mind. The talk of the African abounds in metaphors, figures, similes, imaginative flights, humorous delineations and designations, saws and sayings. These have so interwoven themselves with his daily speech as to have become an unconscious and essential part of it.[93]

That fancy talk is originally pidgin/creole rather than Black appears, however, from examples from islands like St. Helena. In *Islands Time Forgot* (1962), Lawrence Green reports many creolelike features of the dialect of the island and observes:

> Occasionally they invent words, with amusing results . . . "All right," said the islander, "I'll leave the wordification to you." . . . in the islander phrase, "in the before days."[94]

Influences like these produced linguistic results on the frontier that one historian described in these terms:

> They [the Northwestern trappers] developed a spoken language which was so interspersed with idioms that it was difficult for the uninitiated to understand.[95]

It seems clear, however, that what was developing on the frontier was not a group of "regional" patois as in Europe. Rather, the varying groups of the frontier tended to develop trade or professional registers ("slang" or "jargon") that ranged over wide areas and were comprehensible only to the "in" group. Groups like the trappers of the Northwest, who had left "civilization" far behind, were exposed to and picked up many new modes of communication:

> The Indians had a universal sign language by which members of the different tribes who could not understand each other's speech could converse readily for hours. Often by way of practice trappers sat conversing by this method, and it was reflected in the sparsity of words of their conversation.[96]

The taciturnity of trappers, the familiar point of many a stale joke,[97] apparently has some historical basis. But in addition to sign language the trappers undoubtedly learned Pidgin English, its major competitor as the frontier lingua franca.

From the beginnings, British-derived Americans were carpenters or trappers, not East Anglians or Yorkshiremen. When a Vermonter or a Virginian migrated West, he identified himself more as a cowboy or a miner than as someone from his home state. For some, of course, being Quaker or Puritan or Mormon might be still more important. But the historical records yield no indications that the regional groupings in the East were carried to the West. And there are no indications that the new dialects formed in the West were essentially regional in nature.

In a quite traditional, quasi-historic treatment of American English, Thomas Pyles classified three major characteristics of Frontier English as Tall Talk, Turgidity, and Taboo.[98] Taboo, which is the force that made for the use of circumlocutions like *top cow*, *seed cow*, or even *boy cow* for the blunt *bull*, may be traceable to the influence of the Puritans and other sex-conscious religious groups. Turgidity, meaning what perhaps Pyles only knows, could come from anywhere; possibly it just means that Frontier English was not the kind of which the schoolteacher approved. But Tall Talk almost certainly came from the pidgin/creole and language contact traditions. It was part of the basic processes that gave the real character to the American English spoken farther inland than the effete East Coast.

A recent writer on American English, looking at one group in the West, the mountain men, has written of

> their vital and independent way of living, their relations with Indians and Spaniards, and their highly colorful mountain jargon.[99]

It is only one step, which this writer did not take, to the assertion that the "relations with Indians and Spaniards" might have had something to do with the "colorful mountain jargon." There has certainly been more than enough of the suggestion that the frontiersman's talk resulted in some mysterious way from his "vital and independent manner of living," as if there had been no linguistic input to his way of speaking.

What Mencken called "the American Vulgate" was in a sense really an *American* vulgate, although the diversities from group to group were greater than Mencken indicated.[100] The "minorities"—who, taken together, would constitute a majority of our population—seem, on the documentary evidence, to have been more important in the formation of that vulgate or those vulgates than the part of our population that came directly from England. On the frontier, the inherent linguistic competence of "disadvantaged" groups like the Blacks and the Indians asserted itself. To the extent that the frontier linguistic spirit has not been overwhelmed by the schools and the media, their influence is still felt in American English.[101]

V
TAKING STOCK,
OR, WHERE IS
YOU ENGLISHMANS AT?

———————◆•◆ ————————

WHEN THE ENGLISHMEN WHO MIGRATED TO THE EAST COAST OF the United States (then the continental colonies) or their descendants decided to move farther west, they did not travel in a vacuum, in terms of either population or language. Whatever the Pilgrims may have thought before they left Nottinghamshire, or even when they left Holland, they were involved in all kinds of foreign and maritime language contact processes before they found their way to Plymouth Rock. And if they dreamed of establishing a little bit of England in the American wilderness, they were never quite able to do so. Change was involved in every step of the movement, whether by land or by sea.

If we read what the establishment has written about the

155

history of American English, we may be led to believe that American dialects were put together out of made-in-England materials on the East Coast and traveled in the direction of the West Coast with almost no further complicating factors. The most that is allowed is that an occasional member of the Northern migrating group strayed down into the Midland group, or an occasional Midlander into the Southern group, and produced a little "dialect mixing." Thus, for example, a Midlander can find his *slop bucket* getting mixed up with the Northerner's *swill pail* and coming out *slop pail* (of *swill bucket* we hear nothing).[1] Anything more basic to the language than this change is apparently beyond the limits of consideration.

Charged by the dialect-geography establishment with explaining the party line to the National Council of Teachers of English, Roger W. Shuy provided a good sample of what that body and its students were supposed to believe:

> Since the American population shift generally has been from east to west, dialect boundaries are more apt to run horizontally than vertically. People from, say, western New York who moved to Michigan, Wisconsin, northern Illinois, and southern Ohio took their western New York dialect with them. Population shift is affected by the opening of new travel routes, by the invention of new means of transportation, by the development of industry, and by other aspects of American history. And speech patterns are thus moved and changed. For instance, the steamboat ushered in a whole new concept of American migration, allowing New Englanders and the more recent immigrants to move west across the Great Lakes.[2]

All this sounds very pretty, and it is certainly innocuous and noncontroversial. But the more careful and critical reader will note that Shuy's "aspects of American history" do not include slavery and the dispossession of the Indians from their lands. In fact, they conveniently exclude minority groups and the less praiseworthy aspects of American history altogether. In all of Shuy's *Discovering American Dialects*, you will not find one word about a Negro or an Indian, although you will find a few Germans, Irish and Dutch if you look very carefully.[3] Shuy's dialects move "horizontally" or "vertically" because he, like all dialect geographers, thinks about maps, not people. If you look at the record of what the people actually did, you'll find that they moved vertically-horizontally, horizontally-vertically, ziggag and backtrack, clockwise, counterclockwise and antigoglin—presumably taking their "speech patterns" with them.[4] The neatly laid out scheme that Shuy pictures does not exist. The historical evidence is that it never did exist.

Like the emigrants from England, the westward migrants did not, as a rule, travel as regional groups. That is not the usual pattern of migrating, since people who migrate generally hope to *change* their social group and social status. There were, of course, a few exceptions. The Cajuns who moved from Nova Scotia to Louisiana went as an integral group, and it may well be that they retained their dialect.[5] But much more often people went as occupational groups. Dialect geographer Alva L. Davis, describing the alleged migration of regional features to form the dialects of the Great Lakes region, gives inadvertent evidence of this trend:

> Within the Great Lakes Region are two important small areas distinctive in the composition of their population: in southeastern Ohio, the Marietta colony, *founded in 1788 by the Ohio Company*, from Massachusetts, and in northwestern Illinois, the Lead Region *settled in the 1820's by miners from all parts of the country*. [emphasis added][6]

Among the supposedly distinctive dialect forms of these groups, Davis placed the miners' term *spider* for a cast-iron frying pan. In fact, Davis asserted that the word "becomes as real as the use of the Cape Cod lighter or the hip-roofed barn."[7]

It is quite difficult, perhaps impossible, to characterize the profession of mining or the fact of employment by the Ohio Company in terms of either "horizontal" or "vertical" characteristics. But even if that inconvenient fact is overlooked, there are other problems as to where all those "vertical" and "horizontal" people came from. It you believe Professor Shuy, they were all Englishmen, except for the few aforementioned Germans, Irish, and Dutch. No Blacks or Indians need apply—not even any Frenchmen. Shuy tells us, most authoritatively:

> The first American settlers, of course, came from England. At the time of the earliest settlements in Massachusetts, Virginia, Maryland, and Rhode Island, dialect differences in England were even greater than they are today—and today they are still more striking than ours. Speakers of these various dialects crossed the Atlantic Ocean and settled, dialect and all, on the eastern coast of America. The various colonies of the New World found communication very difficult, and the mixed dialects of English settlers who inhabited each colony gradually became distinctive in themselves. The infrequent visits from "outsiders," the lack of safe and efficient transportation methods, and the tendency of each colony to act as a social unit did much to make their dialects distinctive.[8]

There is not a shred of documentary evidence to support any one of the statements about language and dialect history in the above quotation. Compare the statement on how "the various colonies of the New World found communication very difficult" to the travelers' statements about astonishing uniformity quoted in Chapter II. Shuy's picture is not description but invention—not history but antihistory.

There is no room in such a picture for contact varieties, nor for the people who speak them. Nor is there room for language innovations on the part of groups like the Blacks, Chinese, and Indians. The migration from England becomes the equivalent of an overland migration in the Indo-European reconstruction tradition—since, of course, there's no room for maritime influences either. English, the world-wide language spoken fluently by perhaps 400,000,000 people and to some degree by some millions more, by people of many races and colors, is looked upon as being the language of a few small Germanic tribes, which happens to have been carried along in their migrations and to have borrowed a few words along the way. Such a model of dialect spread cannot allow for even the reciprocal influence of the cattle herders of Texas and the northern areas like Montana, since they were more nomadic than migratory and eventually most of them returned to home base.

The kind of dialectology of which Shuy and his book are fair representatives has always overemphasized geographic differences at the expense of the many other factors involved in language variation.[9] This is especially true of the picture given of the earlier period of the history of the English language in Britain, where it is often a matter of necessity being made into a false virtue.[10] Very likely, the social component in British English dialects of the late sixteenth and early seventeenth centuries was at least as important as the geographic component, in spite of the fact that textbooks in the received tradition show only geographic differences.[11] Certain linguistic features, selected for no better reason than that a consideration of those specific features promised to yield the preconceived result, were used to determine dialect areas in England.[12] Then, it was assumed, those British dialects migrated to the New World, became American dialects, and in turn distributed their features regionally.

In addition to lacking statistical validity in terms of random distribution, the two sets of language features (British and American) are disjunctive: virtually *none* of the features used to sort out British dialects (with an extreme bias towards geographic distribution) is used in the differentiation of American dialects. There are, apparently, a few trivial exceptions like *angledog* and *caceworm*, British representatives of "the variety of terms for the earthworm which Kurath has found representative of major or minor American dialect areas."[13] More recently, Kurath has presented a short list of British regional terms that are also regional in the United States: *hay-cock* (and the local synonyms *tumble* and *doodle*), *second crop, hay-loft, near-horse, swingle-tree, shafts* (of a buggy), *cow-shed, pantry* (as a variant of *buttry* or *butlery*), *gutters, creek,* and *pet lamb.*[14] Needless to say, this minute list of farming terms does not make its case at all impressively.

Even so conventional a historian of language as Charlton Laird, who breathes no criticism of dialect geography, notes that:

> Immediately, we are in difficulties. Locutions most used to study population movements within the United States cannot be traced across the Atlantic. Their trails stop at the shore, and the reason for this would be, as Lear's fool would have said, "a pretty reason." In marking off American dialects and their westward courses, a rather curious assemblage of words has been most revealing.[15]

The "pretty reason" for the selection of this "curious assemblage" of words is plainer than is realized by Laird, who for all his perception in the above passage continues to think of dialect geography as "something approaching scientific objectivity."[16] As Glenna Ruth Pickford's brilliant critical article "American Linguistic Geography: A Sociological Appraisal" showed us in 1956, dialect geography's sampling procedures were never of professional caliber. It applied procedures used on stable European peasant populations to mobile Americans in a wholly mechanical way, and it "expended vast energies in order to supply answers to unimportant if not to nonexistent questions."[17] Far from being a modern social scientist, the dialect geographer has been more nearly a manipulator of preconceptions, a taxonomic classifier in an old-fashioned academic tradition who guided even his taxonomic classifying by firm presuppositions and shielded them from the glare of empirical light.

Pickford's criticisms were almost exclusively concerned with the way in which the Linguistic Atlas (the mentors and sponsors of Professor Shuy and those who provided the primary guidelines for Professor Laird) dealt with the populations studied. She criticized especially the way in which the atlas workers overlooked complex American migratory patterns and their consequences. Referring to atlas work in California, she wrote:

> There has never been enough stability of population or homogeneity of origin in California to establish the cultural dominance of an aged native sector . . . Out of fifty-three interviews completed [in a preliminary survey for the Pacific Coast Atlas], where aged, life-time Fresnans of American stock were sought, only six qualified—from a community of 150,000 population first settled by white men in 1849. These six showed a complete lack of homogeneity in their individual backgrounds. Their parents and grandparents migrated from over sixteen states, in varying proportions and combinations. The fact that these six were unacquainted with one another further demonstrates that native Californians do not necessarily comprise a cohesive group—do not, indeed, comprise a group at all. (*pp. 226–27*)

Pickford's devastating critique did not need to focus on the "curious assemblage of words," but equal criticism could be directed at that area.

Many of the terms that have figured prominently in American dialect geography will not be brought up in this book. The reason is simply that they cannot be shown to have any direct relevance to historical—and very little to present-day demographic—considerations. *Mudworm, angledog,* and *johnny cake*[18] contribute neither to the argument that pidgins and other contact varieties were important in the history of American English, nor to the notion that migrating British "regional" varieties redistributed themselves regionally within the United States. When the big historical issues have been settled, when we really know what the major trends in the history of American English have been, then perhaps we can begin to fit that "curious assemblage of words" (and the superficial grammatical forms with which the atlas worksheets are concerned, like *dogbit* and *bitten by a dog*) into the general pattern. But we have not yet reached that vantage point, and we will never reach it by trying to fit our inquiries into the pattern of atlas preconceptions.

This does not, of course, mean that there was no connection between British English and early American English. Elements of the former obviously remain in American, and the relatively small amount of reordering that took place was by no means random rearrangement. Nothing so extreme as reversal of order, for example, took place. British *cat* became American *cat*, not *tac* or *tca*. But this order of the elements (phonemes) of the word belongs to English in general, not to any "regional" dialect of British English. Survivals of this kind do not mean that British patterns of variation also survived in the New World.

It would be well to hesitate before assigning every meaning of American *cat* to British. David Dalby has shown that Black English vernacular *cat* "man" has a very likely West African origin.[19] According to the glossary in *Pimp: The Story of My Life* by Robert Beck (pseudonym Iceberg Slim), *cat* also means "female sex organ" in the lexicon of Black pimps and whores. Little, however, in the vocabulary of prostitution is in any significant sense African. There is a British origin (or better put, an international origin) for that meaning. Wright's *Dictionary of Obsolete and Provincial English* cites the use of *cat* meaning '[female] pudendum' and traces it to "a common use of the French *chat*" in that sense. The basic meaning and some figurative meanings of *cat* have British starting points, but they are not reflected in *regional* American differences today. Furthermore, even Wright, who apparently never thought of the possibility of anything but regional distribution, indicates no area of England to which *cat* meaning "sex organ" could be considered specific. In this, as in many other cases, the picture of "regional" British forms becoming "regional" American forms masks rather than clarifies the historical picture.

Many of the most interesting developments are not elucidated by the emphasis on origin and transmission. The special uses Iceberg Slim makes of *a rare cat with that extra dimension* ("a four-inch cone of jet hair between her thighs") and [a] *cat unique with that extra dimension* in *Pimp: The Story of My Life* may be traceable to the general vocabulary of prostitution, to Beck's own inventiveness, or to innovation within the pimp community. Certainly these uses were never regional within the United States, and their development can't owe anything to regional distributions in England.

A certain amount of continuity within a professional or underworld group, like that of prostitution, would be expected to carry over from England or Europe to the Americas. The vocabulary of pimping and prostitution, whether used by Blacks or not, has nothing especially African or Creole about it, any more than the profession itself. But some of the contact language vocabulary may have been introduced into the vocabulary of prostitution through the Blacks. An example is *trick*, 'an episode with a customer' or 'the customer himself'. The first meaning would seem to be the original one, and it may originally have been nautical. C. W. T. Layton's *Dictionary of Nautical Words and Terms* contains the entry:

> *Trick*—a spell of duty connected with the navigation of a vessel.[20]

Eliminate "connected with the navigation of a vessel" and you have what "trick" means to a prostitute. It is a simple act of transference to apply the same term to the customer with whom one performs such duty.

Other Black slang that has been popularized in recent years turns out to have British origins. Most of it tends to relate to some kind of professional jargon rather than to Africanisms or Creolisms. The now-popular *bread* for money very probably comes from the rhyming slang which is conventionally associated with the Cockney (*bread and honey*: *money*; *apples and pears*: *stairs*).[21] Since not even those who insist that Black English vernacular came from Irish overseers on the plantations have ever suggested that Blacks had much contact with Cockneys, the transfer was probably made through generalized street talk. There are a few obsolescent Harlem jive expressions like *yam*, 'eat' (related to West African and general Caribbean *nyam nyam*, to Papiamentu *jomi jomi*, and probably to "infantile" *yum yum*) which have African roots, but these are the exception rather than the rule.

The point is, however, that British *regional* varieties did not re-form themselves in the North American colonies or the United States. Socially identified speech communities like the Black ethnic group, occupations and professions, and even the rackets were more persistent than communities based upon the accident of geographic proximity, and those speech communities have been a more effective way of transmitting language patterns.

Even in the regionalists' picture of the development of American English, it is conventional to admit some slight influence from foreign-language groups. Shuy, in the article already referred to, points out:

> German pronunciations and vocabulary are still found in Grundy County, Illinois; the linguistic effects of the Irish are present on Beaver Island in Lake Michigan; the Dutch influences, in Holland and Grand Rapids, Michigan; and Briticisms, in many American communities which were settled directly from England (such as Albion, Illinois, and New Harmony, Indiana).[22]

The Jews are perhaps the most important group omitted from Shuy's list. And the reasons may not be hard to deduce. For one with regional preconceptions, foreign-language groups like the Germans of Grundy County, Illinois, are much more convenient. They are "local" in nature and fit Shuy's preconceptions about local dialect patterns. The Jewish contribution, on the other hand, has been national; it is centered around the electronic media, not around some island conveniently isolated in Lake Michigan.[23]

Apart from the Yiddishisms of the relaxed part of media speech behavior (like comedy programs and commercials), the language of the media is the "common" dialect, which obviously has its roots in the koiné. Referred to as Network Standard,[24] it has been shown to be the dialect preferred by diverse groups of Americans. Psycholinguists Lambert and Tucker found that Black college freshmen in the Deep South and their largely white counterparts in New England showed an overwhelming preference for that type of speech over other American dialects.[25] Since almost everyone in the country has contact with the electronic media, it is a part of the language life of nearly all of us. And since radio and television waves do not need a geographic locale but are notoriously mobile, there is very little about the media dialect that correlates with place.

One of H. L. Mencken's most cherished insights was his perception of what he called General American. Incidentally, (this was something quite different from what he called the American Vulgate, a kind of conglomerate of all the "bad" English forms used by Americans, which lacks the validity of his other conception.) Shuy and other dialect geographers have found that, by using research procedures that would not be permitted to a student in any other department in any graduate school, they can draw isoglosses[26] in any part of the country. They have concluded, without justification, that because they can find some variations everywhere, there is no supraregional dialect of the type Mencken described. But Mencken's perceptions seem, to judge by the results of the tests given by Lambert and Tucker,[27] to be more sophisticated than the results of mediocre research performed by dialect geographers. There *is* a dialect that is recognizably American, which, in one form or another, is part of the language behavior of all but the most disadvantaged adult Americans, and which does not correlate with any region.

Neither, as far as that goes, does it correlate with class or caste. Very important research of the past decade has shown how stratificational differences are reflected in the dialects of native English speakers. The most famous work in the field is William Labov's *The Social Stratification of English in New York City*,[28] published in 1966 which, despite some flaws that have been revealed in the past seven or eight years, is still perhaps the masterpiece of American social dialectology. In fact, that discipline may be considered to have had its beginning in the United States in Labov's work, although the spadework had been done by researchers like John Gumperz,[29] who found dialects in India correlated with caste. Still, there are some general trends, like Network Standard, that are affected only by the extremes of social stratification (in that only the superordinated are above their influence and only the extremely disadvantaged lack some participation in them).

The media (especially if we include newspapers and magazines) have had a great deal of influence upon what has come to be in general use in American English. While some German words may have spread out to the surrounding areas from Grundy County, Illinois, the flood of Germanisms in World War II did not come from any such rural groups. *Blitzkrieg, panzer, Luftwaffe, Stuka* and other such military terms came into our vocabulary even if we had never met anyone from Grundy County. We don't have to look for a colony of Russians near our birthplace to explain how we learned the word *Sputnik* in 1957.

Although many Americans are not aware of it, two of our most characteristic words, *hamburger* and *frankfurter*, come ultimately from German. Describing the lower culinary and nutritional end of our national eating habits, they probably reflect scornful naming practices of Germans; that is, a "hamburger" would be the kind of thing a person from another city would accuse a native of Hamburg of eating; a "frankfurter" would be an equivalent aspersion on the tastes of a resident of Frankfurt (*frankfurterwurst* = 'Frankfurt sausage'). *Hot dog*, as is well known, was originally a metaphor for the "dachshund" appearance of the latter.

In spite of the fact that the suffix-*burger* would mean, if anything, 'resident of a city' in German, it came to have a very different meaning in American English. Discarding local associations, Americans used it for the characteristic products of low-grade eating establishments catering to the dietary habits of teenagers and others more interested in filling the stomach than delighting the palate. There was a fad, now largely past, of making new compounds: *Chickburger, nutburger, fishburger, crabburger, shrimpburger, cheeseburger, pizzaburger, steakburger,* etc. There even developed *beefburgers,* although the original hamburger was supposedly made out of beef. The situation became so confusing that a national magazine ran a cartoon in which a small lunch stand was shown with signs advertising the many kinds of burgers. The counterman was saying to a customer, "We got one made out of ham, too; but we don't know what to call it." So far were Americans from thinking in terms of regional origins that the first syllable (*ham-*) had transferred its meaning from the place to a type of meat. Most of us are as little aware of the function of *Limburg* in the naming of *Limburger cheese* as we are of the role of Hamburg and Frankfurt in the name of the sandwiches.

Many people of the rural United States learned the term *Vienna sausage*—to stick to relatively German matters for a few moments—off a can, and pronounced the first word

/vayIna/, not even connecting it to the capital of Austria. Laird, true to his basic dedication to dialect geography, emphasizes the German words which became "traditional in some communities": *Sangerfests, apfel strudel, beer soup, zwieback*.[30] Localisms can be manufactured; we could point out that the German club at the University of Texas in the 1950's was called the *Eulenspiegelverien*. But the media words that came from German because the newspapers and the radio newscasts were full of the Nazis and their war machine (which many of us learned to call the *Wehrmacht*) were transcendently more important than those localisms.

Within special communities, borrowings have special channels. When one hears a speaker of American English using the word *Festschrift*, he can be pretty certain that he is listening to a college professor—or to a student who aspires to be one. But he cannot make the wildest guess as to where the professor is teaching now or where he was born or grew up. *Zeitgeist* is a rather different type of word—the type that the author of a letter to the editor uses in order to impress his readers. Some of the less effete academicians are now a little embarrassed by it; its user is likely to be a literary critic, and often one whose aspirations exceed his accomplishments.

Another interesting case of a questionable localism is *cafeteria*, which came from the Spanish and may first have been borrowed in the Southwest. The word, which means a coffee shop in Spanish, came somehow to designate a self-service restaurant. But American users knew *café* as a word in its own right, and they assumed that *-teria* must have some independent meaning. During the heyday of the term, there were washaterias (now called laundromats), bootaterias, gasaterias, habeterias (for haberdasheries, according to Mencken, Third Edition), and grocetiterias or groceterias. There were even coffeeterias, a full circle from the suffix's original Spanish function. Mencken describes the word *cafeteria* as "once a California localism," but also cites a correspondent who told him that the first cafeteria was in

Chicago. However that may be, the word enjoyed almost immediate national circulation because it was picked up by the media; and the compoundings could not be localized in California or anywhere else.

The tendency to overrate geographic distribution continues to the present time. William Labov, regarded by many as the most supermodern of the sociolinguists, calls "the positive *anymore*" ("We go to the movies anymore") a "regional feature strongly entrenched throughout the Midland area."[31] But the college student who explained the structure (a blend of *We don't go to the drive-in anymore* and *We go to the movies*) to me in 1967 was a lifelong resident of Potsdam, New York. Young people in their late teens and early twenties use the grammatical pattern in most, if not all, parts of the country. It may be merely accidental that dialectologists have happened to hear it in the Midwest. In the absence of any real research, it is as likely to be an age-graded as a regional form.

The, until recently, almost entirely unquestioned assumptions of the dialect geographers provided the intellectual climate in which such assumptions could be made and could pass for "science." Obviously, however, different observers' anecdotal observations are at variance, and some real research is needed. Anyone who looks into "the positive *anymore*" might also look at *you oughta be,* which means 'you should consider yourself.' (*You oughta be lucky* = "You should consider yourself lucky.") That's another one that might prove to be either late teen-age or Midwestern in distribution.

Certain groups may be more influenced by national factors than by local contacts. Sawyer's article on Spanish and English in Texas, referred to extensively in Chapter IV,[32] shows how "Latin bilinguals in Texas are more likely to know *corn husk* and *wish bone* than the terms used by the local 'Anglos': *corn shuck* and *pulley bone.*" They are also unlikely to know *roas' nyears,* a form of *roasting ears,* although Texas whites and Negroes as far away as North Carolina use the term.[33] As in many other cases, geographic proximity has been outweighed by more important considerations. Since the "Latins" and "Anglos" don't mix on kitchen levels of intimacy (which is not to say that they don't wind up in the same bedroom sometimes), they have not learned the same words for these homey items related to food. For the Latins, books were a more important source for such vocabulary.

But a San Antonio "Anglo" and a San Antonio "Latin" who had an interest in recorded music might learn a great deal of the same vocabulary from newspapers and audio magazines. In English, they would both refer to the *turntable, tone arm,* and *cartridge*; to *monophonic, stereophonic,* and *quadrophonic* reproduction; to *solid state, preamp, amplifier, woofer, tweeter, mid-range, damping, moving coil, electrostatic, crossover network, hysteresis, synchronic, elliptical* and *conical styli,* and to *tracking force.* Their records would be *33⅓'s* (*LP's*), *45's,* or *78's.* They might be very much concerned as to whether the recordings were made at a *live* or *studio performance.*

Although the electronic media concerned themselves with nonkitchen vocabulary, they spread words more rapidly than either kitchen contacts or printed media. Thus words from radio and television are highly unlikely to show local distributions. Of course, it is true that since the early days of radio a great deal of the program material has come from New York and Los Angeles. In radio, for example, much was made of the *coast-to-coast hookup,* a term few of us were likely to encounter otherwise. It was considered a great trick to have the engineers on a station that was broadcasting from New York "try" to get Los Angeles. Los Angeles, some of the more skeptical of us were beginning to suspect, may have been there all along. But it impressed us in the beginning. And there's a kind of lesson for all domains[34] of American vocabulary in all this: if there's a *geographic* source of electronic media vocabulary, it is New York–Los Angeles, a "locale" spread over 3,000 miles. One would love to see Professor Shuy deal with that one, perhaps in terms of migrants going east from Los Angeles and west from New York—taking their radios and their dialects with them.

No matter where we came from or where we lived, if we listened to the radio we heard about (and talked about) *soap opera, quiz show, static* (for the radio listener, a sound and not a type of electricity), *announcer* (specialized semantically in the sense that the announcer was a man with a special personality who did much more than just "announce"), *station break, sign-off, comedy hour,* and *give-away program.* Except to the most selective of listeners, phrases like *Fibber McGee's closet, Jack Benny's Maxwell,* and *Bob Hope's nose* were matters of common knowledge and discussion. We didn't have to live near New York, Los Angeles, Chicago, or any other such city in order to talk of these things. On the semitechnical side, and somewhat later, we all learned *AM, FM, transistor,* and *portable* from the media. *Transistor* may have a technical meaning to some speakers, but the meaning "a radio carried around and held to the ear" has been better known to children and teen-agers since the early 1960's.

Some of the terminology of radio, like *serials (daytime serial* was once the more dignified term for *soap opera),* may have come in from the movies. The two media certainly shared some terms. For small boys in the 1930's and 1940's, a *serial* with a cowboy or a jungle man in it was a *continued piece.* In all parts of the country, movie fans at one time or another talked of *bank nights, double features* (or even *triple features) sneak previews* (although the term was not especially meaningful outside of the big cities), *previews of coming attractions, newsreels, shorts* (or *selected short subjects), cartoons, travelogues, Westerns* (which may have been used in novels before that time), *shoot-'em-ups* or *gangster pictures* or *cops 'n' robbers, musicals, tear-jerkers* (perhaps also originally from novels), *screen credits, Acad-*

emy Award, Oscar, Oscar winner, supporting cast, character actor, Technicolor (sometimes applied to the products of its competitors) , *black and white, 3-D, sound track, on location, stunt man, star.* Initially, a diminutive of the last, *starlet,* came to have a very special meaning. A national magazine once ran a cartoon showing a chesty young woman with a big, artificial smile coming into a night club and provoking the remark from a patron, "She's a very famous starlet; they may even put her in a picture."

Television not only carried on a certain amount of the national media vocabulary of radio and the movies, it added a vocabulary of its own. Whether we would be caught dead eating them or not, we all know what *TV dinners* are. Even the aficionados know that the box is often called *the boob tube*—sometimes *the tube* for short. The very slightly technically minded learn of the *Teleprompter* and of *Telestar,* the artificial satellite used in transmission. We know also of *prime time, talk shows, the late show, snow.* It's a fair bet that the residents of the Hudson Valley, whatever their ages, are more likely to know any of these terms than they are to know *olicook,* a doughnut, even though the Linguistic Atlas says the last is characteristic of their dialect and doesn't mention the others.

Although *rerun* may not have come into the language just when television started reusing the same programs in the summer, more of us associate it with television than with anything else. And a *channel* is a number on a dial, not what a river runs through. The British may abbreviate the name of the medium as *telly,* but for Americans from any part of the country it's the *tee-vee.*

The telephone also brought us an essentially national vocabulary. The British call the girl who operates the system a *telephonist* whereas we call her a *switchboard operator* (when not in a mood for viler names), and Americans all picked up the latter term and dropped *central* at about the same time. The Bell system brought into our lives "Number, please"; "The line is busy"; "You have the wrong number"; "Your three minutes are up"; and even "Don't call us; we'll call you." "Give me a ring" had an entirely different meaning before Bell's invention. We expend a great deal of our vocal energy on phrases like *long distance, person-to-person, station-to-station, local call, toll call, direct dial, area code, dial tone, busy signal,* and even *nuisance call* and *obscene call.* Without the telephone, the one-upmanship of *unlisted number* and the scorn of *party line* would have been impossible, and neither *directory* nor *yellow pages* would mean what they mean today.

Again on a national scale, the attempts of brand-name companies to make their products household words have often been strikingly successful. In some cases, the success was too great; the proper noun became a common noun—to the loss of the advertiser. The Eastman Company propagated *Kodak,* only to find to its dismay that the word was coming to mean any camera, except perhaps more expensive Japanese and German imports. Likewise, *Kleenex* could soon be applied to any kind of tissue—at least to any that wouldn't provoke titters if seen outside the bathroom. *Frigidaire* and *Hoover* encountered the same problems of being likely to be used for any refrigerator or vacuum cleaner. The process could work backwards, too: in the mid-sixties a poor old man of my acquaintance acquired a television set made by "the Console Company." But even more typical was what happened to the Coca-Cola company, which found that *coke* meant any soft drink and that "Gimme a coke" was not necessarily the sign of profits entering the company's till. Pepsi Cola, Royal Crown Cola, and even for a time Cleo Cola became almost homonymous competitors in the 1930's; and even drinks with artificial fruit flavors had a nationwide vogue as "cokes."

Trouble with the national vocabulary was perhaps nowhere as important a factor as the differences between the Black English vernacular and other varieties. Experienced carhops in the roadside cafés of East Texas (and perhaps of part of western Louisiana) in the 1930's and 1940's had to explain to new employees that the occasional Black customer who asked for "a Ah See Cola an' a spreadwide" wanted a R[oyal] C[rown] Cola and a large candy bar, which the carhops themselves called a *peanut patty*, and which their modern replacements call a *praline*. The large cola drink of the time made enough for two, and the sugary candy bar could be broken in two and made into a stopgap meal for a couple.

Media words are a good illustration of the nationalizing tendency of American English, especially for those portions of the population that have not been repressed by caste barriers or the more extreme class divisions. Rather than determining the national characteristics of the language, however, it is probable that the media *reflect* these tendencies. After some improvement in the national situation with regard to racial inequality, the television networks hired former Black basketball stars on their sportscasting teams and thereby probably inadvertently produced a diglossic situation in which one sportscaster is, even when unseen, obviously white, while the other, who is usually assigned the job of giving background commentary and who handles the half-time interviews, etc., is just as obviously Black. While the media reflect, there is not much evidence that they initiate. There is no proof, for example, that they have any particular influence on the child who is in the process of acquiring his first dialect.

It is commonly believed that the ghetto child watches television constantly and therefore should be especially proficient in the Network Standard dialect. But one cannot interact effectively with a television set, and the ghetto child, like all other children, learns more language from his peers than he does from any other source.[35] The familiar claims that children from Harlem and Bedford-Stuyvesant sit glued to the television set all day seem never to have been quantitatively substantiated. But even if the claims were true, nothing much would follow about the dialect these children bring to school. Those who really need to learn the unmarked, national dialect are the adults who begin to deal with members of other communities on a business-peer-interaction footing.

The problem of the ghetto child is the major thorn in the side of the established, received picture of the history of American English as sketched in the quotation cited earlier from Shuy. The east-to-west migration picture, with the transmission of dialects intact, is derived entirely from a not wholly credible consideration of the white population of the United States. Unless Blacks match (or derive from) whites, the whole conception is suspect.

It has always been known that there are a few major exceptions to the Anglocentric formation of American English dialects. The most striking is Gullah, also called Geechee,[36] the English Creole of the Sea Islands of South Carolina and Georgia. Along with Louisiana French Creole ("Gombo"), Gullah provides an obvious break in the simplistic pattern. As I tried to show in *Black English*, a generalized Plantation Creole, based on an even more generalized Maritime Pidgin English with a heavy admixture of African influence, provides an even greater exception to the putative pattern. With the additional demonstration of the existence of a colonial koiné, I hope to have shown that the formerly received picture is almost totally invalid. Without the existence of Black English, however, probably no one would have thought of looking for the other kinds of patterns.

Besides being in itself a major challenge to the establishment historical viewpoint, Black English and its antecedent, Plantation Creole, provide a further contradiction to the traditional disbelief in their influence on Southern white speech. This is, in fact, beyond any serious question; only the degree remains to be determined. As I pointed out in *Black English*, the possibility of a Black-on-white influence is strengthened by the most important possible sociolinguistic facts: Southern white children were quite likely to enter into peer relationships with Black children (even the children of slaves), although their elders were not likely to do so with Black adults.

This statement is in direct conflict with the opinions that most linguists, a great many English teachers, and others concerned academically with language acquired in graduate school or elsewhere. Most of these opinions, however, have never been subjected to examination. College language teachers believe in dialect geography and the reconstructive tradition the way young children believe in Santa Claus, and their reaction on reading anything that challenges it is anger —it is the linguistic equivalent of an attack on Mom's apple pie or the corner drugstore.

A hypersensitive Black academic trained in dialect geography, Juanita Williamson, was incensed by statements about Black English (or Nonstandard Negro English) from the very first. Soon realizing that the records of the Linguistic Atlas of the United States and Canada did not disprove the existence of a specifically Black-correlated dialect (they do not, in fact, either prove or disprove anything), she set about collecting such materials herself from white Southerners.

The materials she gathered corroborate the influence of Black English (especially nineteenth-century Plantation Creole) on Southern white English. She recorded, from Southern white informants:

This be all right.   (Customer in a department store)

She be fifteen in November.   (Man talking to clerk in department store)

Think how cool you are and you be cool.   (Customer in department store)

That be all?   (Clerk in a supermarket)

From Southern whites, Professor Williamson found not only the relatively insignificant (because it can be readily accounted for in terms of the [phonological] deletions of casual speech styles), "I been sleeping with a pistol by my side" (secretary, state university), but the strikingly significant (because it cannot be derived by any such process) "I been had it" (a bus driver).

Although many of the Williamson examples are meaningless, revealing only the not very surprising fact that white as well as Black nonstandard speakers use *ain't*, *don't*, and *they is* for *there is*, the examples quoted above suggest a crucial problem about the origin of "Southern" language forms. Used as the primary language variety of Black children and by Black and white Southern adults in relaxed styles, they look like nothing from England, Scotland, or Ireland but are easy to derive from Plantation Creole through the process of decreolization.[37] Furthermore, there is a vast amount of historical documentation of that process.[38]

But the thesis—quite reasonable in itself, and quite in accord with widespread folk typologies and beliefs—that Plantation Creole had an influence on the English of white speakers in the South has been the one repellent to the internal-reconstructionist establishment. James Sledd (who is, by the way, a rabid opponent of teaching Standard English to Black children by any method whatsoever) propounded perhaps the most extreme defense against that theory, some years, it is true, before the actual academic articulation of the theory.[39] According to Sledd, Southern white vowel articulation is traceable to the "breaking" and "umlaut" processes characteristic of the Old English period. This would mean that phonological processes that had run their course in England well before the period of emigration to the Americas have somehow reappeared among the whites of the American South.[40] (Sledd does not specifically mention Southern Blacks, but he apparently believes that the English they acquired was a direct imitation of that of the white man.) It is not clear what causal agency Sledd would credit with the sudden revivification of an essentially medieval phonological process—surely it was not the warmth of the Southern climate which awakened the dormant seeds of "breaking" and "umlaut."

Tracing American English forms to exclusively British "folk" sources has its greatest cost, in terms of complexity of formulation, in the analysis of Black English vernacular. For this reason, those who support the British "folk" origins theory have been, first of all, eager to divert attention away from Black speech patterns; then defensive in regard to the origins of the features of that vernacular. In some cases, this defensiveness has led to extremes of archaizing absurdity. For example, some extremists trace the possession-by-juxtaposition feature that produces "Mary hat," "my friend aunt," "Mr. Jackson car," etc., back to Middle English forms, like the Prologue to Chaucer's late fourteenth-century *Canterbury Tales*: "In hope to stonden in his lady grace."

Such derivation presupposes, of course, that Middle English grammatical forms, which disappeared from the language in general four or five hundred years ago, have turned up in American English, apparently having lain in a state of suspended animation (perhaps in the deep freeze, like *Li'l Abner's* General Bullmoose) all that time.[41]

But there are other structures to which this kind of reasoning, unimpressive as it may be, cannot be applied at all. The preverbal *been* of "I been ate the chicken," "Bill, you been know that," "I been had it a long time" is not grammatically the least bit like the nearest thing in Middle English:

Somme been of tree, and doon hir lord servyse.
   (Wife of Bath's Prologue)

I sey nat this by wyves that been wyse,
   (Wife of Bath's Prologue)

Although Middle English *been* and Black English vernacular *been* are lexically similar, the former is a present tense whereas the latter is a rather emphatic past.

Those oriented toward the reconstructive tradition were most excited by that feature of the Black English vernacular grammar called the "zero copula," the "absence" of a linking verb as in:

> They good
> Who that?
> (You don't know) who Brenda Weston.

The reason for such concern was probably that unlike what could be claimed about *been*, provided no grammatical analysis was performed, there was no way to claim that the "zero copula" was represented in Early English sources. This was, of course, a severe threat to the established view of American English history—although not so great as that posed by the preverbal *been*, once its grammatical structure was understood.

Some attempt has been made to account for the zero copula as a "spontaneous" development, but the attempts are far from convincing.[42] The simple theory of phonological deletion can derive *I'm right* from a simple contraction of *I am right* and *he right* or *you right* from a further deletion stage (just beyond ordinary English *he's right* and *you're right*), but it cannot account for *I'm is (right)* without some real contortions of rule-forming.[43]

Once it was pointed out that there were extensive records of the use of Pidgin English in the United States (as, for example, those cited in Chapters I, III, and IV), there predictably arose a concerted attempt to trace pidgin/creole features like the *-um* transitivizer, zero copula, possession by juxtaposition, and nonredundant pluralization to spontaneous generation from "language universals." Presumably no transmission has to be proved for language universals; they are likely to jump out anywhere people are talking.

If it is true that the language contact features (including Pidgin/Creole) that can be found in American English—especially in earlier historical stages, in those circumstances in which speakers of a large number of languages have been in contact—are the result of a kind of linguistic spontaneous combustion, then the appeal of the Pidgin/Creole theory is weakened. But so is any other theory of transmission. If those forms of American Black English vernacular that match the Pidgin English of West Africa and the Creoles of Surinam can be said to have arisen spontaneously from "language universals," why cannot the same thing be said about those features that happen to match British "folk" or "regional" dialects? Surely the theory of "language universals" and its application to language history should be more than simply a device to dismiss every challenge to establishment preconceptions.

Insofar as language universals are concerned, it seems much more sensible to consider them limiting factors, within which all linguistic change can take place, than immediate causal factors. If British English forms a question from "John goes to town every Saturday" by a rather complex process, which yields "Does John go to town every Saturday?" it is a fairly safe bet that English in no one of the British colonies will produce the question form *"John go to town every Saturday does?" Furthermore, it is fairly certain that no "daughter" dialect of English will form its passive by turning "John killed the lion" into *"Nohj dellik eht noil." That is, no grammatical structure is formed merely by reversing the order of elements in another. But beyond such theoretical limitations, users of descendent dialects have some potential for changing the original constructions, including the wholesale type of remodeling that characterized pidginization.[44]

Since the absence of such "complete reversal" permutations is presumably a linguistic *universal*, it would have been impossible for emigrating Britons to reshape their syntactic structures in terms of such processes. Both their language and the other languages with which they would come into contact would have to fall within the set of linguistic possibilities.[45] But such a statement leaves the question of what happens in language contact up in the air; we know no more from it than that the contact languages did not have any grammatical design properties that "normal" languages do not have.[46] The set of possibilities for syntactic influence, or for influences, can perhaps be determined, and impossible developments excluded, by speculation, intuition, and mathematical formulation.[47] But the decision as to what particular developments took place *within* that set of possibilities is an historical issue, to be resolved by consideration of historical records.[48]

Those records suggest that the contact situation in the United States was the major factor in the development of differences within American English and in its difference from British English. (It should always be remembered that, according to the doctrine of language universals, the "deepest" parts of language—those reflecting the basic nature of language design—are not subject to change under *any* conditions.) The varieties most important for that contact situation, especially on the frontier, included Pidgin English, Creole varieties which developed when Pidgin became the first language of children born in mixed communities, and the koiné. The conflict between the highly useful Pidgin/Creole varieties and the very prestigious koiné was the most important linguistic feature of the advancing frontier.

Theories of linguistic change often combine such contact factors with what is called "psycholinguistic change"; in some extreme cases, contact factors are conceded minimal influence or excluded altogether. The psycholinguistic theory assumes that changes take place between generations. The child alters the rule structure of his parents' language, perhaps because of maturational changes in the brain. Obviously, a great many children speak differently from their parents, even to the point that the parents may speak a language the child doesn't know or the child learn a language the parents don't. But a simple version of the "brain groove" theory overlooks the important fact that the peer group is almost always more important to a child's language development than his parents.[49]

It is currently fashionable to explain pidgin varieties in terms of some such psychological processes.[50] It is frequently asserted, especially by those who have something to lose professionally if pidgin transmission across the United States is established,[51] that on-the-spot pidginization takes place. Thus it would be asserted that it took place independently among the Algonquian Indians, the Seminoles and the Plains Indians, in spite of the fact that there was the common factor of contact with escaped Black slaves for all of them.[52]

It is strange, however, that in observable contact situations where people from different language backgrounds come together in the absence of a lingua franca, there is no such immediate solution from "language universals." The position taken here is that pidgins, like other contact varieties, share in language universals just as much as and no more than any other kind of language—they certainly do not contradict any universal laws of language,[53] but they are no closer to "language universals" than any other language or variety. When a monolingual speaker of English tries to address a monolingual speaker of Chinese, their communication is not going to be furthered by the fact that their languages are designed according to the same set of abstract principles. It may do each speaker some good, in terms of human relationships, to realize that they stand at the same distance from language universals, but there is no reason to believe that they could effect communication on the basis of that knowledge. When, as Asbury relates in *The Barbary Coast*, a Chinese named Lem Duck was able to warn his friend George McMahon, "Georgia man! Georgia Man! Highbinder stealum whistle!" he was able to communicate because of a long language contact tradition going back to Chinese Pidgin English and probably even to the Portuguese Trade Pidgin.[54] Asbury may or may not be right in attributing *hoodlum* to Chinese Pidgin English *huddle 'um* (that is, with the transitivizer); but the word did show up first, as he says, in San Francisco around 1870–71. The *Oxford English Dictionary*, which provides this information, offers no theory of its etymology. It seems, however, impossible that the word should have sprung up spontaneously as a "natural" designation for a thug or rowdy.

If such pure innovations are a priori unlikely, there remain more problematic matters of changes of meaning. Some varieties of American English seem especially prone to picturesque changes. One of the most interesting of such varieties is "Boont," of Boonville, California, which utilizes many vocabulary innovations clearly made on the pattern of English.[55] In that special small-town California variety (almost all the speakers seem to be able to speak ordinary English), *speak* has become *harp, the Boonville dialect* has become *Boontling* or *Boont* (shortened forms of *Boonville Lingo*), and *to burlap* means 'to make love to,' supposedly in memory of a general store clerk who was found with a young lady on a pile of burlap bags.

There are fairly easy explanations for all these developments, none of them indicating a special ability to penetrate to the "universal" layer of language on the part of Boonville residents at any time in the past, and none of them requiring any particular connection with British regions. It also appears that the practitioners of Boont constitute a restricted social group in Boonville, adult to middle-aged males. *Harp* for *speak* seems innovative; but we must remember that ordinary English also uses the word to mean *talk* in the special sense of 'to dwell upon in speech or writing'.[56] To explain the exact factor that removed it from special, metaphorical usage to ordinary usage in Boonville would be a desideratum for historical linguistics; but then so would the explanation of thousands of other words that are not considered out of the ordinary.

The use of the name of the town for the name of the language variety is perhaps the oldest way of all to name a speech type. Schoolchildren whom we interviewed in the Cameroon in 1964 regularly listed the name of their home village as that of their native language—which produced many designations you won't find in any work on African language classifications. The use of final *-t* (*Boon* + *-t*) fits into a common English pattern, although it is sometimes slightly obscured by surface irregularities of the spelling system:

high   height
weigh   weight

Nonstandard dialects regularly produce such forms (not all of them having any additional meaning), which are promptly condemned by schools and other agents of authority:

once   oncet
twice   twicet
close   clost

The form *Boont*, seen in such a context, is far from an absolute invention. Historical omniscience, if we had it, would allow us to explain each individual development of this type. Since we don't have it, there is probably no reason to let such individual developments distort a reasonably clear general picture.

Other developments, less exotic than "Boont," are perhaps more characteristic of the regular process of language change. On Martha's Vineyard, sociolinguist William Labov, mentioned often before in this book, found interesting correlations between the pronunciation of the /aw/ diphthong (the way some of us pronounce the vowel of *cow*) and the age level of the speakers. He found a regular correlation between the speaker's age and the frequency of centralization (pronunciation as /əw/, the latter increasing as the age level decreased. It was concluded that the centralization of the diphthong of *cow, crowd*, or *house* served to mark native status on the island. The nearer the pronunciation was to /aw/ (which is approximately the way the elocutionist may have told you to pronounce it), the less likely you were to be an old-timer of Martha's Vineyard who kept aloof from the tourists. The least "local" pronunciation pattern was that of high-school-age youngsters who planned to find work on the mainland.

The change, according to Labov, began in a not surprising group, considering the pattern of influences on American English we have seen already. Yankee fishermen were apparently the first to use the "centralized" diphthong, and the change spread first to others of the same ethnic group regardless of other factors. Later, this change spread to the neighboring Indian groups and finally to the Portuguese who lived on the island. As "foreigners," the last were, in a familiar pattern, eager to conform to the native norms of the area. They became linguistically more Yankee than the Yankees.

However they originated, certain other tendencies in American English have undoubtedly been accelerated by the desire of outsider groups to pass for native or even supernative.[57] Many structures, such as the verb plus preposition, are as commonplace for "ethnic" Americans as for descendants of true-born Englishmen. Expressions such as *build up*, 'exalt', *start up* (an engine), *brew up* 'instigate', *fall for, lose out*, etc., which have often been compared to the German verb plus separable prefix, belong to a type that in much more restricted use goes back to Old English times. In their superabundance, however, they are very typically American; probably, since they became less frequent during the eighteenth century in England and then proliferated in the Americas, they were part of the American koiné described in Chapter II.

In particular, the two-preposition compounds are characteristic of American but not of British English: *miss out on, carried away with, go away with, get* [a task] *over with, mix up with, cuddle up to* or *with, make up with* [someone], *take up with, put up with, go along with, sit down to, go out with, go up on* [prices, for example], *carry on with* [another woman, for example], *catch on to.* Here, again, the English Creoles have tendencies in common with ordinary American English. In Antigua, for example, there is a shibboleth, "He's from so far back in the country he still says *devel it up.*" More urban speakers say *develop it,* of course, as they approach Standard English more nearly in other aspects. Joel Chandler Harris makes some of his characters, speakers of a form of Plantation Creole, say *gallin' the horses up* (for *galloping the horses*), and Jamaican informants tell me that the same expression is still commonplace on that island.

Virtually nothing is more characteristic of American English, urban or rural, than the verb-preposition compounds. Some of these have even acquired multiple meanings. *Live it up,* for example, can mean not only 'celebrate without restraint', but also 'expend [one's funds] in the purchase of food, housing, etc.' (especially if one has no immediate source of income).

Again, as is well known, *do* (or *does, did*) is used in question structures in both American and British English; but there is a certain difference in their use with the main verb *have.* British "Hasn't he blond hair?" is normal, whereas American (in anything except Anglophile speech) is, "Doesn't he have blond hair?" The tag question form also differs in this type of possession, sometimes called "inalienable possession."[58] Whereas the typical British form would be, "He has blond hair, hasn't he?" Americans generally find it more normal to say, "He has blond hair, doesn't he?" And

a certain type of conjoined question shows the difference
even more markedly:

British: Has he blond hair or hasn't he?
American: Does he have blond hair or doesn't he?

Of course, within the twentieth century the American expression has become somewhat more widely used in England;
and there were always some Americans who affected British
usage. One can say, however, as a kind of obvious minimal
historical statement, that American English has—for some
reason and by some process—carried a modern English syntactic development[59] (use of "do support" in question formation) further than British English, applying it to a verb
(*have*) to which it is not usually applied in British English.

It is interesting, and it may be significant, that Black
English and the English Creoles offer a much greater deviation from the British form—in the same direction as that of
ordinary American English but more extended.[60] Where
ordinary American English has "He has got blond hair" in
casual usage) and treats *has* like any other auxiliary verb,
producing the question form, "Has he got blond hair?" Black
English vernacular has not only "He got blond hair" and
"He gots blond hair," but even "He don't got blond hair."[61]
The question forms are:

Do he got blond hair?
Don't he got blond hair?

What may be involved historically in the Black vernacular
"deviation" is indicated by something in the usage of many
Black speakers. Shown a picture of a plate of food and asked
to describe it as part of a regular language-elicitation procedure, a child from Washington's Adams-Morgan community
responded, "He got cheese, bread, cake . . ." (This means
'There is cheese, bread, cake . . .', since the picture did not
contain a picture of any "he.") This usage is strikingly paral-

lel to other Creole structures, like *get/have*, 'there is', in Hawaiian and other English Creoles, Portuguese Creole *tem*, 'it has; there is', and French Creole *li gagne*. In ordinary French, the last would mean 'he gained' or 'he got', but in Creole it is the ordinary way of saying 'there is' or 'there are'. Considerable evidence supports the thesis that the Black English vernacular forms of today represent convergence with the ordinary American English forms, having started in much more Creolelike structures.[62] Of course, the whites' usage was to some degree influenced by the Creole. It does *not* seem that Blacks started out with white usages and then extended them (by analogy or something of the kind) to arrive at still more nonstandard forms. It indicates, rather, that the general historical principle has been the approximation of the speech of Blacks to that of whites, causing them to leave behind some of the more "extreme" creolisms.

The speech of American whites has been changing, too, as all language changes. Some of the whites have, because they learned Black English in childhood, been strongly influenced by it.[63] But early white "settlers" in the United States had another kind of linguistic sharing with the captives from West Africa: both groups used Pidgin English extensively in the complex frontier contact situations. If, as I have tried to show in Chapter IV, the frontier situation was the primary locus of "nonstandard" (i.e., nonkoiné) grammatical usage, then it might be expected that the "deviation" from British usage, as evidenced in the auxiliary structure with main verb *have*, is part of the quite early American English variety.

A kind of re-Anglicization did take place for some American speakers, especially the urban residents of the eastern seaboard. Among upper-crust Bostonians, you might be able to hear "He has a nice British accent, hasn't he?" or even "Has he a good British accent or hasn't he?" But the rest of the country has been more independent than that—linguistically and otherwise. In most of the country, even English teachers have given up their Anglicization projects. Teachers aren't all that important where language is concerned, anyway.[64]

According to Labov (his conclusions are based on unpublished research, which I have been unable to see), New York and other U.S. seaboard cities were *r*-pronouncing (in words like *card, barn*) in the eighteenth century and became "completely" [sic] *r*-less in the nineteenth.[65] Labov's researchers have attributed this Eastern seaport *r*-dropping (in New York, Boston, Charleston, Savannah, and other ports) to "the model . . . of the prestige pattern of New England and London."[66] This may be true; but there are other explanations for Savannah and Charleston.[67] At any rate, the historical pattern reported by Labov fits perfectly into the picture of maritime influences on American English. Furthermore, since it appears that London dialect was formed by the koiné-izing process, it is one more indication of the importance of dialect leveling in language history. And nothing whatsoever suggests that the *r*-pronouncing situation was affected by the bringing of "regional" British dialects to America.

All recent developments in historical study indicate that the methodology of Shuy and his colleagues will not do, and that their results are not reliable. The history of American English is full of processes that did not come in from British "regional" dialects, and no one feature of our language is explainable only in those terms. The paleontological method of reaching back, cafeteria style, to the Linguistic Atlas of England to find the putative origin of any language feature that happens to turn up on the Linguistic Atlas of the United States and Canada yields results that are directly contradictory to what is revealed by an examination of the historical documents. The methodological implication is that the observational powers of men (even of those who may have been affected by snobbery and by various types of prejudice) is superior to the reconstructive powers of the machine (internal reconstruction). And the intuitions about variation that the average speaker of the language has (although he would have trouble articulating them) are superior to the revelatory power of the isogloss bundles in which the study of American dialects has been tied up for the last forty years.

In no way whatsoever will the two mismatched sets of features used to trace geographic variation in British and in American English recapitulate even the British immigration into the colonies and the United States. If we *really* judged by the results of dialect geography's reconstruction, we would assume that they were all lost at sea. And of course we would have to assume that the immigrants from other lands never made it and that the Indians did not exist at all. Even if we take what Pickford called "an unrepresentative, uncohesive, minor segment"[68] of the total national population as a group that miraculously appeared, without antecedents, on the East Coast and trace them, Linguistic Atlaswise, across the continent, we would get them, by such methods, only about as far as Illinois. Arizona and California would remain howling wildernesses, peopled only by nonprimates. Of course, some people believe that this is indeed the case.

VI
PUERTO RICO:
BICOLONIALISM AND BILINGUALISM

———————◆•◆◆————————

THE HISTORY OF AMERICAN ENGLISH DOES NOT STOP WITH THE
spread of American immigrants to the Pacific Coast. In addition to the more or less internal developments like borrowings and innovations, there have been important recent
external developments. Noteworthy among these is the
world-wide increase in numbers of speakers of English. The
British began using English as an international language, and
by the nineteenth century they had carried it around the
globe. But in the second half of the twentieth century,
Americans are the most effective agents in spreading it. To
some degree then, it is American English that is becoming a
world language.

In this hemisphere, the spread of American English is

part of the same competition with other languages, especially Spanish, that took place on the frontier. It is a continuation of the language struggle between colonialist powers that has brought English to formerly Spanish colonies like Guam, the Philippines, the Canal Zone, and Puerto Rico. In fact, there was a considerable overlap between the dominance of English in the American Southwest and its imposition in the overseas territories.

By the twentieth century, the pidgin contact stage was a matter of the past. Either an "Anglo" or a "Latin" who asked the other, "You savvy?" risked being punched in the nose. For this reason alone, the history of American English has been considerably different in the twentieth century.

Hardly had westward continental expansion been completed—at the expense of the Spanish and the Mexicans, especially in California—than Manifest Destiny found it necessary to carry the blessings of "democracy" to other places, especially islands, beyond the North American continent. The year 1898 marked the greatest step in American colonialism. Admiral Dewey took Manila; Theodore Roosevelt stormed San Juan Hill in Cuba; and U.S. troops landed virtually unopposed at Guanica in Puerto Rico. In these islands, where Spanish was already one kind of colonial language, the new language of English was soon imposed. In Puerto Rico, the imposition began in earnest in 1917, when a unilateral act of Congress conferred U.S. citizenship on Puerto Ricans.

In each of these places, the relationship between Spanish and English was about that of the third stage of contact in the Southwest (Chapter IV). That is, aloofness from Spanish influence was already a part of the linguistic attitude of the "Americans" who entered these formerly Spanish colonies. Spanish speakers were expected to be able to use English but not vice versa. The political implications of this are obvious enough. And as in most colonial situations, the oppressed themselves took over the main job of oppression and became most insistent that they learn English rather than having the outsiders learn Spanish.

Puerto Rico makes an interesting test case of the effects—linguistic as well as political—of the extension of English overseas. It is somewhat closer to the United States than Guam or the Philippines, it has not broken all relationships with the United States like Cuba, and it is bigger than the Canal Zone. Furthermore, the millions of Puerto Ricans on the North American continent, especially in New York City, bring home to Americans the problems and complications of trying to incorporate a population with a different culture and a different language.

As a commonwealth, Puerto Rico enjoys—or suffers—an ambiguous status. In Spanish the term is *Estado Libre Asociado*, 'free, associated state'. Independentistas have long since seized upon the punning possibilities of such a self-contradictory term: *No es estado, no es libre, pero si es ensuciado.* (It is not a state, it is not free, but it *is* dirtied [a pun on the slight resemblance between *asociado* and *ensuciado*]). The adoption of English was never wholehearted in Puerto Rico. The islanders still vary between resentment at being expected to learn English and pride in being able to express themselves in a second language, and it is not hard to detect the influences of that ambivalence in what has happened to English in the Caribbean commonwealth.

The most immediately obvious victims are *Americanos* who come to the island either in the hope of learning Spanish or to do business with groups who use that language. For a person who fancies himself a bit of an interpreter, to be told "Mister, I will traduce for you" is sobering if not outright humiliating. Yet the "continental" (the Puerto Ricans' name for what is called an "Anglo" in the Southwest) who remains on the island for very long is sure to hear many a "traduction."

To paraphrase Byron on Coleridge, continentals often have reason to wish that the interpreter of a given occasion would traduce the traduction. For the hybrid language most Puerto Ricans insist upon using with outsiders contains a rather large amount of Spanish, at least below the surface. The new arrival on the island is likely to be asked, "Is this the first time you are ever outside the States?" Anyone who has had a semester or so of Spanish can recognize this as being traceable to the differences in the way English and Spanish handle the time relations of the immediate past; English would require . . . *you have ever been* . . ., in this context. Some anonymous namer at an unrecorded time had the obvious name for this hybrid between the two languages—Spanglish.

Perhaps this is always understood, after a double take or two. Background knowledge allows for communication even in the case of structural breakdown, at least some of the time. It is doubtful, however, that a monolingual speaker of English would understand "You can stay with the original [copy of a report]" if he did not know the Spanish idiom *quedarse con*, 'keep', a more literal translation of which would be 'stay with'. When it comes to the direction, printed on a rental office:

See Mr. Alfaro on the Yellow House.

the very probabilities of human location carry us through, whether or not we know that Spanish *en* may be translated either *in* or *on*. Generally, we resist the temptation to shout:

"Come down from there, Alfaro! I want to talk about renting a house."

In the same way the familiarity of the Christmas-New Year slogans allows us to understand GREETINGS SEASONS, a sign actually observed in a small store in Hato Rey.

When it comes, however, to a direction that the building you're looking for is "six apples down Mahogany Street," you're lost unless you know that Spanish idiom has *seis manzanas* as one way of saying 'six blocks'. In this case (this actually happened), the street was *Calle Caoba*. In a city like San Juan, where streets often have English names, my friend, who was looking for a specific building, did not know whether he had reached "Mahogany Street" or not.

This is one of the more common phenomena in a situation where rapid acculturation is taking place. It can be paralleled in many other countries. Calling Calle Caoba "Mahogany Street" might be called *overtranslation,* and it is one of the many complexities in language contact. Among other things, it helps to show how a simple substratum or adstratum explanation is an inadequate theory of language change.[1]

It happens elsewhere when two languages are in contact. In the Americas, overtranslation is especially characteristic as the reaction of a Spanish speaker to contact with native speakers of English. The executive director of the Fulbright Commission in Quito, years ago, was proud of his English and refused to use a word of Spanish—even in a name—to American Fulbright professors. New arrivals were greeted at the airport, taken to their hotels, and told to report when convenient to the Fulbright office on "Tenth of August Street." The name of the street was, of course, *Diez de Agosto* (after the date that the Ecuadoreans revere as Americans do the Fourth of July). Taxi drivers in Quito could understand that name, even if pronounced with the most execrable accent, but hardly a one knew what to make of the instruction "Tenth of August Street." There were some—in retrospect— amusing mix-ups as a result. The same confusion may accrue to the visitor to Puerto Rico who is told about "Snake Island" and for a time may fail to identify it as Culebra (especially if his school Spanish course taught him that *serpiente* was snake). Newsvendors who try to sell the protest newspaper *Claridad* to gringos under the overtranslated name *Sunshine* don't help clarify the linguistic confusion very much.

In Puerto Rico, where acculturation goes ahead at a some- times breakneck speed, incidents like this are a daily part of one's linguistic experience. For the sociolinguist and the historical linguist, the Puerto Rican experience has special interest because of the very accelerated pace. For the historian of American English, the island is also an indispensable part of the total picture, since the Puerto Rican learns English for two highly practical reasons: (1) to communicate with the tourists who come to the island; and (2) to provide for mobility back and forth between the island and the continent, especially New York City. The island experience also argues against any simplistic, behavioristic principle like need fulfillment as an adequate explanation for language change, since Puerto Ricans quite demonstrably use English when no native speakers of the language are present (i.e., among themselves) and since hyper-Anglicism is everywhere apparent.

The test case of Puerto Rico does, however, provide fuel for those who say that where bilingualism comes into existence there is a strong tendency for diglossia to develop.[2] During the second decade of the twentieth century, a condition developed in Puerto Rico that was almost perfect diglossia, in which English was the "H" language and Spanish the "L" language. After a period of vacillation beginning in 1900, English was the required language of instruction in the schools from 1917 until 1938. It was used almost exclusively for public functions, while Spanish was reserved for the private side. Militant action by Hispanists brought about some changes, but the tendency toward diglossic distribution is by no means a thing of the past.

The instinct to use English for public functions is so great that even some Independentista political leaders make occasional speeches in English—not without irony. At a boxing match involving a well-known Puerto Rican middleweight who was for a time champion, the announcer thought it appropriate to begin, "Ladies and gentlemen." After a few minutes of booing, he corrected his error, and the correct form of address was produced: *"Damas y caballeros."* Yet if a Puerto Rican figure in whom there is some local pride had not been a participant, the change might not have been necessary.

Diglossia has its more unpleasant side as well as its lighter side. A typical bar may have the sign:

WELCOME. HAPPY HOUR 5 TO 7

along with:

NO SE ADMITEN DAMAS SOLAS.

The second sign, written in smaller letters, means "Unaccompanied ladies are not admitted." It is a flagrant proclamation of the harsh socioeconomic fact that girls who are able to speak English are not so likely to be forced into prostitution as are those who speak only Spanish. Or a store significantly named BEBITA'S SUPER LIQUORS [sic] STORE may have a sign:

PARKING PARA CLIENTES SOLAMENTE
EVITE SER DENUNCIADO

which suggests that customers are more likely to speak English but that people who park in the wrong place and risk getting tickets are more likely to speak Spanish.

There are those who react, sometimes bitterly, against this imputation of linguistic status to English. It is one of the acrimonious political issues of the island. But those who take that side are mainly the Independentistas, who have not gotten 10 percent of the vote in any recent election. The majority of Puerto Ricans adapt themselves to the diglossic situation. A few seem to revel in it, like the man who was selling doggerel entitled "Bilingual Joys" (first line: "It is good to know some languages") on the streets of San Germán in 1960. And although some of them become near "perfect" bilinguals,[3] many others show a strong Spanish influence in their English. This is particularly true of the poorer, working-class people who have not been able to go to private schools. These are also, ironically enough, the ones who are most likely to have to migrate to New York City in search of work.

Asked what he does by an Anglo-American, such a
Puerto Rican will reply that he works in a "fabric" (from
Spanish *fábrica*, 'factory'). If he carries anything in his
hands, it is a "packet" (from *paquete*, 'package') or a "bult"
(*bulto*, 'burden' or 'package'). His children in school ask their
"mister" (teacher) about their "notes" (*notas*, 'grades'). And
if a Puerto Rican asks you, "What is your direction?" he is
asking you where you live (Spanish *dirección*, 'address').
Expressions like these are easy to deal with—in comparison
at least, with "Whatsa matta for you, Mister?" which a small
girl once shouted to me from a passing car. I'm still trying to
figure out what an answer to that could have been.

This particular brand of Spanglish is a way of keeping
separate from *Americanos*. If these speakers knew the terminology of sociolinguistics, they would say "You speak the
'H' variety; speak it, and stay away from me and my 'L'
variety." This is not a relationship on the level of intimacy
(to understate it), and there is little permanent effect on
Spanish in a situation in which Puerto Ricans translate their
Spanish nouns and verbs to near-English by eliminating the
inflectional endings (*langost* from *langosto*, 'lobster'). The
device is effective in keeping *Yanqui* tourists and the few
semipermanent residents from the Puerto Rican inner group,
but it takes more than that to have a lasting effect on a language.

There are, however, other relationships which come close
to solidarity. In fact, the kind of relationship involved is one
that the distinguished Puerto Rican philologist Washington
Llorens has called *germanía*—virtually "brotherhood."[4]
Among the groups who have a *germanía* relationship are drug
addicts, and Llorens shows how English has completely penetrated their Spanish vocabulary:

> chutazo 'shot'
> chutiar 'shoot'
> esnifiar 'sniff'

estofa   'stuff'

juquearse   (from *hook*) 'inject oneself'

cortar   (translating English *cut*)
'adulterate the drug'

Other gang terminology, not necessarily associated with addicts, participates in the same process:

deque   'deck' (of cards)

jolope   'hold up'

pana   'partner'

tofete   'tough'

blofear   'bluff'

These have the sanction of the *germanía* relationship, a much more important factor than how many native speakers of English come to the island over a given period of time, who they are, or where they come from.

When a Puerto Rican uses English forms with other Puerto Ricans, not just with someone he takes for a tourist, then real language influence can occur. And that is what has happened to our fictional workman. He may tell a *compadre* the way to an address on *Ehtop* (English *Stop*) *Dieziocho*, even though the street signs (before they were removed a few years ago) read *Parada 18*. If he goes to a restaurant, the waiter probably brings him *el ticket* ('the check'), although he does not use *un ticket* to go to the movies. When he is sick, he is more likely to go to an *oficina de doctores* (a direct translation of *doctors' office*) than to the more puristically Hispanic *consultorio de médicos*. If he goes to buy furniture on credit, he may find the following offer:

USE NUESTRO PLAN DE LAYAWAY

although the sign may also read:

USE NUESTRO LAYAWAY PLAN

or:

USE OUR LAYAWAY PLAN

199

Spanish has *Sepárelo* or *Separación* for the layaway arrangement so there can be no question of "inability to express the concept."

For some Puerto Ricans, the distinction between English and Spanish is blurred. There is the interesting anecdote of a visiting Spanish lecturer who asked a workman at the university, "¿Donde queda el paraninfo?" (Where is the auditorium?) only to be met with the somewhat hurt rejoinder: *"Por favor, señor, no hablo inglés."* (Sorry, Sir, I don't speak English.) When the dignitary, who did not speak English any too well himself, explained what a *paraninfo* was, the workman replied, *"Eso en español, llamamos el asemblijol."* (In Spanish, we call that the assembly hall.)

The last anecdote may be apocryphal, but I myself have heard a waitress in a tourist-frequented coffee shop, having been asked for *pastel de moras* ("blackberry pie" in some forms of Spanish), turn to an older woman present and ask, "Señora, ¿como se dice en español *pie de blackberries?*" (How do you say *blackberry pie* in Spanish?) Actually, the customer, a gringo trying to show off his Spanish, had a continuum of forms to deal with if he wanted to communicate with Puerto Ricans:

> pastel de moras
> pie de moras
> pie de blackberries
> blackberries pie
> blackberry pie

The first and last forms above are not usual in Puerto Rico. The first would be used only by a self-conscious Hispanist—say, a professor at the Departamento de Estudios Hispánicos of the University of Puerto Rico. (*Pastel*, in fact, is not characteristically Puerto Rican at all, although *pastelillo* is used for a kind of pastry dish that is not a pie in the same American sense as Mom's apple pie.) The last might be used by an unacculturated *gringo* or an *agringado* Neorican. The three inner forms come closer to what an ordinary Puerto Rican would use. Guillermo's Restaurant recently advertised *apples pie, pineaples* [*sic*] *pie.* (In pronunciation *apples* contains two syllables, *pineaples* three.) Unless you do your drinking at the fancier tourist hotels, you're more likely to go into a *Cocktails Lounge* than a *Cocktail Lounge.*

This kind of mixing of languages has some comic possibilities, which are perfectly all right, if done in the right spirit. The late newspaper writer and night-club comedian Eddie Lopez made it a regular part of his career. He developed a fictional character named Candid Flowers (Candido Flores), who said things like "You are the brassiere of your family" to his friends. In Spanish, *el sostén* means either 'brassiere' or 'support'; the pun is quite a meaningful one for the bilingual Puerto Rican. Lopez's characters also did things like thanking benefactors for "overcoating" them. Spanish *abrigar* means 'protect, support', and *abrigo*, a derivative noun, means 'overcoat'.

One can play this game at great lengths. For example, "I have the grasshopper that everything will turn out all right" makes sense in the bilingual situation if one knows that *la esperanza*, 'hope', is often used for 'grasshopper' by Puerto Ricans. English teachers on the island can relax from a sometimes rather grim job by asking each other mock questions like "Do you fume?", since Spanish *fumar*, 'smoke', is etymologically related to English *fume.*[5]

Far from all of this mixing is intentional, however. The young Puerto Rican who was once a member of the English Department in Humanities at the university should have known better than to speak of "a meeting of the faculty cloister [Spanish *claustro*]," since many of them are not especially cloistered. And the English verb-preposition compounds like *pick up* and *fill out*,[6] which are difficult even for Spanish speakers whose English is relatively fluent, produce such confusers as:

Please fill this form.
I have to pick my children.

Overconfidence in the vocabulary-producing device of Spanglish can produce such really problematic questions as:

What is the mark and serie?

What the speaker probably wanted to know was the brand name (*marca*) and serial number (*serie*); but in a case where neither was required (placing an order for recording tape), communication was disrupted for a time.

After a few years, one begins to lose one's grip on just what is English rather than Spanglish. El Monte, an apartment complex in a city with a largely gringo clientele, advertises in the San Juan *Star* that it offers "Elevated Buildings," and some of us are not quite sure any longer whether or not that is "continental" English for a building with elevators. (It doesn't help a bit to know that the elevators don't work very well.)

Probably nowhere is the mixing so complete as in the area called the Condado, the beach resort area which contains the best-known tourist hotels (including the Caribe Hilton) and some of the more expensive beach-front property. There, Puerto Rican waiters take orders from continental tourists (given in English) and relay them to the cooks in some weird combinations. I have heard:

"Tengo dos cheeseburgers trabajando"
(I have two cheeseburgers working)

Un jamón sandwich (A ham sandwich)

and other combinations equally uncharacteristic of either English or Spanish. A first-semester high school Spanish student is likely to learn that *trabajar* is not used with inanimate objects, that he should use *funcionar*. But *No trabaja* is regularly used on out-of-order coin machines in Puerto Rico, even at the university.

Besides being the language of technology, English tends to mediate between Puerto Ricans and foreign populations. The average Puerto Rican's reaction to any other language but Spanish is not just Anglicizing but hyper-Anglicizing. Visiting European professors at the university are sometimes amused, sometimes aghast, at their students' persistent efforts to use English with them, even if the professors happen to be better at Spanish than at English. Even an occasional Argentinian or Ecuadorean visitor finds that many people take his accent for an English accent and persistently use Spanglish with him. And some strange things happen to German and French words, like the time Löwenbrau beer appeared on the price list of the faculty club (University of Puerto Rico) bar as "Lower Braun." When German pianist Georg Demus appeared at the university recital hall, announcements were split about equally in spelling his name *Jorge* and *George*. One local barber has solved that problem by calling his establishment *Gorge's Barber Shop*.

French is used on the island for only the very restricted purpose of snob appeal for tourist shoppers. We find, therefore, a smattering of stores and other establishments with names like MAISON BLANCHE GUEST HOUSE, or:

MATTY'S BOUTIQUE
BRUNNY'S BOUTIQUE
CARMEN CHIRINO'S BOUTIQUE
INTERNATIONAL BOUTIQUE
TU-TU BOUTIQUE
SAN JUAN BOUTIQUE

The apostrophe, of course, indicates the association with English. In fact, these names and others like them could be said to be snobbish English rather than French. Perhaps the all-time champion insofar as rampant apostrophes were concerned was the tiny bar in Santurce with the crudely hand-lettered sign SAN'S SOUCI'S. French as such is no more functional in that context than it was in the small Arlington, Texas, bar that proudly announced MARDI GRAS EVERY WEDNESDAY.

What is even more obvious is that whatever Gallicism is used is aimed at the American tourist:

PETIT NIGHT CLUB
DA VINCI BOUTIQUE (across from Hotel DaVinci)
JUL D'OR JEWELER

and perhaps the most significant of all: THE FRENCH SHOPPE.

Combinations of French and Spanish elements with English (e.g., La Siesta Guest House) serve precisely the same purpose that they do at Miami Beach.[7] In fact, the Condado, formerly a magnificent stretch of natural beach front, is now little more than an imitation Miami Beach. Jul D'Or Jewelry advertises *perfums*, apparently wanting the French touch but not daring to deviate from English so far as *parfums*; and Pinokkio Boutique is a rather striking example of the Condado's language-without-a-country approach to exoticism in names. Like the "French" words with apostrophes, these slightly more sophisticated names can in effect be said to represent English influence in Puerto Rico as surely as Mama's Italian Restaurant (formerly Mama's Little Italy).

The apostrophe tradition has invaded Spanish in Puerto Rico, confounding those who talk of the match between spelling and sound in Spanish. One guest house has a circular with Spanish on one side:

CELEBRATE LAS TRADICIONALES DE
SAN JUAN BAUTISTA EN LOS GARCIA'S
BRISAMAR GUEST HOUSE

and parallel English, which suggests that the traditional festivities of St. John the Baptist be celebrated

AT THE GARCIA'S BRISAMAR GUEST HOUSE

Examples are everywhere.

Anglicization affects certain words that have similar spelling in English and Spanish. *Garage* is regularly used in Puerto Rican car shops; I have never seen the fully acceptable alternative *garaje*. Although *restaurante*, which would also evoke continent-based linguistic snobbery, is used, the more familiar device is the abbreviation REST (KIKI'S BAR & REST). *Dry cleaning* has displaced *limpieza en seco* or *lavado en seco* completely in San Juan, judging from the entries in the yellow pages of the telephone book. And *lavandería* has been almost completely displaced by laundry (giving rise to one wonderful name: LAUNDRY EL BROTHER) and, somewhat more frequently, *laundromat*. Laundries and dry cleaning establishments display the familiar "One Day Service" and even "One Hour Service" claims, apparently imported from the States and quite as meaningless as they are in New York City.

Café is used hardly at all, because of its homophony with the Spanish word meaning 'coffee'. And Anglicization cannot displace the meaning 'coffee house' for *cafetería*. For what continentals call *cafeterias*, which have become abundant in the larger cities, Puerto Ricans have adopted the name *self service* (like the now defunct *La Ronda Self Service* in Miramar). This is frequently combined with Spanish words: La Española Self Service or El Típico Self Service. The term is, of course, not unknown in the States; but it is much more frequent in Puerto Rico.

A somewhat greater mystery is the abundance of small cafés with the name *quick lunch*. (An example is Bony's Quick Lunch, which may make a continental think of someone who *needed* a quick lunch. The more prosaic answer, which a Puerto Rican but not necessarily a South American will recognize, is that the proprietor is named Bonifacio.) *Quick lunch* is almost a prestige designation on the island: Bankers' Quick Lunch, Time [sic] Square Quick Lunch. It is often explained as being a transfer of New York City practices, but there seem to be no such names in New York. (Furthermore, lifetime residents of New York have assured me that it was never very popular there at any time in the recent past.) It may be a replacement, in the process of acculturation, for *Come y Véte* (eat and go), an older naming pattern still seen in some parts of the island.[8]

Language-mixing is very much the order of the day in Puerto Rico, whether it is in the more obvious way that incorporates *on time* (*a cuenta*) in an otherwise monolingual Spanish advertisement on a bus wall, or in subtler manifestations like:

SUITS CITY

THE BARGAINS CORNER

500 COFFEE SHOP CLAMS HOUSE

Even a person with a good English accent who asks for your "phone" probably wants your telephone number (Spanish *teléfono*). Mothers who teach at the university and who have been interested in reading introductory works on linguistics regularly object that the book said that children in bilingual (or polyglot) situations learn both (or all) languages "perfectly," whereas in actuality their own children are mixing the two.

It is not entirely true that all Puerto Ricans speak Spanglish, or that all children of continentals who are being reared on the island mix the two languages; but it happens often enough to be worthy of note and study. Those Puerto Ricans who speak "Standard" English are almost always from middle-class homes and the products of private schooling. Many of them have spent a major part of their childhood in the States. It would be a serious mistake to use such exceptional cases to dismiss the more typical (and, to some, rather embarrassing) Hispano-English of the majority of Puerto Ricans from the working classes who usually migrate to the United States. Yet Puerto Rican image-makers are likely to do just that. Here, one thinks of the Black American analogy; whenever the Black English vernacular is discussed by linguists or by educators, there are always those who will point to the examples of Blacks who speak totally Standard English, as if the existence of this minority somehow did away with the necessity of dealing with the nonstandard dialect of the vast majority of Black Americans.

The analogy goes further in that those who would avoid the issue of class and ethnic-group differences often invoke regional factors as the explanation. Despite listener reaction tests, which show the opposite, Black-white differences are often still explained as the difference between Southern dialect and Northern dialect.[9] In like manner, public statements often refer to the alleged fact that "Puerto Ricans" speak both Spanish and English, without reference to the immediately obvious differences in the speaking of English by different groups of Puerto Ricans.[10]

Just as they have done with the vernacular of Black Americans, many educators and educational psychologists have viewed the Anglo-Spanish and Hispano-English of Puerto Ricans as simply "bad" Spanish and English, or even incompetent language usage.

Here, the existence of Puerto Ricans who speak normatively "correct" Spanish and English is important. For like those Black Americans who speak "correct" Standard English, they demonstrate—if demonstration is needed—that those who speak "correctly" do so for noninherent reasons.

The reasons usually given for the alleged linguistic incompetence on the part of Puerto Ricans (and again, the Black American analogy is striking) are either that the psychological effect of growing up in a lower-class rural or slum environment is such that efficient language-learning is impeded, or that the psychological effect of domination by Americans (cf. by whites)[11] has produced a sociopolitical situation that denies such children the opportunity to develop "good" language.

While such explanations may offer valid reasons as to why children do not learn Castillian Spanish or Standard English, they are of questionable value as explanations as to why the children fail to develop well-formed language, because as any linguist knows, such varieties as Anglo-Spanish, Hispano-English, and Black English, while regrettably low at the present time in social prestige, are nevertheless perfectly normal and structurally well-formed languages. Indeed, historical linguistics is quite capable of supplying documentation, and descriptive linguistics, structual evidence, that makes it clear that such language varieties are the product of normal social processes, rather than being inadequacies on the part of their speakers. This has been done for Black English,[12] but it remains to be done for Anglo-Spanish and Hispano-English.

Those who take the mixing of languages by Puerto Ricans as evidence of incompetence in language often cite the fact that while Puerto Ricans do mix their two languages, others in somewhat similar language contact situations do not. It is certainly true, for example, that educated (often only at high-school level) natives of Curaçao in the Netherlands Antilles manage to speak Dutch, Spanish, and English without much mixing, in addition to their native creole language, Papiamentu.[13] Why does the Puerto Rican creation of "Spanglish," half seriously considered by some as a new language,[14] take place there? Why does nothing comparable take place in Curaçao?

A number of possible answers suggest themselves, and perhaps all of them are partly true. The most obvious is that, as the institutional dominance of one culture and language wanes and that of another waxes, there is a period when for either both or one of these, the prestige of the "pure" form will not be great enough to insulate it against influences from the other. Here a European example comes to mind—the period in the contact between Anglo-Saxon and Norman French that produced the hybridization now codified in modern English.[15] Perhaps an influential factor here is whether the society in question is moving toward internal uniformity or toward pluralism; another factor is the relative prestige per se of the languages in contact.[16]

In this regard, an interesting aspect of the Curaçao example, given earlier, is that one of the four languages used there does tend to undergo hybridization. This is Papiamentu, which constantly incorporates Dutch and Spanish elements, as well as some English. An advertisement in the newspaper *La Prensa* for April 17, 1962, for example, read:

> Haci BO CAS bunita pa PASCU di RESURECCION, cu un DINETTE SET y un set di SALA di Curacao [sic, without cedilla] Trading Company. Prijsnan drásticamente reducí. Condicionnan di pago mash faborable y bo por scohe for diferente model.

> (Make YOUR HOUSE pretty for EASTER with a DI-NETTE SET and a LIVING ROOM set from Curacao Trading Company. Prices drastically reduced. Very favorable payment terms, and you choose among different models.)

In this passage, besides the obvious English of "Dinette Set" and the hybrid English-Spanish-Papiamentu of *set di Sala*, there are Hispanized words (*resureccion, drásticamente,* the article *un*) and *model,* a word it would be folly to try to tie down to one language. Such passages, along with ads and articles in Dutch, Spanish, and English, were commonplace in *La Prensa* until about 1968, when puristic and standard-izing attitudes toward Papiamentu began to exclude other languages from the paper.

It should be stressed that this is no invidious comparison between Puerto Rico and Curaçao. The latter is by no means a linguistic paradise, and educators have not found that problems have disappeared because of the prevalence of four languages. There is no reason to believe that the literacy rate is any higher than in Puerto Rico, that literary culture is any more advanced, or that any other great advance has been accomplished. Educators in Curaçao frequently complain that too many of their people are "semiliterate in four languages." One instructive experience is to watch ordinary airport workers in Willemstad buying magazines in English: comic books and movie magazines.

It is also noteworthy that Papiamentu, which has some interesting similarities to some varieties of Puerto Rican Spanish, is a Creole language in contact with relatively standard varieties of European languages.[17] Since language-mixing, in some sense of the term, is at the historical root of the Creoles, the fact that Papiamentu tends to hybridize more than Dutch, Spanish, or English might be explained in part by a continuation of this mixing tradition.

Lastly, Papiamentu is the native language of Curaçaoans, theirs to do with as they please, in contrast to Dutch, Spanish, and English, which are the languages of economically important and politically dominant outsiders, to be used as those outsiders specify. It should be stated in passing that these factors in the hybridizing tendency of Papiamentu, opposed to their relative absence in Dutch, Spanish, and English as used in Curaçao, are not necessarily incompatible. Indeed, they may all be involved with and may reinforce one another.

Returning to the Puerto Rican situation, it may be more accurate to compare the use of Spanish there with the use of Papiamentu rather than Spanish in Curaçao. It is certainly possible that the increasing domination of English in Puerto Rico (not entirely the product of political domination by the United States, but also of the rise of English as a world language) has caused Spanish to lose prestige and, in some psychological sense, to "destandardize," so that it can be modified with impunity by its speakers, especially in the direction of the more prestigious English.

It is also distinctly possible that the same kind of Creole language-mixing tradition as that involved in Papiamentu is a motivating factor in the hybridizing tendencies of Puerto Rican Spanish. Although most Hispanists have treated Puerto Rican Spanish as a direct and virtually unmodified extension of the Spanish of Spain to the Caribbean,[18] the historical and linguistic accuracy of this view is open to a great deal of doubt.[19]

The demonstration of an African component in Puerto Rican Spanish (paralleling demonstrations of African forms in Creole languages) by University of Puerto Rico linguist Álvarez Nazario and others has been an impressive one, and there is no longer any historical or linguistic reason for doubting that African languages influenced the formation of Puerto Rican Spanish. The appeal of the older view of the language as "pure" continental Spanish in Caribbean mouths has always been a sentimental one, based on well-intended but misplaced ethnocentrism. Like the residents of other Caribbean islands, Puerto Ricans are pathetically eager to find a high incidence of physiological pathology in the speakers of "folk" Spanish. "He's tongue-tied" is a not-infrequent explanation for the language of a very nonstandard speaker.

Other explanations are, however, much more likely linguistically. Even the best-known Puerto-Ricanism, *chévere*, is—like its Anglo-American approximate counterpart, *okay*[20] —African in origin. At the same time, there has been very little demonstration of an African influence beyond the vocabulary of Puerto Rican Spanish. There is certainly no use of actual African languages in Puerto Rico today, as there is in Cuba, Brazil, and Trinidad.[21] It is not, however, to be expected that African linguistic influences in Puerto Rico would take a direct form. Puerto Rico, after all, participated in the same kind of language contact situation as the rest of the Caribbean and even parts of the continental United States in the early period. In addition to African and European languages, there was at least one Amerindian language in Puerto Rico.

In this polyglot situation, the lingua franca typically became first a pidgin and then a creolized variety of the dominant European language, which in turn became the "folk" dialect of a large segment of the Black population in such areas and often influenced the speech of whites as well. This was obviously the origin of Creole English and Papiamentu.[22] The latter's Hispanicity in vocabulary—together with apparent Creole traces in the present-day Spanish of Puerto Rico and other Caribbean islands, especially among the Black population—suggests that there was once a "Spanish-affiliated pan-Caribbean Creole,"[23] from which Puerto Rican Spanish may descend, at least in part.

There is, indeed, documentation of the existence of such a Creole Spanish in Puerto Rico itself. José, the "Negro bozal" (often translated "Negro fresh from Africa," but more literally "muzzled Negro") in *La Juega de Gallos, o El Negro Bozal* (1859), speaks a "bad" Spanish which is as Creole as it is Spanish or African:

> *Yo ta lucu lucu,* 'I was very crazy.' (Standard Spanish,
> '(*yo*) *estaba loco loco*' or '*completamente loco*')

José's speech has the prime Romance Creole characteristic that the object pronoun follows rather than precedes the verb:[24]

> *Yo ta queré mucho a ti,* 'I love you very much'
> (Standard Spanish *Té quiero mucho,* to which *a ti* can be
> added for emphasis)

In the last sentence, *ta* is suspiciously like a form in Papiamentu which is spelled the same way. It can hardly be a reduction of the Spanish *está.* Aside from the fact that the first-person singular pronoun (*yo*) would demand *estoy,* the verb *querer* "want" or "love," adds the auxiliary 'to be' only in very special circumstances. The Standard Spanish sentence *(Yo) te estoy queriendo mucho (a ti)* is only marginally grammatical. The verb form is, however, quite regular in the speech of José: "*Mi corazo ta sufril mucho!*" [My heart is suffering very much].

The important consideration here is that the Puerto Rican language may preserve certain language-mixing tendencies from this earlier stage, in which Creole coexisted with more conventional Spanish. If this was the case, then the "hybridization" tendencies of Puerto Ricans have a sound historical background and are not the result of any kind of pathology in recent times. U.S. colonialism in Puerto Rico is an established fact, as is the guilty conscience that a great part of the mainland feels when it thinks of the island—if it ever does. But it is not committing oneself one way or the other on the issue of Puerto Rico's status to assert that no pathology has been produced in the language-mixing process.

In this connection, it should be remembered that colonialism in Puerto Rico did not begin with the United States's entry in 1898. As Juan M. Garcia-Passalacqua wrote in *The New York Times Book Review* in October 1973:

> The Puerto Ricans are a people born from the wedlock of hunger and colonialism. These two forces have shaped our 500 years of history. During three centuries of stagnation under Spanish rule, the local population clawed a subsistence living from the land while a Spanish elite in the capital guaranteed the island's perpetuation as a strategic military bastion in the Caribbean.

The island was one of the few colonies of Spain that did not revolt in the mid-nineteenth century, despite a movement aimed at bringing Puerto Rico into the general Latin American independence movement. The incident in Puerto Rican history known as the *Grito de Lares* (Cry [for Independence] of Lares) is central to the ideology of many Puerto Rican patriots. In Lares, a small town in the mountainous interior where folk belief places a high proportion of Indian population, a few South American agitators gathered a following, a large portion of which may have been Black, or Black and Indian.[25] The revolutionary leaders were said to be able to appeal to this group because *A cada individuo se le hablaba en su lenguaje* (Each person was spoken to in his own language).[26]

Just what "his own language" would be in this case is difficult to say. It would not have been worth mentioning if the South Americans spoke to the Puerto Ricans in Spanish, since that was presumably the native language of all of them. Were there still some *bozales* like José, and maybe even a few who spoke African languages? Did the Indians (perhaps now thoroughly mixed with Spanish and African "blood") speak a variety of Arawak still? It is easy to find allegedly authoritative denials of all these hypotheses. But the case of Black English should make us wary: it is also easy to find "authoritative" denials that there is any such dialect of American English.

There are some physical matters of relevance to the language situation in Puerto Rico. It is a large island—not so large as Cuba, but still large. Its size permits a certain amount of socioeconomic diversification, including a great deal of subsistence agriculture by the *jíbaros*, as the country people of the inland mountains are known in Puerto Rico. This is not possible on a small, arid island like Curaçao. As on the island of Jamaica, which is more nearly the size of Puerto Rico, mountainous terrain has made possible fugitive and hide-out groups; the government in San Juan is not completely sure what part of the country it controls, and Washington is even less so. Surviving groups of Arawaks, perhaps joined by escaped slaves (as in the case of the Jamaican Maroons), would not have wanted the attention of the Spaniards and would have felt quite the opposite of neglected if European visitors to the island had failed to write about them.

Quite apart from Spanish-English bilingualism, then, there is considerable linguistic diversity in Puerto Rico, even though the Linguistic Atlas methods that have been used on the island in the past have not shown it.[27] The extremes would be the Hispanicized intellectuals in the capital and the universities and the poorer inhabitants of the *barrios* and rural areas. Even among the poorer group, there is considerable difference between the Blacks of low-lying coastal areas and the mountain *jíbaros*. There is more dialectal variation within the Spanish of Puerto Rico than there is in the Papiamentu of Curaçao; in other words, there is a different kind of diversity in the language of Puerto Rico, not necessarily *less* diversity (if something as complex as language diversity can be measured quantitatively in any meaningful sense).

There is also the less tangible matter of a feeling of national unity. In spite of its bicolonialism, there is a more independent national spirit in Puerto Rico than in Curaçao. One of the obvious reasons is Puerto Rico's lesser dependence upon such economic windfalls from the outer world as the tourist dollar. "One Nation, One Language" is not an absolute; but there are tendencies in that direction. In some sense, the "mixed language" may express the Puerto Rican national spirit better than either "pure" Spanish or "undefiled" English—or a "perfect" bilingualism in the two of them.

If the majority of Puerto Ricans who migrate to New York and other parts of the American eastern seaboard are not the graduates of expensive private schools, which provide a near-native mastery of English, neither are they members of the still smaller group that has studied in Spain and been more or less re-Hispanicized.[28] The tendency to mix languages is still very great among New York Puerto Ricans. They are famous for the vocabulary substitutions contained in their favorite example:

> *Está reinando sobre el rufo*, 'It is raining on the roof'.
> (Standard Spanish: *Está lloviendo sobre el techo*.)

Their Spanish changes in some superficial grammatical forms, too, perhaps because of the lack of standardizing influence from education and from use in formal domains.[29] The irregular first-person singular *quepo* (from *caber*, which means, among other things, 'fit into') may become *cabo*, which causes raised eyebrows from educated speakers of

Spanish (more or less like the reaction to an English speaker who says, "I goed.")

Vocabulary substitutions, which represent that part of the results of the language contact situation that is within awareness and considered discussable in polite circumstances, are, of course, commonplace in situations like that in New York City. Italian-Americans in places like New York City did the same thing, developing neo-Italian forms like *minuto* for *minute, ponte* for *pound, storo* for *store, barra* for *bar, giobbo* for *job*, etc. Italo-Americans have even reported the amusing example of *baccauso*, 'toilet', from *back house*, which they found to be English and not Italian only after visiting the home country. There may even have been, at one time, some sharing of such forms between Puerto Ricans and Italians in New York. Some Puerto Ricans have reported depending upon Italians, as speakers of another Romance language and therefore easier to communicate with than English-speaking Americans, in their early years in New York City.

Yet the Neoricans, like the Spanglish speakers on the island, do other things that are not regarded as picturesque and that are not so suitable for discussion in polite conversation. These things are, however, linguistically more significant, involving grammatical systems rather than vocabulary. They produce

> I didn't meant it.
> We didn't called it a game.[30]

A teacher on the island who has instructed a student, "Now repeat after me: He didn't want to go," may receive the unexpected answer: "Meester, you are wrong. It is past tense: He didn't wanted." Sometimes it takes a pretty good debater to come out of that particular class period with everyone convinced that the teacher was right.

In New York's Spanish Harlem, as on the island, it is easy to collect "Spanglish" sentences like the following:

Take slow the car.
The Jets win again the Super Bowl.
It doesn't matter the age.
It doesn't make any difference the outcome.
She's married with my cousin.
He did a mistake.
He has much friends.
He's baseball player.
The Los Angeles has a good team.
The onion is good with a meal.[31]

Particularly among those Neoricans who have a lot of contacts with Black playmates, a great many Black English vernacular patterns can be heard:

He took five book.
The other teacher, they'll yell at you.
I want to know did he go somewhere.
They were hoping to go someplace, which
    they didn't succeed.
The cannon say boom.
The water say whoosh.
I been here for hours.
He gone home already.
Sometime he be here and sometime he don't.
He be here in a few minutes.
If he could, he be here.
the boy hat
This is mines.[32]

Many of these forms, like the possessive pronoun and the "absolute" possessive in the last two examples, are strikingly different in ordinary English and in the Black English vernacular. Neoricans pick up the Black forms if they play with Black peers, as do, especially, those larger Puerto Rican boys who play basketball with the high school teams that are dominated by Black players.[33] They also indulge in some of the same kind of hypercorrection:[34] "Jack's Johnson's car."

The Black English vernacular verb system, which marks

the past tense nonredundantly,[35] leads also to some overcorrection when used by Black or Neorican speakers:

> He speaked to the man.
> He taked his money and left.
> I seened the man.
> He tooked a long ride.[36]
> He threwned the ball to me.[37]

Like the Black American, the Puerto Rican has kept his own linguistic identity even under considerable pressure to do otherwise. In the case of the Puerto Rican, pressures have included colonialism, residence in the slums of American cities, and a school system dominated by *Yanquis* to the extent that if he looks for Cervantes's works in the university library, he must look under *S* for *Spanish* rather than *E* for *Español*. But there is some evidence that he kept his linguistic independence in the past, when the colonialists were Spanish rather than Anglo-American. Whatever the purists may think, it is to some degree his native and inherent self-reliance that allows him to produce "Spanglish."

He still suffers in the schools, however, both from Hispanists who used to post (up to 1964) the sign on the University of Puerto Rico campus:

DISTINGUASE. HABLE BUEN ESPAÑOL
(Distinguish yourself. Speak good Spanish.)

and from the missionary American English-as-a-second-language teachers who scream, "They *need* English!" University of Puerto Rico students who hope to become teachers in the public schools of the island must carry an extra heavy load of English classes, including a pronunciation course that attempts to stuff the still not entirely familiar (and to many still unpleasant) vowel sounds of English into unwilling mouths. It is, in fact, ridiculous that a young man or woman who wants to teach in elementary school cannot do so in his or her own language without having to bother about some strange foreign language. This is especially true when the native language is basically Spanish, one of the world's great culture languages and the medium of expression of some of the world's greatest literature and thought.

There are prophets of doom insofar as Spanish in Puerto Rico is concerned. Author José Luis Gonzalez, for eighteen years a resident of Mexico and now a citizen of that country although born in Puerto Rico, recently reported that, although he had published short stories in Spanish, he felt that he had begun to learn the language only after he moved to Mexico. According to Gonzalez:

> Mexicans know the language much better than Puerto Ricans because they're taught the language much better. Also, there's not such an interference [sic] by a foreign language.[38]

Although some exaggeration for political and rhetorical effect may be suspected, remarks by people like Gonzalez indicate something about the differences between Puerto Rican Spanish and other varieties of the language. The intuitions of native speakers, no matter how nontechnically expressed, are important indicators of such relationships. And the opinion of a distinguished littérateur carries even more than the ordinary amount of weight. But it seems a pity that a major part of Puerto Rico's educational effort is not devoted to the relationship between Puerto Rican and other kinds of Spanish—without any disparagement of the former.

Possibly some Puerto Ricans *do* need English. With English becoming a world language, citizens of almost any nation do. But this isn't the same as saying that no person can feel that he's educated until he speaks English, or even that one's education and status in life correlate with his English accent. As speakers of a world language, Americans have certain responsibilities, and those responsibilities are not met simply by insisting that everyone try to learn *our* language.

One component of a solution would be to become more selective in the teaching of English to Puerto Ricans. The University of Puerto Rico has a new master's degree program in translation, which seems a major step in the right direction. Whatever the major part of the population needs of *Yanqui* talk and publication can be translated into Spanish. But the same university has a requirement that those of its students who make an especially low grade on the English entrance tests, or get a D in the course called Basic English, must take a course in English composition. That is, those who have demonstrated over a period of twelve years of taking English that they lack the interest or the ability (probably, in most cases, the former) to profit from an English composition course are forced to take one. Surely this is linguistic imperialism, if not downright linguistic idiocy. And surely the American educational system is broad enough to be able to realize that the ability to write in English is not identical with the ability to write.

The problems of colonialism and its aftermath are big ones where the United States has expanded abroad, in Puerto Rico and elsewhere. We have a big debt to pay for the injustices we have in many cases forced upon people who were quite happy with their own languages. It is too late, however, to restore the islands and territories to the days when they were uninfluenced by English. (Similarly, efforts to make Black Americans into speakers of African languages, disregarding or even scorning the Black English vernacular, are impractical even if they are theoretically justifiable.) Furthermore, English has undergone some changes from the colonial experience, and it will probably keep them.[39]

However we may feel about such matters, it is hard to keep from deploring the waste that has taken place in Puerto Rico and other foreign-language-speaking dependencies of the United States. Puerto Rico has functioned less as a link to Latin America than as an extension of New York City slums. The "window on the world" has turned out to be no wider in its view than the airline trip from San Juan to New York. The mixing of English and Spanish, the demotion of Spanish to an "L" status diglossically, and all the rest of it are the linguistic correlates of the process that has meant not so much acculturation to U.S. values as deculturation from Puerto Rican values. The only salve for our consciences is that we may justifiably wonder whether the Spanish would have done any better.

Colonialism and Yankee imperialism are the ultimate causes of the situation in which Puerto Ricans who speak an English heavily influenced by Spanish are required to do so, whereas it is virtually taboo for a *gringo* to speak Spanish with an accent. There are many more immediate, currently effective causes, however, which are not so directly linked to colonialism. If Puerto Rico became independent, it would still not eliminate the American English influence and "restore" a purely Iberian form of Spanish. In fact, there probably never was a time when all Puerto Ricans spoke such Spanish.[40]

There are many lessons in Puerto Rico (and undoubtedly in Guam, the Philippines, the Canal Zone, and elsewhere) for those who would teach English as a world language. For one thing, the "repeat after me" or "direct" method of teaching, which stresses performance rather than understanding, is probably one of the reasons for the great amount of Spanish influence in Puerto Rican English, because the Puerto Rican's confidence in his own ability to "speak the English" is often not justified. The behaviorism-inspired drills used to an absurd degree on the island breed overconfidence, even if they avoid the opposite pitfall of the language learner who is afraid to open his mouth for fear of making a mistake.

On the other hand, those in positions high above the classroom teacher have a great deal to learn from such experiences. Success in a program of cultural exchange with, say, an African country is not very closely correlated with the number of professors who go abroad, the number of students they have, or the number of American cultural patterns (including language patterns) those students learn. Even in the seemingly simple matter of teaching English, planning is required. The effects of an intensive program of English teaching on the students, the educational system, and the country must be considered. The people of many—perhaps all—countries have worked out their own lingua franca in a way that has nothing to do with school systems, Fulbright commissions, or "Teaching of English as a Second Language" organizations. To tamper with these solutions may be to do a great deal of harm to the country. It may even rebound to the disadvantage of the U.S. Department of State and the American businessman who is trying to profit from the establishment of a diplomatic sphere of influence. I still remember one Puerto Rican woman, almost perfectly bilingual, who fervently wished that she didn't know any English.

VII
A WORLD LANGUAGE-
AND HOW TO
UNDERSTAND IT

———————◆•◆———————

IN THE PAST FEW DECADES, THE STORY OF HOW ENGLISH HAS become the world's second language has been told many times.[1] In the nineteenth and even into the twentieth century, this could be traced to the colonial expansion and naval might of Great Britain; the world looked to British English, although only a small part of the people spoke it in a readily recognizable form. Even today some West African nations send the sons of their most affluent and powerful families to Oxford and Cambridge, and an "Oxford accent" is still highly prized in India, but the emphasis has been shifting with the decline of British military and economic power. More and more, American power and influence are being felt throughout the world; and it is American English

223

that now provides the initiatory power for the world's lingua franca.

The spread of English, whether British or American, had to do primarily with the military and commercial might of England and then of the United States, rather than with any special characteristics of the language. Some of the older historians of language thought otherwise. Some of them argued that the lack of inflectional endings, compared with Latin and Greek, made English especially well adapted for world language use. It is true that Latin's verb conjugations and noun declensions are rather difficult for speakers of the relatively uninflected English. But one wonders what a speaker of a Bantu language that has inflectional *prefixes* (e.g., *muntu*, 'person', *bantu*, 'people'; *mukara*, 'man', *bakara*, 'men') would think about the alleged simplicity of English and its putative advantages over a language like Latin or Finnish.

Although histories of the English language have carefully overlooked the point, it appears that the use of English as an international lingua franca was foreshadowed by developments in the British Isles in the late medieval period. Scotsmen, Welshmen, and other Celtic-speaking groups had to use English as a second language from as early as the fifth century A.D. The Norman Conquest in 1066, which made French the dominant language in England proper, delayed the process; but English, however strongly influenced by French, was reestablished in the fourteenth century. Evidence from sources like Shakespeare's *Henry V* shows how English became the medium for a kind of British unity under the leadership of England. Captain Fluellen, a Welshman, Captain Jamy, a Scotsman, and the Irish Captain Macmorris discuss the strategy of the Battle of Agincourt:

MAC. By Chrish, la, tish ill done! The work ish give over, the trompet sound the retreat . . .

FLU.   Captain *Macmorris*, I beseech you now, will you vout-
safe me, look you, a few disputations with you, as
partly touching or concerning the disciplines of the
war . . .

JAMY   It sall be vary gud, gud feith, gud Captens bath, and I
sall quit you with gud leve, as I may pick occasion.
That sall I, mary.

The Scotsman's *sall* for *shall* and slightly different vowels
were by this time, of course, merely part of a well-recognized
dialect of English; the Irishman's *tish* for *tis* and *ish* for *is*,
scarcely less so. Fluellen, a highly competent military man who
seems to have replaced Falstaff in the confidence of King
Henry, is not in any way the object of ridicule for his accent.
Once, when he attempts to discourse of Alexander the Great
and produces "Alexander the Pig" (Act IV, Scene 7), there
is some fun with his accent. But Shakespeare seems to link
language and politics, as the "quips and quiddities" of
Falstaff's verbal brilliance give way to the military practi-
calities of Fluellen's stylistically limited but work-oriented
Welsh dialect.

Like Fluellen, the foreigners with whom the trade-minded
Englishmen and later the Americans dealt generally left the
mark of their native language on the English they used. It
has made very little difference whether the English used for
export purposes was American or British. In point of fact, it
has been the "International Lingua Franca" variety that has
been spread abroad.[2] In many an "overseas" area, English
is a usable language of wider communication. But it is often
a great help to be able to understand the English that is
actually produced rather than what is aimed at; in many
cases, this involves knowing something about the native languages of the users. That Fluellen's native Welsh does not
distinguish initial *b-* from *p-* is enough to explain his apparent confusion of *big* and *pig*. Apparently, some shakiness in
his control of English vocabulary would account for his fail-

ure to distinguish *great* and *big*. Thus, by the mid-fourteenth century, a condition that can now be observed virtually around the world was beginning to develop.

In only a few cases, where large blocks of Americans or British have been transported overseas more or less intact, has there been any real influence from the "local" or other dialectal varieties of England or America. Liberia is an outstanding example of such influence. The people sent to that West African country in the mid-nineteenth century were Black ex-slaves. The "repatriation" process was generally carried out without any real regard to what part of West Africa the ancestors of the slaves might originally have come from. Groups of liberated American slaves were transplanted to Liberia in a large enough quantity to have a major influence on the speech of the country. In a real sense, a variety of English that was to some degree genuinely American was transported overseas.[3]

Liberian English of today closely resembles Black English of the continental United States, although the really deep linguistic affinities are rather to the pidgin/creole varieties of other parts of West Africa.[4] Even many of the American inner-city slang terms that have become part of general urban lore in the past few years are paralleled in Liberia. Thus, Liberian use is attested for

bad mouth	'foul or uncomplimentary language'
he zootin'	'he is all dressed up'[5]
fine	'beautiful'
no way	'things are at an impasse'
sweet mouth	'flattery'

A few of these, although well known in inner-city Black vernacular, may be thought of as "Southern" rather than characteristic of Black-imitative groups like the hippies. On the other hand, some of the Liberian terms are even more strongly reminiscent of rural Black usage:

dollbaby	'doll'
He can run, but he can't hide	'He will eventually be caught'
He carry her home	'He walked home with her'
I chunk the rock	'I threw the rock'[7]
tote	'carry'[8]

Other usages are closer to West African varieties, especially those of the Cameroon and Nigeria. With these, it is almost impossible to tell whether they were carried to America and then back to Africa in repatriation, were picked up by the newcomers to Liberia from the West African Pidgin English still in use on the west coast, or both.

That humbug me	'that bothers, annoys me'
dash	'reward, tip'
we reach soon	'we soon arrived'
fufu	a starchy dish
juke	'stick, poke, puncture'
josna ("just now")	'right away'
ju ju[9]	magical practice
one-one	'separately'
one-time	'immediately'
palaver	'talk, trouble, discussion, argument'
too much	'very'

A few Liberian terms like *stink-mouth*, 'abusive or bad talk', are even reminiscent of Hawaiian Pidgin English (*talk stink*).

The American or Briton who travels to Liberia risks misunderstanding and being misunderstood, even though the official language of the country is English. The U.S. Fulbright Commission, for example, issues warnings to its prospective lecturers about the confusing nature of "African idioms" in Liberian English, and the Peace Corps has prepared glossaries for its volunteers.[10] The problem is, in fact, essentially the same as that of the Cameroon, where Peace Corps volunteers were given actual training in Pidgin English.

Pidgin English is, however, not the official fashion in

Liberia; and it is now held in relatively low prestige throughout the world. But it is not dying out anything like so rapidly as some authorities would have us believe. Melanesian Pidgin English, in particular, seems quite healthy. However, the pidgin varieties are no longer spreading around the seacoasts, ports, and islands of the world as they did in the sixteenth, seventeenth, and eighteenth centuries. Perhaps the fact that travel is no longer by sea but by air, which is both more rapid and more transitory, has something to do with the changed situation. The "bad" English you struggled to understand on your last guided-tour vacation was not Pidgin. More than likely, it was something quite different—more nearly the vocabulary of English superimposed on the grammar and phonological system of the other speaker, with whatever approximation to the English system he could manage.

Sometimes it all works quite well, but each of us has his own list of incomprehensible "English" writings and utterances. My favorites include an item on the menu of the Hotel Torarica in Paramaribo, Surinam, which advertised "selectable French toast" along with "golden brown waffers." Friends have tried to help me with those, but we haven't been very successful in riddling them out. One thing I'm sure of: the English word aimed at couldn't have been *delectable*—I ordered the stuff one morning.

A rather typical incident at the same hotel showed what is happening to English on a nearly world-wide scale. At the table next to me were a Belgian gentleman and his young son. It happened that they were talking together in French, but the man—like many Belgians—was quite as proficient in Dutch. The waiter, who was also quite proficient in Dutch, could just struggle along in English (as distinct from Sranan Tongo, the English Creole that was his native language). Nevertheless, the waiter, like many another the world around, insisted on using English with *all* his customers. He and the Belgian had a terrible time communicating, even at the level of ordering meals, and the Belgian threw up his hands in comic despair after each such encounter, but the waiter's decision that English must remain the language of ordering was unalterable. The same kind of insistence is to be observed in many kinds of activities in widely dispersed areas.

One can be addressed as a user of English in the strangest conceivable ways. In Bujumbura, Burundi, I was hailed from a passing truck by a man (who I never saw again, of course) who was probably a laborer being carried to his job: "You Spinglish?" Of course, there was opportunity to answer, "Yes, I can Spinglish." Another in the same city yelled at me, "Hee, Yankee, hee!" (apparently attempting "Hey" to attract my attention) and then added "Geu heum!"[11]

We all understand things like this without any real trouble; they are simple, stereotyped messages, and we know the content before we hear the words. It doesn't say any more about the level of mastery of English in Bujumbura than the fact that I understood the first time someone shouted at me *"Mzungu!"* does about my own ability with Swahili. The term means "white man," with some of the same unflattering connotations as English Creole *buckra*, and I understood it probably because I had heard the word before in some forgotten context.[12]

Many of the things the American traveler hears ("Is this the first time you are ever outside the states?") are intelligible because languages have a lot in common, and speakers are able to interpret statements they themselves would never produce. But it helps to know something—even a very little— about the other fellow's language. A Spanish speaker's *He threw me with a rock* is sure to be confusing unless you know *Me tiró con una piedra*, 'He threw a rock at me'. *He likes to take coffee* can be interpreted as involving a propensity for stealing, unless the hearer knows that Spanish *tomar café* translates as "drink coffee." When a Dutch girl in Curaçao told me that a friend of hers was studying "dod" languages, I was happy that, even though I had never studied Dutch as such, I had done graduate work in Old Germanic languages and knew enough to expect a cognate for English *dead*, which might be a kind of compromise between that and German *tot*.

The prestige of English and its lingua franca function have created a world-wide situation in which great numbers of people are striving to learn English and are eager to use what they know. Sometimes such people can be extremely aggressive, like the Japanese just after World War II. One favorite story concerns the Japanese student who took a job as caddy at a golf course frequented by Americans so that he could practice English. When the first player drove 250 yards straight down the fairway, the student asked him, "Is this the first time you have ever play golf?" Another tells how a Japanese passenger on a Tokyo bus spotted an American, pushed past other riders to get to him, carefully stepped on his foot, and then said, "Pardon me."

Such eager practicers of English may be bitterly disappointed, and even violently resentful, to find that their efforts are not appreciated, even that the English speaker knows their own language. Many of them hope to make some money by translating for the American. Other, pleasanter relationships develop when the American directs his efforts toward understanding the foreign-accented English rather than expressing himself in the other language. American capitalists abroad have undoubtedly had a better reception because they knew enough to boost the linguistic ego (if not the economic status) of citizens of the host country. And many an American abroad with an eye for female beauty has found that he gets more attractive dates if he throws in an English lesson as an inducement.

If English "enjoys" the position of being virtually the "H" language in a world diglossic situation,[13] it—or its speakers—are exposed to some suffering as well. Any person who *can* speak English is expected to speak English in many cases, even though his interlocutor may know very little. The traveler who is getting along quite well in French until someone examines his passport, discovers that he is a U.S. citizen and begins the familiar insistence that only English be used, is only going through one of the little agonies that beset a speaker of a world-wide lingua franca. It undoubtedly happened to the Romans during the great days of the empire, to the Greeks earlier and to the French in the early modern period. Even if you handle the other fellow's language better than he handles English, you may make the purchase more cheaply or get the deal done more profitably if you go along with his/her persistence in using English.

Nor is it a very good idea to imitate him, to use his own "dialect" or "accent." In the first place, your imitation probably isn't as good as you think it is. More than that, an accurate imitation may be more "off-turning" than a poor one. If the other fellow speaks Pidgin, or Pidgin-influenced English, it still may be better not to use Pidgin to him. During the summer of 1971 seven students from Hilo College, Hawaii Community College, and Hilo High School combined efforts to draw up a course for new Hilo College faculty members entitled *An Introduction to Hawaii Pidgin*. The course specifically states that the new professors should strive to understand, but not to produce, "the local language."

There is, however, no guarantee that, even with the best of intentions and determination to remain passive and non-ridiculing, the native speaker of American English will understand the foreigners' English at all. The eagerness of the Japanese to learn English has been proverbial, but their confidence in their own achievements has been misplaced at times, as anyone who has read the instructions that come with a Japanese piece of equipment knows. The *New Yorker* magazine used to run selections of Japanese English under the heading "The Mysterious East."

231

EXPLANATION

NAME: Picture and Letter match.

MAKER: No. 1 Toys Industrial Co. Ltd.
          Shiozaki-muri, Sarashina-gun, Naga
          Prefecture, Japan

Materials and Quality:

1. This toy is made of the best qualified wood (ho tree), grows in cold region, which has been Carefully dealt with an artificial drier, so that if it is used for a long time no strain will be occurred.

2. In paintiny [*sic!*] we never used chalk powder on the wooden basis but directly painted the wood three times with lacquar and enamel. Discolouration or dispainting will not be seen. Even if a child is happend to lick it absolutely caused no harm.

How to Play:

1. Picture match
   Children can take out 30 cubic pieces (we calls it a pawn hereafter) from a box scattering them on a table and arrange a piece to piece to form the original picture. Several children can play a game at the same time counting required time to make the picture complete. A child who needs the shortest time is a winner.

2. Letter match
   Children can learn English words in playing with this toy. An alphabet letter is on each side of a cubic pawn. We arrange letters in order on serial pawn in such a way that the letters of A. B. C. D. are on the first pawn, B.C.D.E on the second, C. D. E. F on the third and so on.

3. Building blocks
   We painted the building bricks set around a box and back side of 30 pawns in a box with the same colour children can play a blocks as they like with 43 pieces of bricks in total we do not figne out what blocks will they play but children's parents and brother or sister can help them to train their construction sense or ability.

To childrens' Mathers

> We explained briefly to you the way how to play these toys "Picture and Letter Match," but the first of all we wish to mention is that you must have children put toy to rights in the box as it ought to be by themselves right after they have played with it. also we wish you would think over that a good toy will help them to secure "a good Health," "a good brain," "a good ability" and "a good Sentiment."[14]

It might be almost as easy to learn Japanese as to understand these instructions. And even Chinese couldn't be much more incomprehensible than the following, which the *New Yorker* reprinted from the *North China Daily News*:

> The undersigned hereby announce to the public in representing Messrs. F. Y. Wong, F. C. Yee the representatives among twelve buyers of Metropolitan Motors Ltd. Co.
> on account of ordering from the same twelve American "Studebaker Champion De Luxe" motor cars respectively which as notified by the same are already arrived to Shanghai. As the above mentioned company set an extremely high price on each one of the cars, even they asked the same to deliver the cars to them, yet the same refused to do so. The negotiations between two parties are just in proceeding now. Whoever wants to buy those cars ordered by them is kindly requested to take notice of the above mentioned affairs in order to avoid trouble.
>
> C. Y. TAI,
Barrister-at-Law
>
> Office: 190 Kiukiang Road
Floor 3[15]

It is easier to figure out the English spoken or written by someone whose native language is one of the Romance or Germanic group. Spanish, or Spanglish, is so familiar to most of us that we don't even notice it when we hear, for the *n*th time, "It makes two years that I am here." Although there are differences in the ways in which Spanish and English allot time relationships in the immediate present or immediate past (especially where continuity in the past is concerned), the grammatical systems are comparatively rather close together. In fact, a teacher's main problem is persuading his students that there are differences that must be taken into account.

The cumulative effect of "deep" Spanglish can, nevertheless, be difficult to work out. The *New Yorker* provided this example from *El Ferrocarril*, Lima, Peru:

A ENGLISH SECTION

The want of to make arrived to know the exigence by to build more railways over our territory, us compel at we led all north americans citizens divelling into Perú for to invite we assistance in the compaing by the railroads building.

The basis of the publicity struggle consist in to cooperate with omens of all industry an whole business into our magazine entitling "The Railway" one of the first pictures railroad publicity imprinting in Perú. During the last war our monthly publication "The Railway" she offer a assiduous information of the event warlike, receiving of the northamerican colony only indifference of all the high yankee commerce. One railroad magazine she can not sustain self with the an scanty advertisements. Reason in the another country they can self to obtain luxuriouses magazines?

The cause is very pure. In United States of America, or at any country european, the commerce an industry activities consider an obligation necessary to advertisement at all national magazines, because this publications are committing of to make to knows the natural wealths of the huge territory of the United States of America.

Our rewievs has a resemblance mission, since for it our manager Mr. Paul Lorza Dávila travel a repeat upon the peruvian country with alone reason of to propagate the national strength of the one nations more rich in to south-american continent.[16]

My knowledge of Spanish enables me to understand *One railroad magazine she can not sustain self* as an overliteral translation of (*Una revista* [a feminine noun, therefore the pronoun *she*] *de ferrocarriles no puede sostenerse*), "A magazine about railroads cannot support itself." It is, on mature consideration, only the study most Americans with college degrees have made of at least one or two Romance languages that makes it easier for us to communicate, in English, with a Frenchman or a Spaniard than with a Chinese or a Japanese.

One thing seems very certain: world-wide use of English as a language of wider communication, coupled with the direct method of teaching (instruction only in English, with no translations into the native language), has bred a world-wide assurance that often amounts to overconfidence, even among academic organizations. In 1972 the International Association for Research and Diffusion of Audio-Visual and Structuro-Global Methods circulated an English-language letter that began:

Dear Sir/Madam,

Either because we have heard of your pre-occupations or else because your name has been brought to our notice by a colleague . . .

The Brussels dateline for the letter probably warns most readers not to take the word *pre-occupations* in its literal English sense of 'absorption, or engrossment in one's own thoughts'. Most readers would probably take it to mean 'occupation' or 'previous occupation'. Orally, a strong foreign accent can provide an equally useful warning. But those who learned English pronunciation and intonation, without any special study of larger grammatical or semantic patterns, from the eager, aggressive American teachers of English as a second language who went abroad in the late 1950's and early 1960's sometimes do not give that useful warning.

Perhaps worse than not understanding is thinking that one understands when one does not. Psychologists are especially prone to this kind of blunder, as has been shown in the case of children's Black English, which psychologists frequently dub "linguistic deprivation."[17] A former acquaintance of mine, now a psychology professor himself, was a native speaker of Ilicano, a Filipino language that does not happen to have sex-gender contrast *in the pronoun system.* (Of course, speakers of the language can indicate the difference between boys and girls; they just don't do it with pronouns.)[18] In the early years of his college education in the United States, when the structure of his own language still carried over into his English writing, he was called in for a conference by a clinically minded professor, who took his confusion of *he* and *she* in English writing as evidence of homosexuality! An error of equal gravity was committed by psychiatrist Edwin A. Weinstein, who in his *Cultural Aspects of Delusion: A Psychiatric Study of the Virgin Islands* (1962) saw male dominance in the use of *him* meaning 'he/him; she/her' by speakers of English Creole and in the general term of address *man.*[19]

In the Virgin Islands or elsewhere where languages and dialects are mixed, it is well for the visitor to proceed carefully and to avoid racy, idiomatic talk, which will almost never be understood. My own first experience of this came on my first visit to the island of St. Thomas, when I asked the maid at the guest house, "How do I get to town from here?" In my own particular American speech style, this is an informal request for directions. But the maid took it differently. She stared at me a second, then in the tone one reserves for small children or unintelligent animals, she answered, "Why, man, you just walk."

That experiment was inadvertent, but it soon became

an intentional, if informal, one. I tried it in every English-speaking Caribbean island area to which I went—and was misunderstood every time. It was actually only a few months later that I read the bop joke:

"How do I get to Carnegie Hall?"
"Man, practice!"

With accumulating evidence of the existence of a related chain of Afro-American English varieties, with jive and bop-talk expressions clearly paralleled in such dialects as Liberian English, it becomes obvious that such experiences are more than just isolated events and the similarities more than merely coincidental. One of the more important facts about the early historical spread of English is manifested in the difference in casual usage between continental white American English and the usages of Blacks from Freetown to Los Angeles.

The sword of idiomatic usage is, moreover, double-edged. A woman who was studying at Philippine Women's University liked to dress casually, in a then fashionable American style, so she wore *zoris* (thonged sandals) to class. She was astonished to be stopped one day by the dean, who informed her, "Women are not allowed to wear step-ins on the campus." Of course, the meaning soon became obvious: one *steps in* sandals, but it was impossible to avoid being amused, even though the dean had no reasonable way of knowing that in continental American English *step in* had been appropriated for a very different garment.

The English spoken in the Philippines must be quite strange to American ears if we can judge by travelers' reports and the English of an occasional manual of Tagalog like that of Paraluman S. Aspillera.[20] Professor Aspillera tells us how to say "Happy greetings" in the official language of the Philippines, as well as "Good afternoon, too" (*Magan dáng hápon po namán*). Speaking of meetings and conventions, we must voice our request to speak by saying, "May I lose my courtesy?" ("*Mawaláng—gálang po*"). In more homey domains, we are taught to say "The dress and the pairs of shoes are clean" (*Ang mga bán at ang mga sapátos ay malinis*), and "How many are their children?" (*Ilán-ilán ang mga arak mulá?*) Translation exercises, English into Tagalog, include *We are clean and good* and *Their pencil is long.* The English of these and many other sentences in Professor Aspillera's book is strange and almost exotic, but not difficult to comprehend.

Nor is there more than momentary difficulty in understanding the foreign-English writing of someone like E. R. Goilu, whose *Papiamentu Textbook* (1962) comes an occasional cropper in translations like: *Mi falta dos florin*, 'I am short of two guilders.'[21] The book also contains a rather large number of English examples (for translation into Papiamentu) like, "I have no many friends because I have no money."[22]

But Goilu's charming book perhaps unintentionally performs the greatest possible linguistic service for American readers who wish to learn to communicate in Curaçao: it introduces them to Papiamentu-tinged English, which will be the language they will have to cope with most often while they are on the island. For on Aruba, Bonaire, and Curaçao, where Spanish, Dutch, and Papiamentu are in daily use, volunteer interpreters intent upon aiding Americans to surmount language barriers are even more abundant than on other Caribbean islands. The American who comes to work on Aruba/Curaçao or to enjoy the beautiful beaches may never really need to know what Goilu calls the Papiamentu "conjunctions of copulation" (*i, ni, tambe, no solamente, mi tambe*) any more than he will need to know the language's "conjunctions of separation" (both are listed in Goilu, p. 120); but it may help if he learns to refrain from smiling too broadly if some friendly grammarian undertakes to instruct him in the "conjunctions of copulation."

Foreign-language-interference problems that can lead to

double entendre interpretations are the most memorable, if not the biggest blocks to communication. A quite representative example is quoted from a Filipino speaker in *Sociological Inquiry* for the spring of 1966:

> . . . because I tend to say what I really mean in a contraception of Tagalog, Cebuano, and English.

To a great many foreign speakers (like one of my best students in Burundi), there is no sensible reason why the *secretary is at work* is preferable to the *secretary is in labor.*

The adult learner of English seldom if ever manages much of its phonology, so the sounds of "world-wide English" are endlessly varied and often strange indeed to the ears of native speakers. Usually, however, the sound differences are not great barriers to communication. It is easier for most of us to interpret the French or German uvular *r,* however strange it may sound in extreme phrases like *reactionary Republican,* than it is to articulate it ourselves in *Folies Bèrgère* or *Drittes Reich.* We can learn to place speakers from certain parts of India by their unique postalveolar *t;* but it helps little to read a description like this if you've never heard the sound.[23]

In a few cases, a different phonemic (sound contrastive) system on the part of the speaker of another language renders more words into homophones than are so for native speakers of English. There is the notorious case of Spanish lack of contrast between *b* and *v,* leading to the amusing, if not incomprehensible, statement to the teacher of English as a second language, "Mister, I think my consonants are okay, but I am still having trouble with my bowels." The lack of contrast between *l* and *r,* which is characteristic of Chinese (and of many of the world's less-known languages, including some of those of West Africa) can produce homophony of *very* and *belly;* but barring a contrived utterance like "I am belly full," few occasions are likely to arise on which it severely impedes communication.

Vocabulary differences, often involving what are called false cognates,[24] are another thing. There's always the possibility that a German who offers you a "gift" may be proffering poison. But a Spaniard who says you work for a company of "fabricators" probably just means manufacturers. On the other hand, if a Frenchwoman tells you that your dress looks like chiffon, don't be flattered unless you know she knows the English word. She may mean it looks like a dishrag. Hazards are equally great in the English-to-French direction. An American lady of my acquaintance used to take leave of her French drinking companions each night by saying *Je vais m'accoucher*, 'I am going to give birth', when she meant *Je vais me coucher*, 'I am going to bed'.

The false cognates are hackneyed concerns insofar as linguists and language teachers are concerned, but they still provide a great potential for misunderstanding foreigners' English. A Frenchman who knows a little English may mean bacon when he says *lard*, face when he says *figure*, and wide when he says *large*.[25] Either a French- or a Spanish-speaking lady who speaks of "taking a douche" may have nothing more than a shower in mind. The Frenchman's *travail*, 'work', is a little more likely to confuse an English-speaking person than a Spaniard's *trabajo*; but both Frenchman and Spaniard are likely to say that they "assisted" a meeting when they mean that they attended, and it is no help that the word once had that meaning in earlier English.[26]

Even when there is no cognate relationship at all, chance resemblances in spelling or pronunciation of English words to taboo words in other languages may complicate the communication problem of the traveler who speaks the "world" language. English *sick* sounds just enough like the Turkish verb meaning to have sexual intercourse to cause occasional snickers, and *peach* can be taken for the Turkish word meaning bastard. In print, the English third-person singular present tense verb *condones* looks like the Spanish noun plural for contraceptive devices and could cause embarrassment.

On the other hand, such terms are used rather freely almost anywhere these days and only the very old-fashioned blush. Shakespeare testified long ago to the existence of such problems in the revulsion which Katherine of France felt toward some English words (*Henry V*, Act II). But, significantly enough, she was engaged to Henry the Englishman by Act V.

Possibly the long experience of English speakers with foreign accents has something to do with the fact that we are not really confused by some interference factors. Entries on the menu of an Italian cruise ship (*Leonardo da Vinci,* Italia line, May 13, 1974) like *wines suggestion (sugerencia de vinos)* and *green peas soup (sopa cremosa de chicharos)* constitute no barrier to understanding, although they are immediately detectable as nonnative. Perhaps, on the other hand, it is our sheer willingness to understand that lowers the barrier.

Probably the only insuperable barrier in a bilingual language contact situation is overtranslation, the process that may turn *Calle Caoba* into *Mahogany Street, Mona* into *Monkey Island,* and *Culebra* into *Snake Island.* But a combination of interference and accommodation can produce something almost as insurmountable. The Spanish-speaking student who says, "I cannot get the book at the library, because I have no money," can presumably be straightened out by the explanation that *"Librería* in Spanish is translated by *bookstore* in English; the library is what you call *la biblioteca."* But in a situation in which Spanglish has been institutionalized, the speaker may have been using the expression *the library* for bookstore with native English-speaking peers who have accommodated. One can actually get the answer—I have gotten it—"I know, Mister, but I cannot get the book at the library because I have no money." Spanish-influenced English is by now so widely used that it may have claims to being a variety of its own, not subject to correction by monolinguals. In like manner, Cameroonians, including some children of French ancestry who have grown up there, tend to say *l'aviacion* for *l'aerodrome*; and they will brook no correction from speakers of continental French.

The real beginner, in the full flush of interference, is probably less likely to cause confusion than the intermediate speaker who has attained a certain amount of fluency in English. A Frenchman of the first description may say "a type" in such a way that you can figure out that it means a guy. But the one who has learned just enough English to think that he can get slangy may on occasion believe that it is an acceptable abbreviation for a *typewriter*. (Again, this is a matter of personal observation.)

For the many Americans who have gone abroad in the last few decades, particularly since World War II, there has been little or no instruction in this most vital phase of their communication problems. Herman and Herman have produced *A Manual of Foreign Dialects* for actors, and much of what they have done has had a great practical value.[27] But their material on "Mexican Spanish dialect" contains a great deal that is questionable and inspires something less than confidence in their treatment of the results of more exotic languages.[28] Somehow the American businessman and tourist have managed the difficult (from one theoretical point of view, virtually impossible) job of communication without immediate instruction in how to understand strange brands of English. Their greatest help may have come from the unsung hero of the development of English as a world language, the American foreign-language teacher.

Although a great deal has been said about the American foreign-language teacher, almost all of it has been concerned with his deficiencies. A teacher of French, Spanish, or German for the most part, the typical professor branched off into Russian, Norwegian, or Modern Greek very rarely, and into such exotic languages as Turkish, Mongolian and Mandarin Chinese almost never. He had a brother who taught Latin and Classical Greek and who almost invariably imbued his students with a snobbish attitude toward any language that people actually spoke, along with the dogmatic view that anyone who had trouble translating from Latin must not "really know English." He seldom spoke the language he was teaching with real fluency, and in some extreme cases he had never spoken in that language to a native speaker. From about 1940 onwards, almost everybody who wrote about language and education spent a few pages denouncing him.

American foreign-language teaching was almost universally regarded as "bad" up to World War II at least, and there was a lot of chest-beating and shouting of *mea culpa* from language teachers. It was asserted—truthfully—that college and high school students were not learning to speak the languages they studied; and it was assumed—unthinkingly—that no other purpose could be served by such courses. There were a lot of conferences, paid for from funds aimed at the improvement of education and usually provided by the government or the well-known foundations, on how this regrettable situation could be improved.

Many books issued from such conferences, not the best or the worst of which was Joseph S. Roucek's *The Study of Foreign Languages*.[29] A very typical article was Calvin A. Claudel's "The Changing Aspects of Teaching Spanish," which dealt with lower-level college Spanish in these terms:

> Elementary grammar was covered in one year, to be followed by a review grammar accompanied by literary or practical reading dealing with the culture of Spain or Spanish America. Although numerous texts might be labelled "conversational", in reality their contents and use in class in general paid only lip-service to an oral method. While in many areas a reading knowledge of the language was the main objective, in some areas such as New Orleans, both a conversational and a cultural ability in Spanish were required and ultimately achieved. But this high level of achievement has declined today because of regimentation

into the audio-lingual method which demonstrates "unprecedented activity—although not unprecedented success."[30]

Although Claudel and the other contributors did not consider the possibility that such "inadequate" language teaching was useful for a student whose future language experience might be primarily in terms of the Spanish-influenced English of Spain or Spanish America, they documented the fact that American language teaching was undergoing radical changes. Peter F. Oliva attests that "modern trends" in foreign-language teaching were at an "all time low in the 1940's" but came into "national prominence in the 1960's."[31] The government aided in the process with Title VI Language Institutes and Title III equipment for foreign-language departments in public schools.[32] Prior to World War II, ability to read the foreign language had been the goal, but now a speaking knowledge was their aim.[33] Oliva is very sanguine about the change to audio-lingual methodology, the use of such "advanced" methods as contrastive analysis,[34] and the continued growth of enrollments in foreign-language classes.[35]

The Northeast Conference on the Teaching of Foreign Languages would probably not share Oliva's optimism. In 1972, only four years after the publication of Roucek's book, it was necessary to set up a task force on the problem of teaching another language as part of another culture.[36] One reason why it was found advisable to take this step was a thorough disillusionment with the audio-lingual method as a device for teaching a foreign language. More than that, however, it was becoming clear that mere mastery of a foreign language, without familiarity with the culture of the speakers, was not really adequate for communication—assuming that the acquisition of the language under such circumstances was actually possible. And there was a third, highly practical motivation for an organization whose membership was almost entirely foreign-language teachers: enrollment in foreign-language classes in high schools and even more in colleges was declining rapidly. In these days of specialization in such matters as computer "languages," even an occasional professional linguist feels that he does not need any real fluency in a second "natural" language.[37]

This was a strange development from the point of view of Roucek's contributors and the many others who shared their feelings. Oliva asserted that "barring a great war or depression, Americans will continue to travel in unprecedented numbers,"[38] and he seemed to regard it as axiomatic that such travel would increase their awareness of the need to speak foreign languages. But perhaps he failed to take into account that such American travelers would be met by increasing numbers of students of English as a foreign language who would insist upon "traducing" for the Americans.

Among the post–World War II tourists and traveling American businessmen were no doubt many who had studied foreign languages in the "bad" old method—and most of them probably did as well in actual communication, since there were virtual taboos against the use of any language except English where Americans were present. Although few of them may have realized it, what they had been given in college may well have been just exactly what was needed for the kind of communication problem they faced as they traveled, for business or pleasure, about the world that spoke often fluent but frequently flawed English and was often grimly determined to use it. No one, so far as I know, has recently suggested going back to the old grammar-translation method of language teaching; but it might fill up a few more classes than the methods currently practiced, since a lot of students resent those weekly hours in the laboratory. Genevieve Delattre, one of the contributors to the Roucek volume, did have a few good words to say about the text by Fraser and Squair, in its various editions, for grammar/translation-oriented teaching of French.

The use of English as a world language seems to be increasing rather than diminishing, even if England and the United States do not have the dominant position in world affairs they had only four or five years ago. Americans, who *will* probably continue to go abroad in great numbers in any foreseeable future, will need a great deal of linguistic sophistication in order to understand this world use of "their" language. They will need to know something about their language and the variation that takes place in it, although it is unlikely that a study of dialect geography will help much.[39] But, most of all, they will need to be able to repeat the performance of their predecessors in World War II and immediately thereafter, to understand English with all kinds of foreign accents and interferences. It may seem terribly reactionary to suggest that some of the same kind of language training might not be inappropriate. But if the experience of the past is to teach us anything, it may be that a study of foreign languages is the most useful step toward understanding the English of the many millions for whom it is not a native language.

In the preceding chapters, I have tried to show how little is revealed about even American English by a consideration of what rural corner of England a particular verb form or turn of expression may possibly have come from. In fact, it elucidates American English very little to place it within the conventions of the reconstructive tradition.[40] Even less is revealed about the world language of many, many Africans, Asians, Semitic peoples, and non-Germanic Europeans if we trace English back to the hypothetical three Low German tribes (Angles, Saxons, and Jutes) who may have effected a crossing to the British Isles somewhere around 449.[41] Significant as it was in its own way, that crossing would not amount to a heavy day's traffic on the Staten Island ferry today. The extensive use of English by groups that would more than dwarf those three Germanic tribes has removed modern English from that historic tradition and placed it, whether we like it or not, in an international context in which rural England and nearly prehistoric Germany seem exceedingly trivial.

It is conventional to moralize about usage a bit at the end of a work on the history of the language. A dozen or so histories of English (mainly of Old and Middle English) have wound up with a supermodern admonition to school-teachers and their ilk that users of the language—even Americans—are having their own way with English and that not much can be done about it. It was something of a triumph to establish the principle that American English is all right, that it isn't necessary for Americans to keep running back to London (or Oxford or Cambridge) every few years to replenish their language, to reestablish contact with the "real" English. It is only fair to extend that principle, to assert that International English is "British" or "American" only by the merest technicality. If Americans are now the main carriers of English about the globe, there is no law whatsoever that says speakers elsewhere must try to talk like Americans. Most of them will not try, and of those few who do, only a tiny percentage will have any noticeable success. "Foreigners" who find it useful to speak the language—and in the current world situation it is hardly possible to predict how long they will continue to do so—will make their own use of it. They will not come to any British or American dialect, not even to Network Standard, to have their English remedied. Furthermore, there is no more guarantee that an American or an Englishman can understand every variety of International English without special preparation than there was that an Italian could understand Old French or Old Spanish. It seems safe enough to predict that the longer the language continues to be used by other populations, the more variety will come to be subsumed under what we call "English."

Language study is thus an important part of the educational needs of Americans. American English came to be in a highly multilingual context, and many of us—perhaps increasing numbers in the next few decades—use it in almost equally multilingual circumstances. To understand its past, as well as to do what little we can to predict its future, we need to know how it relates to other languages. We also need to know as much as possible about other languages—if only to be able to understand what other populations are likely to believe is our own. There are many ways in which knowledge about other languages and about our own can be acquired. Even the old-fashioned method of sitting alone reading grammar books, although thoroughly out of fashion for a few decades, can have its uses. Perhaps the greatest need in linguistic pedagogy, however, is the avoidance of dogmatism. "You can't learn the language unless you imitate the pronunciation of a native speaker" can be as dogmatically deadly as the older, now probably no-more-repeated, "You don't really know any language unless you know Latin." Furthermore, unless the Arabs' increasing economic power makes their language the next world lingua franca sooner than we expect, speakers of American English will have to go on for a long time understanding foreigners who have not imitated the native speaker very well.

NOTES

PREFATORY NOTE

[1] We are omitting the use of English by native speakers of Celtic languages who remained in Great Britain after the Anglo-Saxon conquest. Obviously, some such use must have predated what is described here. But historians of both the English language and the British Isles have ignored the matter entirely, although they have, of course, dealt with borrowings into English from the Celtic language and from British Latin—essentially the opposite of the process under discussion.

[2] See Leonard Bloomfield, *Language*, 1933, Chapters 18 and 19.

CHAPTER I

[1] (p. 8) This statement is chosen as representative, and not singled out for special criticism. Others have written essentially the same thing. For example, Thomas Pyles, in *Words and Ways in American English* (1952), says, "American English began as seventeenth century British English" (p. 4). Traditionally, work on American English has been full of such statements, and most of its conclusions have been colored by such presuppositions. Works cited anywhere in this book are chosen more or less at random, and never with the intention of a specific attack on any one word or author.

[2] Some idea of these varieties can be obtained from W. Matthews, "Sailors' Pronunciation in the Second Half of the Seventeenth Century," *Anglia,* 1935; "Sailors' Pronunciation 1770–1783," *Anglia,* 1937. Ian F. Hancock ("A Domestic Origin for the English-derived Atlantic Creoles," *Florida Foreign Language Reporter,* Spring/Fall, 1972) compares some of the pronunciations attested by Matthews for the maritime variety to pronunciations in the Krio of Sierra Leone. More of Hancock's observations on the same topic are published in "Nautical Sources of Krio Vocabulary," *International Journal of the Sociology of Language* (forthcoming). Like William A. Stewart, myself, and others who subscribe to some version of this hypothesis, Hancock believes that West African languages contributed a great deal to the creole varieties. But the West African English varieties have too many similarities to varieties like that of Pitcairn Island, where few or no speakers of African languages have been to permit a simple interpretation in terms of "substratum" influences. In some cases, maritime vocabulary was obviously learned by West African speakers:

> Ver fine biggy house, and ab got two deck.
> (W. F. W. Owen, *Voyages to Explore the Shores of Africa, Arabia, and Madagascar,* 1833, II, p. 177)

> Dat nothing; by by you come back, look um nudder deck.
> (*Ibid.,* II, p. 178)

[3] See Chapter II.

[4] Conventional work on American English has been based upon the premise, articulated by Hans Kurath in 1928 ("The Origin of Dialectal Differences in Spoken American English," *Modern Philology* XXV), that British "regional" dialects, or features thereof, migrated to North America and formed the basis of American English dialects—also conceived of as being almost exclusively regional. In Kurath's basic formulaton, Southern forms should have come almost exclusively from Southern British dialects. Under pressure of the challenge of the creole origin of Black English Vernacular, however, dialect geographers have tried to trace features of Southern English to any and all English dialects,

including not only Northern and Western dialects but even Scottish and Irish dialects! For a satirical treatment of those procedures, see my "Principles in the History of American English: Paradox, Virginity, and Cafeteria," *Florida FL Reporter*, 1970.

[5] Since it is an accepted tenet of all schools of language study that languages change constantly (although there is great disagreement about the mechanism of change), no one within the profession of linguistics believes the popularly appealing statements about "Elizabethan English" being spoken in the mountains of Tennessee (or some other suitably remote place). My purpose is to take issue with some of the relatively serious theories that have been advanced, not to knock over that straw man once again. As should be obvious, I am not ascribing any such absurd view to other language historians against whose positions I happen to be arguing. Statements, on the other hand, about "Shakespearean English" being the language of the colonists are and should be subject to check and possible refutation. For Shakespeare's language, Franz, *Shakespeare-Grammatik*, is the standard work. See his materials on "impersonal" instructions dealt with in the text and on other constructions like *is arisen, are entered in the territories*, and *were safe arrived*.

[6] The story of language contact and relationship in Great Britain is told in Kenneth Jackson, *Language and History in Early Britain*, University of Edinburgh Press, 1953.

[7] The most accessible source of Lingua Franca material is the article by Hugo Schuchardt, "Die Lingua Franca," in *Zeitschrift für Romanische Philologie*, 1909). Kahane, Kahane, and Tietze (1958) are especially good on nautical terms from several languages, including Turkish and Greek, in current Mediterranean sailor talk and therefore presumably in the Lingua Franca.

[8] The specific statement that Lingua Franca relationships were to be found in the creole languages, including those of the Caribbean, was first made by Keith Whinnom, "The Origin of the European-based Creoles and Pidgins," *Orbis* (1965). My own *Black English* (1972) and other scattered articles (see Bibliography) consider some of the documentary evidence for the use of the Lingua Franca (Sabir) in the maritime and slave trades. Whinnom was, to some degree, expanding a suggestion made by

Robert W. Thompson, "A Note on Some Possible Affinities Between the Creole Dialects of the Old World and Those of the New," in LePage (ed.), *Creole Language Studies II* (1961). The conference on creole language studies, of which the LePage work represents the proceedings, was characterized by a recognition on the part of all those present of the great similarities between pidgin and the creole varieties of Portuguese, French, and English in West Africa, the Americas, the Indian Ocean, and the Pacific. It seemed obvious to the linguists present at that conference—as it still seems obvious twelve years later—that the striking resemblances in the verb systems (*as systems*, not in terms of phonological or lexical resemblances) of Portuguese, French, and English varieties, and some that are conventionally traced to Dutch and even to Danish, precluded taking seriously the conclusion that they were all accidental parallels, based upon somehow spontaneous developments from "regional" or other dialects of European languages. The scholars referred to above (along with William A. Stewart, whose "Creole Languages of the Caribbean"—see Bibliography—may have been the locus of the first use of the term) have come to be associated with the relexification theory. The outstanding creolist Jan Voorhoeve, in "Historical and Linguistic Evidence in Favor of the Relexification Theory in the Formation of Creoles," *Language in Society,* Vol. 2 (1973), presents what is probably the strongest argument for that position.

⁹ This process was brilliantly described by Paul Christophersen in two articles which were largely overlooked, perhaps because of their modest titles: "Some Special West African Words" (*English Studies,* 1953) and "A Note on the Words *dash* and *ju-ju* in West African English" (*English Studies,* 1959). Christophersen's examplary attention to documents has never been equaled, and certainly not surpassed, by students of Afro-American English. Most recent studies have preferred to do history by speculation, not by study of documents, in spite of the obvious pitfalls of such an approach. Proponents of this type of language history—which involves internal reconstruction and the creation of "proto-forms" in preference to the examination of sources—forget, as Christophersen did not, that reconstructive theory was evolved essentially by philologists who paid very careful attention to their often very

limited documents (like, for example, Wulfila's fourth century A.D. translation of the Bible into Gothic). In one extreme case of simplistic reconstruction theory (Walter Wolfram, review of *Black English, Language,* 1972), all use of documents has been stigmatized as "anecdotal." For further documentary support of the position stated by Christophersen, see Dillard, "Creole English and Creole Portuguese: The Early Records," *Journal of African Languages* (forthcoming).

[10] A reasonably good account of the origin and, especially, the present extension of pidgin languages (Portuguese, French, and English) and their descendant creole languages can be gleaned from Dell Hymes (ed., *Pidginization and Creolization of Languages,* 1971). One of the limitations of this work, however, is that the editor and several of his contributors are overinclined to see direct environmental influence on language change and language development. For criticism of one aspect of Hymes's theoretical position, see Dillard, review of Cazden, Hymes, and John (eds.), *Functions of Language in the Classroom* (*Science,* May 11, 1973).

[11] Even some of the technical literature of linguistics (e.g., Hymes, *op. cit.*) represents pidgins as "originating" in a bilingual contact situation. It is obvious from any historical consideration, however, that their domain is that of multilingual contact. There is, then, very little historical validity to a statement such as:

> As the history of various Creoles shows, the rapid result of sudden contact of two dissimilar structures is frequently the lowest common denominator of both with a strong push towards inflectional simplification.
>
> (William Labov, *Sociolinguistic Patterns,* 1972, p. 300)

As creolists (e.g., those cited in footnotes 8 and 9) are generally aware, but as linguists who have approached language primarily from the point of view of one or another school of psychology are not, a pidgin (as the most typical Lingua Franca) spreads rapidly in a complex multilingual situation. The case of Curaçao would seem to show that stable societal multilingualism is possible up to the level of four or five languages. Beyond that, and especially if a significant group that must be communicated with but does not speak one of the languages of the stable group is involved, a Lingua Franca is a practical necessity. The issue in the use of pidgins and the development of creoles is not, then, that of "uniformitarian" versus "cataclysmic" bilingual contact (Labov, *op. cit.*, p. 265) but the rather different one of working out the contact dynamics of a highly diversified, multilingual contact, whether "cataclysmic" or not. At any rate, the "lowest common denominator" factor in pidgins applies (if at all) only to the comparatively trivial morphological features like number and gender concord.

[12] Since Molière added no translations or explanations, he apparently expected the members of the French court to understand Sabir. The speakers are Turks, and therefore "funny" foreigners to whom it was probably considered appropriate to attribute such language.

[13] See works in Bibliography, discussion in Dillard, *Black English* (Chapter III), and attestations cited below.

[14] See *Black English,* Chapter IV.

[15] On the switch from sign language to pidgin on the part of the plains Indians, see Chapter III.

[16] For an extreme version of this line of reasoning, carried to the point of absurdity, consider the following:

> If the typical situation which produces a pidgin is contact for the purposes of trade between speakers of mutually unintelligible languages, there would initially be a good deal of gesture accompanying speech; this would be reduced, though probably never eliminated, as the pidgin took shape. Gestures would accompany the first exclamations: shouts to attract attention (arm waving), more restrained greetings (salutes, beckoning to approach, signs to stop, parting signs). Exclamations or interjections expressing surprise, fear, amusement, warning, anger, might be accompanied by gestures—which can only be guessed at.
> (Frederic G. Cassidy, "The Pidgin Element in Jamaican Creole," in Hymes [ed.], *Pidginization and Creolization of Languages,* pp. 212–13)

This statement, by a well-known dialect geographer and reconstructionist, is a horrible example of what the reconstructionist tradition was trying to avoid in developing rigorously formal procedures. Imaginative "reconstructions" like this one can, of course, be developed by anyone—and a small child's "reconstruction" of this type would be as valid as that of an experienced linguist. In addition, the statement reveals an almost frightening disregard of relativism in gestural systems, expression of emotion, and so forth.

[17] The case of Pidgin English is, however, in some ways less striking than that of the creoles, which are still obviously Portuguese-based. Creolists who have studied the West Indian language Papiamentu find that they are able to read the Portuguese Creole of Senegal or Papia Kristang (Malacca Creole Portuguese) with only an occasional gloss of a word. For the last and its striking similarity to the Afro-American Portuguese-based Creoles, see Ian F. Hancock, "Malacca Creole Portuguese" (to appear in D. Craig [ed.], *Proceedings of the Conference on Creole Languages and Educational Development,* to be published by UNESCO.)

[18] Because Chinese and Melanesian Pidgin English have been better known to Europeans than the African varieties, many writers have assumed that Pidgin English originated in the China coastal trade. While it seems probable that Melanesian Pidgin English was partly the result of the spread of the Chinese variety (see the quotation from G. W. Turner, note 37), finding the "place" or origin of any pidgin seems almost as hopeless as determining, with present techniques, the "spot" of origin of the universe.

[19] Morrison, *The Maritime History of Massachusetts,* 1961, p. 65.

[20] *Ibid.,* p. 78.

[21] Dulles, *The Old China Trade,* 1930, p. 20.

[22] *Ibid.*

[23] Bailyn, *The New England Merchants in the Seventeenth Century,* 1955, p. 84.

[24] Francis Grose, *A Classical Dictionary of the Vulgar Tongue,* 1785.

[25] John Atkins, *A Voyage to Guinea, Brasil, and the West Indies,* 1737, p. 60, in a list of "Some Negrish Words."

[26] Hans Nathan, *Dan Emmett and the Rise of Negro Minstrelsy,* 1962, pp. 27–28.

[27] *Ibid.,* p. 27.

[28] Black speakers of Creole languages like Krio frequently simplify their language in order to make themselves understood by Europeans. See E. C. Jones, *Sierra Leone Language Review,* 1962.

[29] *The Religious Intelligencer,* 1821.

[30] In addition to Christophersen, *opera cit.,* (discussed above in footnote 9), David Dalby's *Black Through White: Patterns of Communication in Africa and the New World* (Hans Wolff Memorial Lecture, Bloomington, Indiana, 1969) cites many of the relevant documents.

[31] Sir Richard Francis Burton, *Wanderings in West Africa,* 1863, Vol. I, p. 215.

[32] Professor Luis Ferraz of the University of the Witwatersrand (personal communication) informs me that Fanakalo has *mbayi mbayi,* rather obviously an adaptation to the phonotactic patterns of the African languages of the area. Whether the "original" phrase was *by and by* or *by by* (the form used consistently by Owen, *Voyages to Explore the Shores of Africa, Arabia, and Madagascar,* 1933) has not been definitively determined. Cassidy (*op. cit.*), who has a strong predisposition to find Pidgin English forms as close to British dialects as possible, cites forms from Jamaican Creole, the United States (Joel Chandler Harris), Melanesian Pidgin, Pitcairnese, Sranan Tongo, and Beach-la-Mar, with speculation that comparable forms might be in West African forms of Pidgin English. He does not, however, cite any of the attestations in travel literature, etc.

[33] John Reinecke, *Language and Dialect in Hawaii,* p. 285.

[34] Clark, *Lights and Shadows in Sailor Life,* 1847, p. 188. Cf. the use of the term in present-day Hawaii, as attested in John Reinecke, *Language and Dialect in Hawaii,* p. 170.

[35] Beecher and Harvey, *Memoirs of Henry Obookiah,* quoted in Reinecke, *Language and Dialect in Hawaii,* p. 198.

[36] Baker, *The Australian Language,* 1966, p. 310.

[37] G. W. Turner, *The English Language in Australia and New Zealand,* 1966, p. 203.

[38] *Ibid.*

[39] *Ibid.*

[40] R. V. Lendenveld, "Die Chinesen in Australien," in Emil Deckert (ed.), *Globus*, Vol. LVIII, No. 1.

[41] Kenneth E. Read, *The High Valley*, 1965, p. 7.

[42] These are, of course, specifically "Chinese" Pidgin English only in terms of the medium of transmission to the British sailors. Only slight phonological differences would be indicated by *wanchee* and the Surinam form *wantje* (quoted above from Herlein).

[43] For the record, I do not believe that such words can originate or can be taken into Pidgin English through the process of "phonetic symbolism" (a direct equivalence of sound and meaning), which seems to me a complete ghost process insofar as etymology is concerned. That some of the popularity of the forms was due to the similarity to *phooey* or other such expressions is, of course, a distinct possibility.

[44] "Linguistic Hybridization and the 'Special Case' of Pidgins and Creoles," in Hymes (ed.), *Pidginization and Creolization of Language,* p. 103.

[45] George W. Matsell, *Vocabulum or the Rogue's Lexicon,* New York, 1859.

[46] For *hepcat, hip, cat,* and other West Africanisms in American English, see Dalby's "The African Element in Black American English," in Thomas Kochman (ed.), *Rappin' and Stylin' Out,* 1972. For *higo, dago,* and other relevant comparative material on Pitcairn and other island varieties of English, see Ian F. Hancock, "Nautical Sources of Krio Vocabulary," *International Journal of the Sociology of Language,* forthcoming.

[47] *Narrative of Voyages to Explore the Shores of Africa, Arabia, and Madagascar,* 1833, Vol. II, p. 191.

[48] A West Indian proverb is

> Tief tief tief, God laugh: 'If a thief steals from a thief, God laughs'.

[49] "Lexical Expansion Outside a Closed System," *Journal of African Languages* XII, 1973.

[50] Chomsky, *Cartesian Linguistics,* New York and London,

1966, p. 22: "The purely practical use of language is characteristic of no real human language, but only of invented parasitic systems." A footnote adds: "for example, the *lingua franca* of the Mediterranean coast." The "real human" factors involved are, from Chomsky's point of view, psychological rather than historical. It is not known how he or any of his followers would react to the theory of "real human" languages (the Creoles) having developed from a start in Sabir. The issue is of no great importance, anyway; once it is the native language of the speech community, a Creole is not used for "purely practical" purposes but becomes as much a "means of thought and self-expression" (Chomsky 1966, p. 21) as any other language. In fact, the stereotypical reactions of native speakers of Creoles have typically stressed the value of the Creole for "sentiment," "feeling," etc. The relationship of the language of inner monologue to thought is, of course, a vexed and problematic issue, and there are great differences of opinion about it between mentalistic linguists and cognitive psychologists. But the use of Creoles for inner monologue and not exclusively for "practical uses" is as far beyond doubt as any issue that depends upon introspective report could be.

[51] C. H. de Goeje, *Verslag der Toemoekhoemakexpeditie (Tumuchumacexpeditie)*, Leiden, 1908, Betrage 11, Taal 204-10.

[52] William Falconer, *The Mariner's Dictionary* (1805), cites a use of the word in English in 1769. Bense, *Dictionary of the Low Dutch Element in the English Vocabulary*, 1939, who feels that the word was used in English much earlier than the attestation cited by Falconer, cites *camboose, canboose,* and *coboose* in early attestations.

[53] *The Origins and Development of the English Language*, p. 220.

[54] On this matter, the most instructive study is one of the few ever to be performed with adult immigrants in depth, Werner F. Leopold, "The Decline of German Dialects," *Word*, 1959. Leopold found that East German refugees to West Germany used Stage German (if adults) with their new neighbors or became bidialectal (if children). In many cases, however, when for sentimental reasons they attempted to recapture the "old home" dialect, they

found that they had partially forgotten it. Leopold also points out that the East Germans have influenced the use of dialect among the West Germans, who tended to standardize their speech more when confronted with large numbers of speakers of radically different "local" dialects.

CHAPTER II

[1] Such statements are commonplace in sources like Albert Marckwardt's *American English* and Thomas Pyles's *The Origins and Development of the English Language*. Pyles states explicitly:

> All types of American English have grown out of the regional modifications of the British Standard—with some coloring from British dialects—as it existed in the seventeenth century, when it was much less rigid than it is today. (*p. 233*)

[2] Charles M. Andrews, *The Fathers of New England: A Chronicle of the Puritan Commonwealth*, in *The Chronicles of America*, 1919, Vol. 6, p. 6.

[3] D. Plooij, D.D., *The Pilgrim Fathers from a Dutch Point of View*, p. 91.

[4] William Macon Coleman, *The History of the Primitive Yankees; or the Pilgrim Fathers in England and Holland*, p. 44.

[5] Andrews, *op. cit.*, p. 10.

[6] *The Quaker Colonies: A Chronicle of the Proprietors of the Delaware*, 1919, p. 192.

[7] Quoted in Allen Walker Read, "British Recognition of American Speech in the Eighteenth Century," *Dialect Notes*, 1933, p. 323.

[8] *The New England Merchants in the Seventeenth Century*, 1955, p. 84.

[9] *Ibid.*

[10] The basic principle of leveling in the American colonial dialects was well established in Allen Walker Read's "British Recognition of American Speech in the Eighteenth Century," *Dialect Notes*, 1933. Read did not, however, use the term *koiné*. In a later

article ("The Assimilation of the Speech of British Immigrants in Colonial America," *Journal of English and Germanic Philology*, 1938), Read subscribed to the notion, then becoming popular, that the southeastern counties of England—the area around London—had given their basic character to American English. It is occasionally hinted at (see below), but never apparently treated in detail, that the "London" dialect was itself the result of a leveling process. Although it is beyond the scope of this book, there is considerable reason to believe that this kind of koiné-forming process goes well back into English language history. In the Middle English period and in the Renaissance, there were frequent statements about the ridiculing at court of speakers of a noticeable dialect. After discarding the littérateur's notion that Chaucer invented a prestige Middle English dialect, historians generally gravitated to the position that Chaucerian English was the "regional" dialect of London. However, the possibility that the court (like the stage and radio and television broadcast networks later) was the locus of the standard dialect would be worth investigating. If that was indeed the case, the standard dialect can hardly be called "regional" in any meaningful sense of the term. The most important recent treatments of koiné formation in specific situations are Haim Blanc, "The Israeli Koiné as an Emerging National Standard" (see Bibliography), and Nida and Fehdereau, "Indigenous Pidgins and Koinés," *International Journal of American Linguistics*, 1971. The latter treats pidgins, as well as koinés, as "internal" developments in individual contact situations. While agreeing with Nida and Fehdereau that pidgin-using and koiné-forming situations are strongly analogous, I cannot agree that the "Sabir Pidgins" (see above, Chapter I, note 8) at least are special formations. Rather, they were transmitted by maritime routes—and in some frontier situations, like the one to be discussed in Chapter III. The Old English migration (traditionally around 449) to England apparently did not engender this kind of leveling. From such traditional sources as we have—and they are far from the actual date of the reported migration—a possible explanation appears. It would appear that the "Anglo-Saxon" migration was more or less tribal in nature. The American migration was not.

[11] The motivating philosophy behind these attempts is a noble, politically liberal attitude. It is typically represented by a statement in Hans Kurath's "The Linguistic Atlas of the United States and Canada," in D. F. Fry and Daniel Jones (eds.), *Proceedings of the Second International Conference of Phonetic Sciences* (1936):

> Folk speech and cultivated speech are very close together in recently settled and democratically organized America. (*p. 19*)

While one must of necessity feel guilty about criticizing a statement of such high seriousness and noble innocence, it must be immediately apparent to any reader that neither sociology nor dialectology could possibly proceed in any objective terms without at least leaving such a statement open to question. In fact, it was the recognition of the inadequacy of a dialectology based on such virtually gullible preconceptions that first led me to develop an interest in social dialectology. And it is very tempting to quote one of my brighter students, who, after I had just pointed out that the phrase "recently settled" left out the American Indians, asserted, "And the phrase 'democratically organized' leaves out the rest of us!"

[12] According to Kurath ("The Origin of Dialectal Differences in Spoken American English," *Modern Philology,* 1928), a long tradition of writers who held such preconceptions preceded Kurath himself and George Philip Krapp (*The English Language in America,* 1925):

> It is generally assumed—if one may judge by the statements that appeared in print before the publication of Krapp's work—that American English, apparently also in its spoken form, is essentially the Southern English Standard of the Seventeenth and Eighteenth centuries as modified locally in the course of the last century or two. This is the view advanced by Whitney [*Language and the Study of Language,* 1868, pp. 171ff], presumably for American English as a whole; by Ellis [J. A. Ellis, *Early English Pronunciation,* V. 236] for "the eastern United States, New York and Mas-

sachusetts"; accepted by Emerson [O. F. Emerson, "The Ithaca Dialect," *Dialect Notes,* I, pp. 169–73] for the speech of Ithaca, New York; and defended by Sheldon [F. S. Sheldon, "What is a Dialect?" *Dialect Notes* I, p. 293]

Viewed in the context of combating earlier notions that Americans had "corrupted" the English language and of the struggle for legitimacy of American English, the work of Kurath, Krapp, and even Whitney, Ellis, Emerson, and Sheldon has a great deal that is praiseworthy about it. The trouble is that Kurath especially exerted so strong an influence on subsequent dialect research that not only his principles but the details of his presentation hardened into dogma. Although they were in their day leaders and innovators in studying the process of change in American English, Kurath and Krapp strangely overlooked all the evidence for the contact varieties, like pidgins. Indeed, they went so far as to assert that such evidence was false. Krapp, for example, excoriated James Fenimore Cooper for not presenting evidence of a "frontier lingua franca," in the midst of quotations from Cooper in Pidgin English (not recognized, evidently, or at least not labeled as such, by Krapp). The result has been that work in one area of study of the American developments has been not merely inhibited but virtually tabooed.

[13] The strongest claim of this sort was presented by Kurath, "The Origin of Dialectal Differences in Spoken American English" (*Modern Philology* XXV, 1928). Reluctance to criticize an article of that ancient a date is partly alleviated by the iteration of the same position in Kurath's 1965 article, "Some Aspects of Atlantic Seaboard English Considered in Connection with British English," *Communications et Rapports,* Troisième Partie (Louvain 1965). Both of these were reprinted in Williamson and Burke (eds.), *A Various Language: Perspectives on American Dialects* (1971), a collection so narrow in its discipleship to the Kurath position as to make the term "perspectives" in the title a misnomer. See my review in *Caribbean Studies* (1972).

[14] Raven I. McDavid, Jr., "Historical, Regional, and Social Variation," *Journal of English Linguistics,* 1967. See my criticism in "American Negro Dialects: Convergence or Divergence?" *Flor-*

ida FL Reporter (1968: reprinted in Whitten and Szwed, *Afro-American Anthropology: Contemporary Perspectives,* 1970).

[15] The statement is:

> Features of pronunciation now more widely current in rural areas than in the great population centers derive either from British folk speech or from earlier stages of SBE [Standard British English].
> (Quoted in Williamson and Burke [eds.], *A Various Language,* p. 107)

Although the term "folk speech" is ambiguous enough, considered in isolation, to include possible maritime varieties, the article as a whole makes it clear that Kurath was referring to British "regional" varieties.

[16] P. 63.

[17] Orbeck's caveats against uncritical acceptance of British dialect origin for American forms are almost as frequent—and, in retrospect, more important—than the statement and slight bit of evidence he offers in support of such derivations. Consider, for example, these statements from *Early New England Pronunciation* (1927):

> The only piece of evidence about which there can be little doubt is the characteristically Kentish, southern, and southwestern past participial form. On the other hand, there are no examples of the southern development of OE íe . . ., no forms indicating the characteristic southern voicing of final *f* and *s*, no clear examples of western *u*, and the few forms that can be explained as reflecting Kentish ĕ (from OE ȳ) can also be otherwise explained.   (*p. 142*)

or

> Some few features may possibly be of [British] dialectal origin, but they are at present so widely current that it is altogether impossible to determine which dialect is to be credited with them. There are isolated forms here and there which may be explained on the basis of the northern

dialects. On the other hand it should be pointed out that there are no examples in the records of the northern plural. Nor is there much evidence for the typical Scotch scribal habit of representing vowel length by orthographic *i.* (*pp. 141–42*)

or

The northern *sall* for shall occurs in Bradford's *History of Plimouth*; Bradford himself, however, came from southern Yorkshire within the provenience of the midland dialect. (*p. 141*)

All in all, Orbeck presents very little evidence for the presentation of British "regional" dialects, in any meaningful way, in the early town records of Massachusetts. In the context of defending the legitimacy of American English—and of linguistic change—Orbeck and others like him may be considered praiseworthy. Our respect for them should not, however, go so far as to commit us to their rather shaky (and, in the case of Orbeck, reluctantly drawn) specific conclusions about the British provenience of American dialect forms.

[18] Orbeck, *op. cit.,* p. 129.

[19] *Ibid.*

[20] Charles O. Paullin and John K. Wright (1932), *Atlas of the Historical Geography of the United States,* Washington, Carnegie Institution, Plate 70, C and D.

[21] Orbeck, *op. cit.,* p. 145.

[22] *Ibid.,* p. 143.

[23] *Ibid.,* p. 142.

[24] *Ibid.*

[25] "Some Aspects of Atlantic Seaboard English Considered in Comparison with Their Connection with British English," in Williamson and Burke (eds.), *A Various Language,* p. 105.

[26] Orbeck, *op. cit.,* p. 9.

[27] *Ibid.,* p. 141.

[28] Recent studies emphasize ethnic group loyalties, social stratification, and relationships within the peer group as influences upon each individual's choice of a range of linguistic variants open to

him. Certain works of William Labov (*The Social Stratification of English in New York City*, 1966; *Language in the Inner City*, 1972; and "The Linguistic Consequences of Being a Lame," *Language in Society*, Vol. 2, No. 1, 1973) are representative of the change in emphasis. In particular, social stratification, as a factor in dialect variation was given an early, convincing demonstration by John Gumperz, "Dialect and Social Stratification" (*American Anthropologist*, 1958). Ethnic group variation is effectively demonstrated in Haim Blanc, *Communal Dialects of Baghdad Arabic*, 1954.

[29] A caveat against uncritical acceptance of such procedures was entered by W. Nelson Francis, "Some Dialect Verb Forms in England," *Orbis*, 1961. In one of the closest approaches to the description of the koiné ever accomplished by a conventional dialectologist, Francis hypothesized that the Atlantic seaboard regions had probably been "dialectal melting pots" (p. 8). Although Francis did not say so, this would, in the Linguistic Atlas tradition, preclude significant representation of British dialects in the United States, since that tradition assumes that dialects further west represent migration patterns from the eastern seaboard.

Tracing British dialects to America with any confidence would require better sources for historical dialectology than those of Wright (see Bibliography). The deficiencies of such standard nineteenth-century works have been sporadically recognized. Raven I. McDavid, Jr., and Virginia Glenn McDavid, "The Relationship of the Speech of American Negroes to the Speech of Whites," *American Speech*, 1951, warn that "One must, of course, use Wright with caution, since a large part of the evidence on which both the *Grammar* and the *Dictionary* are based was collected by amateurs with uneven training and without any systematic procedure."

[30] One of the most interesting and relevant studies is that of Werner F. Leopold, "The Decline of German Dialects," *Word*, 1959. In the case of East German refugees subject to dialect pressures in West Germany, Leopold shows that considerable "disappearance" of dialect differences (herein it would be called leveling) can take place even within the adult generation that has migrated.

[31] Sydney G. Fisher, *The Quaker Colonies, A Chronicle of the Proprietors of the Delaware,* 1919, p. 3.

[32] Alexander Hamilton, *Hamilton's Itinerarium, Being a Narrative of a Journey from Annapolis Maryland . . from May to September, 1744,* pp. 199–200.

[33] Quoted in Read, 1933, p. 323.

[34] *Ibid.*

[35] "Letters of Rev. Jonathan Boucher," *Maryland Historical Magazine* X (1916), p. 30.

[36] *The Journal of Nicholas Creswell, 1774–1777,* p. 271.

[37] For some of the records of West African Pidgin English, see William A. Stewart, "Sociolinguistic Factors in the History of American Negro Dialects" (1967), and "Continuity and Change in American Negro Dialects" (1968); Dillard, *Black English* (1972), and below, Chapter III. For American Indian Pidgin English, see Douglas Leechman and Robert A. Hall, Jr., "American Indian Pidgin English Attestations and Grammatical Peculiarities," *American Speech,* 1955; Mary Rita Miller, "Attestations of American Indian Pidgin English in Fiction and Non-Fiction," *American Speech,* 1967; and Dillard, *Black English,* Chapter IV.

[38] In a manner crudely prefiguring Chomsky and Halle, *The Sound Pattern of English* (1968), Adams pointed out that inconsistencies between English spelling and pronunciation (from his point of view, apparent deficiencies in the latter) reflected underlying consistency. For example, he pointed out what would now be called a derivational relationship between *bile* and *bilious,* and accounted for the different vowel pronunciations in terms of that relationship. While this is hardly of the level of sophistication of Chomsky and Halle, it does represent an awareness of a relationship that some professional linguists of the mid-twentieth century ignored.

[39] P. 146.

[40] London editor of *Ramsay's History of the American Revolution,* 1782, quoted in Read, 1933, pp. 324–25.

[41] *Ibid.*

[42] For a specific statement on parent-peer influences, see Labov, *Sociolinguistic Patterns,* p. 304.

[43] Cited in Read, 1933, p. 325.

[44] John Davis, *Travels of Four Years and a Half in the United States of America During 1798, 1799, 1800, 1801 and 1802,* New York, 1809; Charles William Janson, *Stranger in America,* London, 1807; J. F. D. Smyth, *A Tour of the United States of America,* London, 1784. There are, of course, very many other such sources.

[45] For a specific application of caste rules to dialect, and some interesting and important generalizations, see John Gumperz, "Dialect and Social Stratification in a North Indian Village," *American Anthropologist,* 1958.

[46] Other partly unassimilated ethnic groups, besides the Blacks, include the Cajuns of Louisiana, the Pennsylvania Germans ("Dutch"), and the Chicanos. It is, of course, commonplace that some Americans regard themselves as overassimilated, or as being in danger of losing a valuable cultural heritage. Linguistically, such effects are perhaps best known in terms of such activities as the attempts of Jewish Americans to preserve Yiddish. See especially the works of Joshua Fishman (Bibliography).

[47] Although some Americans, including many in public life, tend to regard the schoolmarm as a legitimate watchdog of English usage, the position maintained herein is that Standard English is little affected by—and only distantly related to—schoolmarm purism.

[48] One of the better general treatments of language standardization is Paul Garvin, *The Standard Language Question.* Language standardization and dialect standardization are, of course, merely different aspects of the same process. Although Americans have tended to hedge on the matter, Englishmen have been more realistic in judging a "standard" dialect to be free of prominent, stereotypable variations either geographically or socially. Norman W. Schur's *British Self-Taught, with Comments in American* (1973) quotes, with obvious approval, David Abercrombie's statement:

> Not only is it [Standard English] different from the dialects linguistically . . . it differs from them socially and politically also. Unlike the dialects, it is not tied to any particular region of country; but is a *universal* form of English; it is

the kind used everywhere by educated people. This, moreover, is the *official* form of English, the only kind which is used for public information and administration. It thus has a quite different standing in the English-speaking world from the dialects . . . Although it is called "English" it no longer has any necessary connection with England.

(*Problems and Principles*, 1955, p. 375)

One could quibble about the terminology of this statement—insisting, for example, that Standard English is itself a dialect, and therefore cannot be "unlike the dialects." On the whole, however, the statement is so reasonable as to disarm such criticism.

[49] As my discussion above implies, this statement is subject to modification in terms of the problem of just when the koiné can conveniently be said to have "begun." At any rate, the leveling process would have applied to such a first-generation child not subject to restrictive social pressures of the kinds discussed above.

[50] George E. Noyes, in a letter to E. C. Hills, quoted in "Linguistic Substrata of American English," *American Speech*, 1929, p. 432.

[51] *Ibid.*

[52] P. 336.

[53] Descriptions of Australian dialects have been given by (e.g.) A. G. Mitchell, *The Pronunciation of English in Australia* (1946):

There are two well-defined types of speech in Australia, an educated, cultivated professional speech, and an uncultivated popular speech.

(Quoted in Baker, *op. cit.*, p. 436)

Mitchell labeled these two "Broad Australian" and "Educated Australian." Baker himself expands the designation to

Broad Australian
General Australian
Educated Australian

Naïve American reactions typically relate Australian to Cockney; it is often said that "An American can't tell an Australian from a Cockney." Britishers, however, find it quite easy to do so.

[54] *The English Language in Australia and New Zealand,* 1966, p. 163.

[55] *Ibid.,* p. 15.

[56] John Witherspoon (quoted in Mencken, Supplement II, p. 19) associated the same processes with mobility as did Turner:

> The vulgar in America speak much better than the vulgar in Great Britain, for a very obvious reason, *viz.,* that being much more unsettled and moving frequently from place to place, they are not so liable to local peculiarities either in accent or phraseology.

As I hope to demonstrate, this assertion—whether by Turner or by Witherspoon—is not so much wrong as irrelevant. Mobility or a "nomadic" life cannot be said to promote *either* uniformity *or* diversity, unless the circumstances of language contact in the moving about can be stated.

[57] *The American Language,* Supplement I, p. 118.

[58] *Ibid.,* p. 156.

[59] The historical treatment of British influence on the "r-lessness" of American coastal cities is that of William Labov, *Sociolinguistic Patterns,* 1972, p. 145.

[60] Alice Morse Earle, *Child-Life in Colonial Days,* 1899, p. 21.

[61] Marckwardt, *American English,* apparently did not notice this simple chronological division. He asserted that

> early travelers to America and native commentators on the language agree on the existence of regional differences at an early period in our national history. Mrs. Ann Royall called attention to various Southernisms in the works which she wrote in the second quarter of the nineteenth century, and as early as 1829, Dr. Robley Dunglison had identified many of the Americanisms, in the glossary he compiled, with particular portions of the country. Charles Dickens recognized regional differences in the English he encountered in his first tour of the United States, and William Howard Russell, reporting on Abraham Lincoln's first state banquet, at which he was a guest, mentions his astonishment at finding 'a diversity of accent almost as great as if a number of foreigners had been speaking English.' *(pp. 131–32)*

He goes on to compare de Tocqueville's assertion that "There is no patois in the New World," although de Tocqueville wrote in the eighteenth century, whereas all the others were in the nineteenth century. The earliest of them, as a matter of fact, seems to come in the second quarter of the nineteenth century. Marckwardt was, of course, motivated by the bias of the reconstructive tradition, which wanted to see "regional" dialects represented in American English and therefore wanted to see regional differences as early as possible in the United States.

[62] *Men and Manners in America*, 1833, p. 127. Approximately this much of Hamilton's statement was quoted in Read's "British Recognition of American Speech in the Eighteenth Century" (1933). The further statements of Hamilton have, however, a great interest of their own. He continues:

> Even by this educated and respectable class, the commonest words are often so transmogrified as to be placed beyond the recognition of an Englishman. The word *does* is split into two syllables, and pronounced *do-es*. *Where*, for some incomprehensible reason, is converted into *whare*, *there* into *thare*; and I remember, on mentioning to an acquaintance that I had called on a gentleman of taste in the arts, he asked, "Whether he *shew* (showed) me his pictures." Such words as oratory and dilatory, are pronounced with the penult syllable, long and accented; missionary becomes *missionairy*; angel, a-i-ngel; danger, da-i-nger, &c.

> But this is not all. The Americans have chosen arbitrarily to change the meaning of certain old and established English words, for reasons which they cannot explain, and which I doubt much whether any European philologist could understand. The word *clever* affords a case in point. It has here no connexion with talent, and simply means pleasant or amiable. Thus, a good-natured blockhead in the American vernacular, is a clever man, and having had this drilled into me, I foolishly imagined that all trouble with regard to this word at least, was at an end. It was not long, however, before I heard of a gentleman having moved into a *clever* house, of another succeeding to a *clever* sum of money, of a third embarking in a *clever* ship, and making

a *clever* voyage, with a *clever* cargo; and of the sense attached to the word in these various combinations, I could gain nothing like a satisfactory explanation.

With regard to the meaning intended to be conveyed by an American in conversation, one is sometimes left utterly at large. I remember, after conversing with a very plain, but very agreeable lady, being asked whether Mrs. ——— was not *a very fine woman.* I believe I have not more conscience than my neighbours in regard to a compliment, but in the present case there seemed something so ludicrous in the application of the term, that I found it really impossible to answer in the affirmative. I, therefore, ventured to hint . . . This led to an explanation, and I learned that, in the dialect of this country, the term *fine woman* refers exclusively to the intellect.

The privilege of barbarizing the King's English is assumed by all ranks and conditions of men. Such words as *slick, kedge,* and *boss,* it is true, are rarely used by the better orders; but they assume unlimited liberty in the use of "expect," "reckon," "guess," "calculate," and perpetrate conversational anomalies with the most remorseless impunity. It were easy to accumulate instances, but I will not go on with this unpleasant subject . . . I feel it something of a duty to express the natural feelings of an Englishman, at finding the language of Shakespeare and Milton thus gratuitously degraded. Unless the present progress of change can be arrested, by an increase of taste and judgment in the more educated classes, there can be no doubt that, in another century, the dialect of the Americans will become utterly unintelligible to an Englishman.

As Charlton Laird, *Language in America* (1970, pp. 457–58) points out, except for *boss,* these words all had a prior history of use in England and therefore cannot be considered "Americanisms" in the sense that they were innovated or borrowed here. In the interpretation of this chapter, they would be part of the koiné vocabulary.

[63] Ethan Allen Hitchcock, *A Traveller in Indian Territory,* 1930, p. 125.

[64] *Ibid.,* p. 51.

[65] P. 132.

[66] P. 89.

[67] *Thirty Years of Army Life on the Border,* p. 383.

[68] Marcy quoted, for example, a Texas hostess, from the dense forest region of northwest Texas:

> "Wall, now, stranger, my ole man he ar out on a bar track, but I sort-o-reckon maybe you mought get to stay . . . that thar war narry shaw of vittles in the house barrin some sweet taters and a small chance of corn."

> "What my name mought be," "she knowed a heap of Massys (Marcy) in ole Massasip . . . me an him allers 'lowed that them thar Massys was considdible on bar and other varmits." *(Ibid.)*

[69] *The Look of the West,* 1860, p. 207.

[70] See especially Chomsky, *Cartesian Linguistics,* 1966. Chomsky defends some of the more profoundly philosophical grammatical traditions of the seventeenth century against the charge of Latinizing the structure of modern languages (specifically French). It is still true, however, that some early grammarians of English, among them Americans, drew unwarranted conclusions about English structure from Latin and prescribed usages in English on the basis of Latin.

[71] "The Methods of American Dialectology," *Zeitschrift für Mundartforschung,* 1963, p. 11.

[72] As a vehicle for spreading a version of high culture to the frontier populations, the Lyceum movement provided models of "cultivated" English even for those in relatively isolated places.

> The spread of the Lyceum system along the line of westward emigration from New England as far as the Mississippi is one tangible evidence of the high level of popular intelligence.
> (Bliss Perry, *The American Spirit in Literature, A Chronicle of Great Interpreters,* Vol. 34 in the Chronicles of America Series, 1918, p. 175)

[73] On the Chautauqua as a successor to the earlier Lyceum movement, see Edwin E. Sloson, *The American Spirit in Education,* Vol. 33, Chronicles of America Series, pp. 281f.

[74] For a report of a behavioral test (listeners' evaluations) which showed preference for "Network Standard" on the part of both Southern Black students in a Mississippi college and Northern (mostly white) students in a New England college, see Wallace A. Lambert and G. Richard Tucker, "White and Negro Listeners' Reactions to Various American-English Dialects," *Social Forces,* Vol. 47, No. 4 (June 1969), pp. 463–68.

C. J. Bailey, in a review of my *Black English* (*Foundations of Language* 11 [1974], pp. 299–309), objects to the concept of Network Standard and points to phonological patterns called nonstandard in my book used on television by "senators and clergy." In fact, an issue-confusing point often raised by those who oppose the teaching of Standard English is that successful politicians (Lyndon Johnson is most often cited) use nonstandard forms. It ought to be obvious to anyone interested in the sociological distribution of language forms, however, that politicians are frequently superordinated figures not subject to many of the pressures (including pressure toward using the standard dialect) which most of the rest of us feel. Politicians and clergymen are, moreover, hardly a large enough group to sway language-engineering considerations very much. The term "Network Standard," as applied to the only serious candidate American English has for a national standard, has been used regularly to refer to the speech of television newscasters.

CHAPTER III

[1] Marcus Lee Hansen, "The Problem of the Third Generation Immigrant," *Augustana Historical Society Publications.*

[2] The substratum principle has been assumed by some historical linguists to explain certain kinds of linguistic change. Essentially, the theory assumes that when a foreign language is imposed upon a population for some reason like military conquest, the "subject" population learns the conquerors' language but retains some of its native linguistic habits (this is the principle of "interference"—see next note). More generalized theories have

assumed a superstratum relationship (wherein the "conquering" language is influenced by the "subject" language) and an adstratum relationship between adjacent languages that have no such marked political or social relationship. These principles have at various times been in disrepute, particularly in the reconstruction of Proto-Indo-European, in which case the "-stratum" languages are often unknown and in which the very nature of the investigation demands the assumption that as much as possible of the change took place because of internal factors.

[3] Interference is the factor that makes it difficult for a monolingual English speaker to differentiate Spanish *perra*, 'bitch', and *pera*, 'pear', because the rolled *r* is not among his native language habits. Some such assumption has for a long time been the staple principle of instruction in applied linguistics. More recently, under the influence of the linguistic theories of Noam Chomsky, modern schools of linguistics, being unable to accept the behaviorist principle of linguistic "habit," have tended to reject this principle or to insist upon statements with more subtle conditions of application.

[4] Since it is necessary to use written records in a historical approach, it might be well to examine what we know about the use of foreign languages or varieties and how that usage compares with observable modern authors. In many cases, obviously, the two do not match. In order to create an air of foreignness, a novelist may make a Spanish-speaking (for example) character use the words of address, greetings, etc., in his native language:

> *Buenos días, Señor.* I regret that I could not attend your class yesterday.

In actual practice, such a speaker would be sure to use English in forms of address and greeting, and to revert to Spanish only in the more difficult expressions that he had not mastered in English:

> Goods days, Mister. I regret that I could not assist your class yesterday.

Thus, a novelist like Ernest Hemingway (*For Whom the Bell Tolls*) reverses the language-use pattern to that degree. Hemingway did not, however, actually *invent* Spanish words, or represent a character as speaking Spanish-accented English when he would actually have been speaking with a German accent.

[5] For a corrective to this oversimplified approach, see especially Labov, *Sociolinguistic Patterns,* quoted extensively below.

[6] An example of an article based on this philosophy is Arthur Bronstein, "Let's Take Another Look at New York City English," reprinted in Williamson and Burke, *A Various Language.*

[7] "The Depth and Breadth of English in the United States," in Aarons, Gordon, and Stewart (eds.), *Linguistic-Cultural Differences and American Education,* 1969.

[8] In Lancaster County, Pennsylvania, the Amish isolate themselves from other groups and are therefore more conservative in terms of language. Pennsylvania German (and its influence on English) is probably stronger and in a sense "purer" among them. The Mennonites, on the other hand, accept higher education (orthodox Amish refuse to allow their children to go beyond the eighth grade), drive cars, and have founded schools to train missionaries, although, like the Amish, they retain the Plain Dress. They are, as would be expected, more nearly assimilated linguistically. One can still hear a great deal of Pennsylvania-German influence on the English of many of them, however.

[9] See *The Joys of Yiddish,* by Leo Rosten, and *The Taste of Yiddish,* by Lillian Mermin Feinsilver. The latter seems especially valuable and has been drawn upon extensively for this treatment. It is particularly interesting in the amount of borrowing from Yiddish it shows has occurred in radio and television, particularly where advertising is concerned.

[10] E. C. Hills, "Linguistic Substrata of American English," *American Speech* 4 (1929), pp. 431–33.

[11] Labov, *Sociolinguistic Patterns,* 1972, p. 298.

[12] Ralph Wood (ed.), *The Pennsylvania Germans,* 1942, p. 261.

[13] My chief source of information here is a seminar report by Miss Leslie Brown, a native of Reading, Pennsylvania, who was in my course in social dialectology at Ferkauf Graduate School of Yeshiva University in the spring of 1971. Miss Brown, who had spoken Pennsylvania-German-influenced English until about the

age of twenty, had spent several years attempting to eliminate its "accent" from her ordinary English (she had been an English major in college and was suspicious and perhaps even resentful of my early attempts to have her "recover" her childhood dialect). She responded very well, however, after a brief period of indoctrination; when giving the term report, she shifted confidently between the two dialects. Unfortunately, she never presented the paper in written form. Miss Brown was able to demonstrate the fortis-lenis contrast of German *der Hund, des Hundes* (where the realization of orthographic *d* is, of course, not identical to English /d/ and /t/, respectively, as some textbooks would lead the unwary to believe), although she insisted that she spoke no German at all and had never studied the language.

[14] Especially useful for this purpose is George G. Struble, "The English of the Pennsylvania Germans," *American Speech* X (1935), pp. 163–72. The real master of the field, however, and one who has not been accorded the credit due him, is Otto Springer. Among his many articles, see especially "The Study of the Pennsylvania German Dialect," *Journal of English and Germanic Philology*, XLII (1943), pp. 1–39. The reason for the neglect of this variety by dialectologists can be seen by consulting even the rather ludicrous title ("Double Dialect Geography") of Carroll E. Reed's article (reprinted in Allen and Underwood, *Readings in American Dialectology*).

Novelist John O'Hara frequently presents, as in *From the Terrace,* snatches of conversation in the Pennsylvania German-influenced dialect:

> "What did they do with the auto?"
> "She got towed in town with a team."
> "What for make was she?"

[15] John H. Beadle, *Western Wilds and the Men Who Redeem Them,* 1878, p. 19.

[16] Ambrose Gonzales, *The Black Border,* 1964, p. 163.

[17] P. 347.

[18] See especially the Prentice-Hall collection *Chicano Literature.* On the Chicanos in general, see Julian Samora (ed.), *La*

Raza: Forgotten Americans (1966); K. Revelle, *Chicano!* (1969); Henry Sioux Johnson and William J. Hernandez, *Educating the Mexican American* (1970); and Jack D. Forbes, *Mexican-Americans: A Handbook for Educators* (1966).

[19] The best-known statement of this position—and quite possibly the first in the formal literature—was that of E. Franklin Frazier, *Black Bourgeoisie*, 1957, p. 13. In the plantation literature of the nineteenth century, however, such statements are extremely commonplace.

[20] James Patrick Sullivan, *Interference, Integration and Shift: The Genesis of Anglo-Irish*, Ferkauf Graduate School, Yeshiva University, dissertation, 1974, details several characteristic Anglo-Irish English syntactic structures, and the source structures in Irish. Among the syntactic structures are

1. A difference in reflexivization rules:
   And is he come with yourself?
2. The Irish conjugated preposition and the verb *to be*:
   There is on me, 'I have', etc.
3. Nonintonational emphasis:
   But is it mocking me you are?
4. Consuetudinal or habitual present:
   . . . don't be after puffing on us.
   . . . he does always be telling me . . .
   They do be cheering . . .
   Don't be bothering us about Winny's talk.
5. Recent perfective:
   I was after cleaning the house.
   He is after coming in.
   I'm after seeing him this day, and he riding and galloping. (Synge)
6. Verbal noun as gerund:
   She is at milking of the cows.
   Sean is at working.
7. *For to* verbal construction:
   Six yards of stuff for to make a yellow gown (Yeats).
   . . . the way she'd have a cup of goat's milk for to colour my tea. (Yeats)

Of these only *be* (the consuetudinal or habitual present) has been suggested to have any resemblance to the Black English vernacular (BEV). In Sullivan's considerable amount of data, there is no example of such a *be* without a preceding *do* or *does*. Furthermore, this is a consuetudinal *present; She be dancing last Friday,* perfectly grammatical in BEV, is rejected in Anglo-Irish on two accounts—occurrence in the past time (co-occurrence with *last Friday*) and (more trivially) occurrence without preceding *do.* Obviously, the BEV form merges with the Anglo-Irish in the negative (*don't be* V-ing) in those cases where BEV is (incidentally) present in time.

It seems quite significant that BEV emphatically does not have —and the historical records do not report at any time—any of the other Anglo-Irish features. If the plantation slaves "learned their English from Irish overseers," as is often somewhat irresponsibly claimed, it is strange that they learned nothing besides the consuetudinal *be.* And on the evidence available, the historical facts could be accounted for only by the professionally unacceptable statement that they "mislearned" even the *be!*

[21] Labov, *Language in the Inner City,* 1972, p. 51.

[22] For the West African derivation of *de,* see (among many others) Turner's *Africanisms in the Gullah Dialect* (1949) and Cassidy's *Jamaica Talk* (1961). About the only English etymon ever suggested for the form is the auxiliary *do;* a suggestion which —in addition to its implausibility on other grounds—is rendered virtually absurd by the use of *do–does* in another function (although not that of ordinary English emphatic *do*) in many of the same varieties which use *de.*

[23] The addition of *-ing* seems to be obligatory in all varieties of Black English vernacular today. Use of *be V-ing* in Gullah (i.e., a semi-risqué joke involving *I be layin' linoleum*) is sporadically reported. See Carawan and Carawan, *Ain't You Got a Right to the Tree of Life?,* 1967.

[24] *The Black Border,* p. 214.

[25] Richard Lawrence Beyer, "Robert Hunter, Royal Governor of New York: A Study in Colonial Administration," *Iowa University Studies in The Social Sciences,* Vol. X, No. 2, 1932.

[26] For the Surinam relationship, the most useful information is provided in a 1908 report by C. H. de Goeje (see Bibliography).

[27] P. 347.

[28] P. 402.

[29] Leonard, 1910, p. 201; "The New York Slave Revolt of 1741: A Re-Examination," *New York History* XLXIII (1967), p. 217.

[30] P. 127.

[31] The interpretation "white" for *fat* is admittedly conjectural here; but it seems likely, since horses are more regularly identified by color than by weight. In the Plantation literature, phrases like a *fite man* are commonplace in contexts in which no interpretation besides 'a white man' is semantically plausible.

[32] On the day names, see *Black English,* Chapter III. For their use in Jamaica especially, see articles by De Camp and Cassidy (Bibliography).

[33] These include such phrases as *the houses,* interpreted as 'the town', with the explanation that such is the meaning in "the negroes' dialect."

[34] Quoted in Greene, *A History of Colonial New England,* p. 247.

[35] P. 55.

[36] Large numbers of these attestations are presented by G. P. Krapp, *The English Language in America,* 1925, although Krapp was at best ambiguous about the presentation of the material. See also William A. Stewart, "Sociolinguistic Factors in the History of American Negro Dialects" (1967) and "Continuity and Change in American Negro Dialects" (1968).

[37] See my "The History of Black English in Nova Scotia: A First Step," in *African Language Review,* 1973.

[38] Alexis de Tocqueville, *Democracy in America,* 1835.

[39] See my Chapter V in *Black English* and "Black Through White: The Neglected Side of Communication Patterns in the New World" (forthcoming).

[40] See, for example, the transcriptions of the speech of Sojourner Truth made by Harriet Beecher Stowe in her article "Sojourner Truth, The Libyan Sybil," *Atlantic Monthly,* 1863.

[41] Newbell Niles Puckett, *Folk Beliefs of the Southern Negro,* p. 20.

[42] The case for the *Gemein-Bantu* theory and for relatively simple interference phenomena in producing Afro-American varieties (like the more "African" varieties of Puerto Rican Spanish) has

been made in works like Manual Alvarez Nazario, *El Elemento Afronegroïde en el Español de Puerto Rico* (1961). Luis Ferraz (U. of the Witwatersrand) makes a case for the same kind of genesis of the Afro-Portuguese Creoles (personal communication). For a strong case to the contrary, however, see the works of Marius Valkhoff (Bibliography), especially *Studies in Portuguese and Creole*, 1966.

[43] See the examples cited by Elsa Goveia (Bibliography).

[44] Emanuel J. Drechsel, "An Essay on Pidginization and Creolization of American Indian Languages," *International Journal of the Sociology of Language* (forthcoming), discusses in some detail the pidginization of indigenous languages of North America, intertribal trade as a factor, and the existence of Indian trade languages before the coming of the Europeans.

[45] "An Ancient New Jersey Indian Jargon," *American Anthropologist*, 1912, p. 509.

[46] C. E. Campbell, "Down Among the Red Men," *Kansas State Historical Society Review* XVII (1928), p. 659.

[47] *On the Border with Crook*, 1892, p. 339.

[48] See Leechman and Hall, *American Speech*, 1955.

[49] See *Black English*, pp. 143–47.

[50] Greene, *The Negro in Colonial New England*, 1942.

[51] It seems perfectly obvious that Pidgin English acquired "new" grammatical structures of this type under the influence of the native languages of the primary speakers of a given variety. For example, Chinese (and Melanesian) Pidgin English have—or had at one time in the past—a noun classification system, which can be roughly represented by:

one fellow man	'a man'
one piecee table	'a table'

[52] Col. R. B. Marcy, *Thirty Years of Army Life on the Border*, 1866, p. 122.

[53] *Illustrations of the Manners, Customs, and Conditions of the North American Indians*, Vol. II, p. 230.

[54] *Travels in the Interior of North America*, translated by Seymour Feiler, University of Oklahoma Press, 1962, p. 114.

[55] NEA Release, August 24, 1973.

[56] E. C. Campbell, "Down Among the Red Men," *Kansas State Historical Society Review* XVII (1928), p. 659.

[57] *Ibid.*

[58] *Ibid.*

[59] *Ibid.*

[60] P. 201

[61] P. 437.

[62] *Cycles of Conquest,* 1968, p. 440.

[63] P. 173

[64] P. 441

[65] *Chronicles of Oklahoma* XIV (1930), p. 224.

[66] *On the Border with Crook,* p. 473.

[67] Although this poem is cited in many sources, one of the most accessible is Samuel Bowles, *The New West,* 1869, which has a great deal to say about the Chinese, their "Josh Houses," and their "pigeon" (*sic*) English. The opening stanza of the poem, which has many variants, is given by Bowles as:

> My name being Norval, topside that Glampian Hille
> My father you sabee my father, makee pay chow-chow to sheep,
> He smallo heartee man, too muchee take care that dolla, gallo?
> So fashion he wantchee keep my counta me piecee chilo sope he own side
> My no wantchee long that largee mandolo, go knockee alla man . . .

"Topside, Galah!" is notably represented in Mamie Meredith's "Longfellow's Excelsior Done Into Pidgin English," *American Speech* IV (1929), pp. 148–51. This article, despite a certain triviality, deserves some credit as the only academic article before the 1950's to discuss the use of Pidgin English in the United States.

[68] Herbert Asbury, *The Barbary Coast,* 1933, p. 176.

[69] *Ibid.,* p. 177.

CHAPTER IV

[1] See, for example, Hugo Schuchardt, "Die Lingua Franca," *Zeitschrift für Romanische Philologie,* 1909; or the Introduction

to Henry Yule and A. C. Burnell, *Hobson-Jobson, A Glossary of Colloquial Anglo-Indian Words and Phrases, and of Kindred Terms, Etymological, Historical, Geographical and Discursive*, 2nd Ed., 1903.

² The word *caboose* has had a very widespread use, and, as might be expected, other etymologies have been suggested:

> According to MacNamarra, the name was originally the French word "cambuse"—a store room. The *Camboose* shanty served as a dining, sleeping, and recreative center.
> (*Dictionary of Canadianisms*)

The word was recorded in Canada as early as 1835. Within the United States, it was recorded first in 1862 (*Dictionary of American English*) in the present sense of last car on a train. *Caboose*, 'a small house', is in the *Dictionary of Jamaicanisms*; the editors apparently assume that it is obsolete in that sense elsewhere, as they have restricted their dictionary to Jamaican words that do not occur elsewhere, that occurred first in Jamaica, or that are no longer used in the Jamaican sense elsewhere. The American dictionary tradition would support the notion that *caboose* in the sense of "a small house" became obsolete around 1874. It seems obvious, however, that the "small house" was originally the galley on a ship, that it became either the cook shack on a ranch or—probably earlier—a special wagon designed to hold provisions, and then the well-known last car on a train. The maritime associations are certain. In his *Mariner's Dictionary* (1769), Falconer recorded

> Caboose. See Galley.
> GALLEY, is also the name of the cookroom, or kitchen, of a ship of war. In East India ships it is generally termed the cook-room, and on board of merchantmen it is called the caboose.

It is surely no accident that this word belongs to the contact-language tradition as well as to the vocabulary of ranching, since minority-group workers (e.g., Mexican or Negro) were frequently assigned the task of cooking. See Dick, 1948, p. 54.

³ The new Supplement to the *Oxford English Dictionary* re-

jects the attribution of Drake's word to *cache*, 'hiding place'—but, it seems to me, on insufficient grounds. (The reason may be that the newer editors have been unduly influenced by dialect geography and are less capable of accounting for maritime developments than their predecessors.) The Supplement regards *cache* (verb) as "originally U.S." and cites its earliest examples from the Western frontier. Besides the dictionary entries, *cache* (noun) can be found in many frontier sources.

> This is a term used by the Rocky Mountain trappers and Western traders, and is equivalent to the English word *bury*. Furs and other valuables, when secreted in the ground, are called *cached*. The word is an obvious derivative from French *cacher*.
> (George Wilkins Kendall, *Narrative of the Texan Santa Fé Expedition*, 1846, I, p. 205)

> The cavern called "Cache cave" [in Montana, in 1880]
> (Granville Stuart, *Forty Years on the Frontier*, 1925, I, p. 49)

> The Aricaras [1817] ... their caches.
> (John Bradbury, *Travels*)

⁴ Supplement I, pp. 227–228.
⁵ The most important historian who has dealt with the frontier concept in American history is, of course, Frederick Jackson Turner. For the discussion below, the general background of works like his *Rise of the New West*, in *The American Nation: A History* (1906) is assumed.
⁶ Statements are easily found in the better handbooks, supposedly well known to everyone in the field of linguistics. A representative articulation of the principle is that of Charles Hockett:

> Dialect geography, as a technique for reconstructing past history, is obviously limited. It is at its best only under very special conditions (long-settled sedentary population) and when used in conjunction with documentary evidence. Even then it can operate only in a relatively small scale of time and space.
> (*A Course in Modern Linguistics*, 1958, p. 483)

[7] Excellent historical works—unfortunately too little known —have been produced by Jack D. Forbes (*Nevada Indians Speak,* 1967, among others), William Loren Katz (*The Black West,* 1971), Kenneth Wiggins Porter (*The Negro on the American Frontier,* 1970), Philip Durham and Everett L. Jones (*The Negro Cowboys,* 1965), Joshua R. Giddings (*The Exiles of Florida,* 1858), and Edwin C. McReynolds (*The Seminoles,* 1957). There are many interesting and suggestive books (like Philip T. Drotning, *Black Heroes in Our Nation's History*) that lack the documentation that would justify their being classified as "studies."

[8] It is tempting to give West African languages all the "credit" for the changes in the European languages that took place in maritime contact, but it would be inaccurate. The "interference" or "substratum" theory is too simplistic to account completely for linguistic change, although it is often present as a contributing factor. The striking resemblance of varieties like Papia Kristang (the Portuguese-based Creole of Malacca, where there have apparently never been any West Africans) and Papiamentu (the Portuguese-based Creole, strongly influenced by Spanish, of Aruba, Bonaire, and Curaçao in the Caribbean) and of West African and Caribbean Creoles with Pidgins and Creoles of the Pacific (including the somewhat decreolized variety spoken on Pitcairn Island) argues against the acceptance of the African substratum explanation for the total picture. On this issue, see especially Jan Voorhoeve, "Historical and Linguistic Evidence in Support of the Relexification Theory," *Language in Society* II, No. 1 (1973).

[9] See especially the works of Kenneth Wiggins Porter (Bibliography).

[10] P. 343.

[11] Gustav Dresel's *Houston Journal,* 1838, translated from German and edited by Max Freund, Texas University Press, 1954, p. 137.

[12] *Ibid.*

[13] Grant Foreman, "Notes from the Indian Advocate," *Chronicles of Oklahoma* 14 (1926), pp. 76–79.

[14] John G. Burke, *On the Border with Crook,* 1892, pp. 186–87.

[15] See Chapter III, p. 100.

[16] Josiah Gregg, *The Commerce of the Prairies,* 1844, p. 16.

[17] Douglas Taylor, "New Languages for Old in the West Indies," *Comparative Studies in Society and History,* 1961, reprinted in Fishman, *Readings in the Sociology of Language,* 1968, p. 611.

[18] Richard Price, "Avenging Spirits and the Structure of Saramaka Lineages," *Bijdragen tot de Taal-, Land-, en Volkenkunde,* 1973.

[19] George Wilkins Kendall, *Narrative of the Texan Sante Fé Expedition,* New York, 1846, Vol. I, p. 56.

[20] Herbert E. Bolton and Mary Ross, *The Debatable Land, A Sketch of the Anglo-Spanish Contest for the Georgia Country,* 1925, p. v.

[21] Mattie Alice Austin Hatcher, *The Opening of Texas to Foreign Settlement, 1801–1821,* University of Texas Bulletin No. 2714, April 8, 1927. This work is also the source of a great deal of the other background material used herein.

[22] Julia Kathryn Garrell, *Green Flag Over Texas,* 1939, p. 6.

[23] Hatcher, *op. cit.,* p. 144.

[24] *Jonathan Dickinson's Journal; or, God's Protecting Providence, Being the Narrative of a Journey from Port Royal in Jamaica to Philadelphia between August 23, 1696, and April 1, 1697,* New Haven, 1944.

[25] See especially Keith Whinnom, "The Origin of the European-based Pidgins and Creoles," in *Orbis,* 1965. In much of the relevant literature, a maritime variety of Portuguese is given special prominence in the development of the Creoles, even those popularly considered to be varieties of English, French, Spanish, or even Dutch. For the last, see especially Marius Valkhoff, *Studies in Portuguese and Creole* (1966), which deals with the early development of Afrikaans. The most important article in the tradition is, however, Douglas Taylor's "Language Shift or Changing Relationship?" *International Journal of American Linguistics,* 1960, which points out how a variety of Portuguese can "shift" to become, at least in folk typology, a variety of, say, French.

[26] George Catlin, *Illustrations,* 1856, Vol. II, p. 56.

[27] *Mollie: The Journal of Mollie Dorsey Sanford in Nebraska and Colorado Territories, 1857–1866,* Donald F. Danker (ed.), p. 123.

[28] Josiah Gregg, *The Commerce of the Prairies*, 1844, p. 185.

[29] *Swap* is one of the many words that were thought of as American innovations (or even "corruptions") until it was pointed out that they had occurred in earlier British texts. In this way, it resembles the koiné vocabulary discussed in Chapter II. The early occurrences of *swap* in American English tend, however, to be in pidgin contexts. Rusling, *Across America,* quotes a young Ute chief known to whites as Jack Cox, who "spoke a little broken English":

> "Mean Indian swop—pony, bow, quivver, robe, anything!
> Jack Cox no swop!" (*p. 131*)

[30] The citations are from Allen Walker Read, "The English of the Indians," *American Speech* 16 (1941), pp. 72–74. Read drew some conclusions from this evidence that are very different from the ones presented in this book and elsewhere in my work. See my *Black English* (1972), pp. 83–84.

[31] For an excellent survey of those varieties and some material on sociolinguistic attitudes toward them, see William A. Stewart, "Creole Languages in the Caribbean," in F. A. Rice (ed.), *Study of the Role of Second Languages,* 1962.

[32] See *Black English,* Chapter IV.

[33] For some indication of what such a variety might be, see the works cited in note 25 above, and David Lopes, *A Extensão do Português na Oriente,* 1936.

[34] *Western Words,* 1968. In this chapter, all references to Adams are to that work.

[35] The same problem of derivation from Spanish /o/ is encountered in the vowels of *quadroon, octoroon, galoot,* and *caboodle,* to mention only a few of the most obvious examples from the Southwestern contact situation. *Coosie,* 'cook', from *cucinero* (Adams, *Western Words*) offers no problem concerning the stressed vowel but it does offer problems on other grounds.

[36] Julian Mason, "The Etymology of *buckaroo,*" *American Speech,* 1960.

[37] See the examples in Eric Partridge, *A Dictionary of Slang and Unconventional Usage.*

[38] Spanish /bámos/, under the influence of English interfer-

ence, would be expected to give */báhmows/ or even */bǽmows/ but not *vamoose*. (The asterisk marks an impossible or non-occurring form.)

[39] If the Spanish word were */bamós/, English /mows/ or even /mowz/ could be explained, at least insofar as the first syllable is concerned. Nothing in Spanish *vamos*, however, explains the /-iy/ syllable.

[40] Called by the *Dictionary of Americanisms* "a southwestern [American] expression of unknown parentage," the word is asserted in Hancock's dissertation to be "general dialectal," including Cornwall, Ireland, Sierra Leone, and the United States. Barrere and Leland, *Dictionary of Slang, Jargon, and Cant* (1889) would derive it from Italian *galeotto*, 'a galley slave' (thereby, presumably, a man of no cultivation or refinement). Since Italian was an important contributor to the early stages of the maritime Lingua Franca (see Schuchardt, *op. cit.*), there may be a certain amount of symbolic accuracy in this etymology.

[41] The Western use of the expression has been frequently recognized, as in Adams's entry under *caboodle*:

A cowboy's word for the whole amount, the entire lot.

The OED labels it "originally U.S.," which is inaccurate in the light of Hancock's investigations. Some of the more venturesome have attributed it to Portuguese *cabilda*. No authority has, to my knowledge, seriously suggested a Spanish etymology for either *caboodle* alone or the compound *kit and caboodle*. Hancock (1971) looks rather to French *botel, boteau*; German *Baeutel*; Dutch *boedel*, 'possessions'. Multiple etymologies of this sort are, of course, commonplace among Lingua Franca words.

[42] Sir Richard Burton, *The Look of the West*, 1860, p. 313.

[43] Margaret Mead, *New Lives for Old: Cultural Transformation—Manus, 1928–1953*, 1966, p. 92.

[44] Karl Lentzner, *Wörterbuch der Englischen Volkssprache in Australien und einiger Englische Mischsprachen*, 1892, p. 154, cites Cameroonian Pidgin English "Callaboos he no good."

[45] At the present time, this area consists of a small part of Louisiana around St. Martinsville, and Creole is not the only

variety, even of French, spoken in the area. Some migrants have gone as far as Beaumont, Texas, and some few have gone to Houston, where a little French Creole may be heard in the ghetto. There is a strong possibility that the Creole variety was more widespread at an earlier time. See Edward Larocque Tinker, "Creole Comes to Philadelphia," *American Antiquarian Society Proceedings,* 67, 1957, pp. 50–76.

[46] Like *lariat,* conventionally traced to Spanish *la reata,* and *alligator* (*el lagarto*), *lagniappe* has combined the article with the noun base. This is a common word-forming device in many of the Creoles (Papiamentu *lareina,* 'queen', not 'the queen'; Haitian Creole *lakay,* 'house', not 'the house'; Louisiana French Creole *lamezō,* 'house'). *Lagniappe* has been conventionally traced to Quechua *yapa,* with the added article explained no more adequately than with the phrase "from Spanish." Nasalization of the initial palatal consonant is widely observable, even in varieties in which the article has not been incorporated into the noun (Puerto Rican *la ñapa*). The initial consonant /ñ/ is relatively rare in Spanish; the great majority of the words in Puerto Rican Spanish that begin with it are Africanisms, like *ñam ñam* 'eat' (Manuel Álvarez Nazario, *El Elemento Afronegroïde en el Español de Puerto Rico,* 1961, p. 142). It is well known that the Arabic article *al* was incorporated into Spanish (*alcohol, algebra, alferez*); but it is not clear what light this fact sheds on the quite different vocabulary involved in the Southwestern borrowings from Spanish into English.

[47] Spanish contact vernaculars have played an important role in the Philippines since the early eighteenth century, according to Charles O. Frake, "Lexical Origins and Semantic Structure in Philippine Creole Spanish," in Hymes (ed.), *Pidginization and Creolization of Languages,* 1971. See also Keith Whinnom, *Spanish Contact Vernaculars in the Philippine Islands,* 1956, and Douglas Taylor's review in *Word,* 1957. Taylor's review provided the impetus for a great deal of the interest in the influence of the Portuguese contact variety.

[48] An account is given in Baker, *The Australian Language,* p. 312. Baker considers the word "a pidgin corruption of *wood.*"

For *corruption,* we would rather note the typical addition of the enclitic vowel, which makes the word into two syllables, and the substitution of the /a/ vowel which is easier, in a language-universals sense, than the English /ʊ/. These phonological tendencies have a great deal to do with the viability of pidgins in language-contact situations.

[49] Cook, *Fifty Years on the Old Frontier,* p. 17.

[50] *Ibid.,* p. 34.

[51] Documentation of the West African use of *palaver,* its borrowing from Portuguese, and its gradual semantic change can be found in Ruth Fisher, *Extracts from the Records of the African Companies* (1924) and in my "Creole English and Creole Portuguese: The Early Records," *Journal of African Languages* (forthcoming).

[52] They derive it from an alleged "phonetic deformation" of *clabba.* There is, of course, no /kl-/ to /pl-/ rule in the derivational phonology of Jamaican English. See my review in *Caribbean Studies,* 1971.

[53] Sir Richard Burton, *Wanderings in West Africa,* Vol. I, p. 211.

[54] *Diglossia* is used in the sense in which it is employed in Charles A. Ferguson's well-known paper ("Diglossia," *Word,* 1959) as a description of a situation in which two languages (or other language varieties, like dialects) tend to be distributed in function, with one (called the "H" language by Ferguson) used for formal, public activities and the other (Ferguson's "L" language) usually reserved for informal, private communication.

[55] A fairly adequate listing of the Spanish vocabulary of the Texas English of the mid-twentieth century is to be found in E. B. Atwood, *The Regional Vocabulary of Texas,* 1962. The work is, however, done in a doctrinaire linguistic atlas framework; its insights are, historically at least, quite superficial.

[56] English /h/, the phonetically closest phoneme to the /x/ of the Spanish pronunciation, does not occur in post-stressed syllables. It is, therefore, not especially strange within the phonology of English, for the glide consonant /r/ to replace it. This particular substitution shows, however, how little consciousness of Spanish pro-

nunciation, or even of the Spanish origin of the name of the town, is characteristic of the "Anglos."

[57] P. 87.

[58] P. 450.

[59] P. 89.

[60] Archer B. Hulbert, *Frontiers, The Genius of American Nationality*, 1929, p. 135.

[61] Several of the texts cited by Mary Rita Miller, *American Speech,* 1967, have Chinook words and may be suspected of representing Chinook Jargon mixed with Pidgin English.

[62] Stuart Granville, *Montana As It Is*, p. 297.

[63] Inasmuch as the Algonquian languages extend throughout all this territory, independent borrowing is a possibility. But they stop at the Rocky Mountains, and those occurrences in Oregon and Washington must at any rate be the result of transmission. It is hardly possible, furthermore, that the use of *squaw* and *papoose* among Southern tribes like the Seminoles of Florida was the result of any such process.

[64] *Vanguards of the Frontier,* 1941, p. 40.

[65] "Mr." Willson was the otherwise unidentified husband of Minnie Moore-Willson, whose *The Seminoles of Florida* (1910) is an excellent source of American Indian Pidgin English.

[66] Chinese were, of course, employed in heavy laboring occupations in other parts of the West Coast. *Longtime Californ': A Documentary Study of an American Chinatown* by Victor G. and Brett DeBary Nee (1972) describes how they were exploited in the building of the Central Pacific Railroad in the last century and contains considerable evidence of their being exploited in San Francisco today. Although there is relatively little about the English of the San Francisco Chinatown dwellers (the language of those interviewed has apparently been regularized), there is indication in the title itself and in one quotation (p. 41) that Pidgin English was used. There is an occasional statement like, "The men and children in these families speak English, though the men apologize for not speaking better" (p. 402). Studies of the present-day English of American Chinese, as of Indians and (until recently) of Blacks are still to be made.

[67] Among the indications that Chinese may have played the

same role in Australian that they did in American English is the following:

> There is a large number of Chinamen in New South Wales [i.e., Australia], from market gardeners, cabinet makers, "fossickers," etc., to merchants.
>   (G. L. James, *Shall I Try Australia?*, 1892, p. 290)

James also reports that restrictions had been placed on the entry of Chinese by 1892.

[68] Rusling, *Across America,* p. 299.

[69] Richardson, *Beyond the Mississippi,* p. 390.

[70] The term *domain* is characteristic of the work of Yeshiva University sociolinguist Joshua Fishman. According to his own discussion of the term, the concept of domain is an abstraction from cultural notions of appropriate persons, places, and times for given behavior patterns (including language forms). See his *Bilingualism in the Barrio* (1968), Vol. II, 974–75.

[71] "The Position of the Charleston Dialect," *Publications of the American Dialect Society,* 1955. For a criticism of this article, see my "American Negro Dialects: Convergence or Divergence?" *Florida FL Reporter,* 1968; reprinted in Whitten and Szwed, *Afro-American Anthropology: Contemporary Perspectives* (1970).

[72] *The Regional Vocabulary of Texas,* 1962, p. 46.

[73] *Forty-Niners, The Chronicle of the California Trail,* Boston, 1931, p. 187.

[74] Thomas Pyles, *Words and Ways in American English,* 1954, p. 56.

[75] Armstrong, *I Have Spoken,* p. 7.

[76] Leland, *Pidgin English Sing-Song.*

[77] *Words and Ways in American English,* 1952, p. 50.

[78] Thomas Norton's *New English Canaan,* 1632, contains one of the earliest observations about the English of the Indians:

> for this is commonly seene where 2 nations traffique together, the one endeavouring to understand the others meaning makes the both many times speak a mixed language, as is approved by the Natives of New England, through the covetous desire they have, to commerce with our nation, and wee with them.

[79] George Catlin, *Life Among the Indians,* 1874, pp. 83–84.

[80] See Virgil J. Vogel, *American Indian Medicine,* 1970.

[81] P. 72.

[82] George A. Crofutt, *Crofutt's Trans-Continental Tourist's Guide,* 1871.

[83] E. C. Campbell, "Down Among the Red Men," *Kansas State Historical Review,* Vol. XVII (1928), p. 660.

[84] Ian F. Hancock, "Lexical Expansion Outside a Closed System," *Journal of African Languages,* 1973, gives the following examples from Krio, the English-based Creole of Sierra Leone:

Jakas-os	(*jackass* plus *horse*)	'a glutton for hard work'
cher-cov	(*tear* plus *curve*)	'take a stroll'
han beli	(*hand* plus *belly*)	'palm of hand'
big yai	(*big* plus *eye*)	'covetous'
swit mot	(*sweet* plus *mouth*)	'flattery'
do klin	(*day* plus *clean*)	'daybreak'

Many of these can be paralleled from the other pidgin-creole situations and from dialects of English influenced by creole varieties. Hancock cites *beli-han,* in the same meaning as Krio *han beli,* from Trinidad. *Sweet mouth* may underlie *sweet talk,* which is well known in Southern and general American English. *Do klin* is paralleled in Gullah and in several other English-based Creoles.

[85] *American English,* 1958, p. 102. Marckwardt also cites some "tumid and turgid vocabulary" in Nathaniel Ward's *The Simple Cobbler of Aggawam* (1647), with a suggestion that it is an indication of the transition from Elizabethan usages to frontier tall talk. The suggestion does not seem very convincing. Furthermore, the time gap cited by Laird (see below) is reduced insignificantly if at all.

[86] Charlton Laird, *Language in America,* p. 353.

[87] Josiah Gregg, *The Commerce of the Prairies,* 1844, p. 189.

[88] Archer Hulbert, *Frontiers, The Genius of American Nationality,* 1929, p. 156.

[89] *Illustrations,* 1856, Vol. II, p. 93. For fancy talk, see *Black English,* Chapter V.

[90] *The Southwest by a Yankee,* 1835.

[91] P. 245.

[92] Samuel Alfred Beadle, *Adam Shuffler*, 1890, p. 6.

[93] J. W. Harrison, "Negro English," *Anglia*, 1884.

[94] P. 94.

[95] E. N. Dick, *Vanguards of the Frontier*, 1941, p. 69.

[96] *Ibid.*

[97] Perhaps the best-known concerns the two trappers who were marooned in a cabin together by a heavy snowfall for an entire winter. After two months, one of them said, "Lousy weather we're having." A month later, the other replied, "If I'd knowed you was such a chatterbox, I'd've got me another podner."

[98] *Words and Ways in American English,* Chapter VI.

[99] Claude Hubbard, "The Language of Ruxton's Mountain Men," *American Speech*, October 1968, p. 221.

[100] Mencken's "The Declaration of Independence in American," which begins as follows

> When things get so balled up that the people of a country have got to cut loose from some other country, and go it on their own hook, without asking no permission from nobody . . . (*Third Edition, p. 398*)

has been widely stigmatized as a composite that represented the actual usage of no one person or group. From even the short passage quoted above, it becomes apparent that Mencken the iconoclast rather than Mencken the insightful (if amateur) linguist was at work on the passage. Among other things, he failed to take into account that any group of human beings of social organization complex enough to frame a Declaration of Independence would certainly have a formal style as well as the more informal styles ("colloquial usage"). On the other hand, Mencken's distortions seem, in perspective, less than those perpetrated by language historians who have asserted that no such thing as an American vulgate exists—and that Mencken's slight distortions of emphasis are *proof* that it does not exist.

[101] On Western talk, the observations of contemporary observers are relatively clear and unambiguous. We find, for example, the statement of Burke, *On the Border with Crook*:

> One could pick up not a little good Spanish in a pack train in the times of which I speak—twenty-one years ago—and there were many expressions in general use which presented all the flavor of other lands and other ideas. (*p. 152*)

It is impossible to say as much of works in the reconstructive tradition. In Williamson and Burke (eds.), *A Various Language,* in which dissertations in a conventional American dialectological framework are summarized, one work (Elizabeth Hope Jackson's *An Analysis of Certain Colorado Field Records with Regard to Settlement History and Other Factors,* University of Colorado dissertation, 1956) deals with the English of the Western states.

CHAPTER V

[1] A great deal is actually made of these terms by Gary N. Underwood, "Vocabulary Change in the Upper Midwest," *Publications of the American Dialect Society* 49 (1968), pp. 8–28.

[2] Roger W. Shuy, *Discovering American Dialects,* National Council of Teachers of English, 1967. The section quoted here is reprinted in Virginia P. Clark, Paul A. Eschholz, and Alfred R. Rosa (eds.), *Language, Introductory Readings,* 1972, pp. 344–48. It is chosen for examination and rebuttal for the specific reason that it has been regarded as a kind of model of writing about American English for presentation to educated but nonprofessional readers.

[3] Other works for the educated layman share in this particular lack. Other works in American dialectology have conventionally assumed that Black speakers everywhere adjusted themselves, immediately and without incident, to white speech patterns. This is in spite of well-known difficulties in acculturation in other aspects of behavior, and in direct disregard of evidence of West African cultural survivals in the tradition of Melville J. Herskovits's *The Myth of the Negro Past* (1942). It is especially unfortunate that the only works that have paid any special attention to Black English have been works with a psychological tinge, like Frederick Williams (ed.), *Language and Poverty,* 1970. Almost by default, works that discuss at least the possibility that Blacks have

language (and even mental) deficiencies have had the field to themselves as far as the average reader is concerned.

[4] Glenna Ruth Pickford's excellent 1956 critical article (see Bibliography) points out that "the whirlpool caused by continual mixing, moving, and intermarriage of peoples of heterogeneous origin renders a sociological analysis by groups of common origin patently impossible" (p. 226).

[5] Among the rare works on "Cajun" is an article by an outstanding phonetician who was also one of the pioneers in work on the Black English vernacular, Claude M. Wise. His article, "Specimen of Louisiana French-English; or Cajun Dialect in Phonetic Transcription," appeared in *American Speech* for October 1935. Since that time, very little if any attention has been given to the Cajuns.

[6] "Dialect Distribution and Settlement Patterns in the Great Lakes Region," *Ohio State Archeological and Historical Quarterly*, 1951, pp. 48–56. The article is reprinted in Williamson and Burke (eds.), *A Various Language: Perspectives on American Dialects*, 1971. It is thus apparently to be taken as an ideal statement of this kind of philosophy of language change and dialect distribution. As a matter of fact, although the Williamson and Burke collection apparently subscribes to the Davis thesis, there is no other article that bears directly upon traceable migrations within the continental United States in the book.

[7] P. 365.

[8] Shuy, *op. cit.* No evidence is offered, either here or in any other work known to me, for the statement that "the mixed dialects of English settlers who inhabited each colony gradually became distinctive in themselves." In the same excerpt (included in Clark, Eschholz, and Rosa) Shuy states, "Nor are regional dialects organized along state lines." Since modern "regional" dialects, which are *not* organized along state lines, are said to derive from colonial dialects, which *were* "distinctive in themselves," Professor Shuy apparently assumes that there is little or no connection between the original colonies and the eastern seaboard states of today. Otherwise, he is obviously indulging in self-contradiction. It is particularly puzzling in that Shuy correlates dialect spread with natural barriers like mountain ranges and rivers. The implication

of his two statements, placed side by side, would seem to be that the location of those natural features has shifted within the past 250 years or so.

[9] Work by professional dialectologists, rather embarrassingly few of them Americans, has shown that dialect variation may correlate with age grade, sex, professional or occupational group, religious affiliation, ethnic group, and even preference in sports. (See Silverman and Wolfram, Shiels, and Fasold in the Bibliography for works that show how a preference for basketball over baseball on the part of New York City Puerto Rican teen-agers correlates with their acquisition of Black English vernacular forms.)

[10] It is one of the best-known philological commonplaces that the scribes who copied Old and Middle English documents, and whose linguistic practices are assumed to have influenced whatever variations can be found in comparable manuscripts, were young men of relatively good family (although not of the nobility) who entered minor clerical orders and were assigned to the scriptoria. Speakers of Old and Middle English who are represented in the writings of the periods are, therefore, of quite limited class, sex, and age groups. It is no wonder that a student trained primarily in those periods is predisposed to find regional variations. It is an accident of history that little or no evidence for any other kind of variation is available for those early times, and a dialectologist who works on those periods can hardly deal in anything but regional variation. It is quite another matter, however, to insist that the only patterns that can be found in early English dialects must also be found in modern times, when a great deal of evidence of many other kinds is available. Unfortunately, the dominant members of the Linguistic Atlas of the United States and Canada were trained in the philological tradition, with a great deal of emphasis on Old and Middle English (and Old High German, Middle High German, etc., where the comments above about the scribes who produced the manuscripts apply equally well). We therefore have a bizarre reversal where the unknown (older periods of language history) has not been conceived in terms of what we can find out about the known (present-day distributions), but vice versa.

[11] Collections and textbooks that, tacitly or overtly, reflect this orientation are (in addition to the Williamson and Burke collection discussed above) Malmstrom and Ashley, *Dialects— USA,* 1963, Malmstrom, *Language in Society,* 1965, Carroll E. Reed, *Dialects of American English,* 1967; and Shuy, *op. cit.*

[12] See E. Bagby Atwood, "The Methods of American Dialectology," *Zeitschrift für Mundartforschung,* 1963.

[13] McDavid and McDavid, "The Relationship of the Speech of American Negroes to the Speech of Whites," *American Speech* 26 (1951), note 1.

[14] Hans Kurath, "English Sources of Some American Regional Words and Verb Forms," *American Speech* 45 (1970), pp. 60–68. Kurath also claims regional British origin for the American nonstandard verb forms *see* or *seen* (instead of *saw, catched* (past tense of *catch*), and *took* (past participle of *take*). It is hardly necessary to comment that these attributions are not impressive.

[15] Charlton Laird, *Language in America,* 1970, p. 160.

[16] *Ibid.,* p. 145. But there is little even "approaching" scientific objectivity in the fantasy with which Laird follows this statement:

> We should probably assume that Nantucket folk tended to go to sea more than to the west, but that somebody from Nantucket took *masculine* [as a euphemism for *bull*] with him to West Virginia.

This imaginative story about "someone" going from Nantucket to West Virginia is about as scientific as the story about how a lisping Spanish king "originated" the Castillian pronunciation [θ] in *cazar.*

[17] P. 212. Pickford states explicitly, even bluntly, that dialect geography "falls short of the standards of social scientific inquiry (*Ibid.*)." Although the Pickford article is well known in American academic circles, no one of the works referred to above contains any reference to it.

[18] These words, not one of which may be familiar to the average reader, play a prominent role in the worksheets of the Lin-

guistic Atlas of the United States and Canada. Pickford and other critics have repeatedly pointed out that this emphasis upon rural terms distorts the picture of language variation in an essentially urban nation:

> By their selectivity, the cartographical surveys would deny the extent of the spread of urbanization in America. (Pickford, *op. cit.*, p. 228)

[19] "The African Element in Black American English," in Thomas Kochman (ed.), *Rappin' and Stylin' Out,* 1972. Dalby directs attention to Wolof *hipikat,* the second element of which is the probable source of Black ethnic slang *cat* and the first of which probably explains *hip,* 'aware'.

[20] Wright's *English Dialect Dictionary* does list *trick,* 'Intercourse, dealings; trade, business, traffic,' from Yorkshire, Lakeland, and Lincolnshire. The Lakeland source, however, dates from 1898, the Yorkshire from 1883, and the Lincolnshire from 1866. There is, then, no special historical depth to Wright's materials. The Cafeteria Principle regularly assumes that English "regional" distribution during the nineteenth century can be projected back to the period of emigration to the American colonies, but there is no rational basis for that belief.

[21] Rhyming slang is described by Schur (*British Self-Taught,* p. xxi) as "the peculiarly cockney game of replacing certain common words with phrases which end with a word that rhymes with the word replaced." He gives the examples:

boat race   face
daisy roots   boots
etc.

Boat race is then shortened to *boat,* which means 'face' in the rhyming slang. Amusing examples, like *"Jenny* for *window (Jenny Linder* is the full form of the name, and *window* is pronounced 'winder') are given by Leonard R. N. Ashley, "Scoff Love: British Words for Food and Drink," *Names,* Vol. 16, No. 3 (September 1968), 238–72.

²² In the collection by Clark, Eschholz, and Rosa, p. 344.

²³ Feinsilver's *The Taste of Yiddish* (1970) is a gold mine of such influences. No small number of examples can illustrate the importance she shows Yiddish-influenced English to have had on the American English vocabulary, especially in advertising and the media. See also her commentary on the spread of Yiddish terms in novels and in other literary sources (pp. 296–99).

²⁴ William A. Stewart used the term in public lectures in the early 1960's (see W. Nelson Francis, *The English Language, An Introduction,* 1963, p. 247).

²⁵ Richard G. Tucker and Wallace Lambert, "White and Negro Listeners' Reactions to Various American-English Dialects," *Social Forces,* Vol. 47, No. 4 (June 1969), 463–68.

²⁶ A representative definition of an *isogloss* would be "the geographical boundaries of usage" (Hockett, *A Course in Modern Linguistics,* 1958, p. 473). Winfred P. Lehmann asserts:

> To represent linguistic units the term *gloss* is used (based on Greek *glossa* 'word'), and isoglosses, which depict the boundaries within which items are attested, are determined. Any linguistic characteristic may be mapped with isoglosses. (*Descriptive Linguistics, An Introduction,* 1972, p. 240)

Hockett, however, warns:

> The conclusions which can validly be drawn, about speech or any other facet of human behavior, purely from geographical distribution are remarkably limited. A number of patently unworkable assumptions have been used, tacitly or overtly, in this connection. (*op. cit.,* p. 478)

Linguistic geography, with its isoglosses, has long been an embarrassment to linguistics, since the geographists work with individual "items" in language (like the *s* or *z* sound in *greasy*) without regard to their place in the language system. Linguists, since the origin of the discipline, have insisted that the systemic relationships are important, not the items themselves. An early attempt to bring dialectology within linguistics proper was made by Uriel Weinreich, "Is a Structural Dialectology Possible?" (see

Bibliography). A more extreme view is expressed in my "Lay My Isogloss Bundle Down: The Contribution of Black English to American Dialectology," *Linguistics*, Vol. 119 (January 1974), pp. 5–14.

[27] A side effect of the Tucker and Lambert study (cited in note 25) is that it was the first of the tests that showed that listeners were able to identify the race of Black or white speakers from the same region, from tape-recorded cues only, about 80 percent of the time.

[28] Washington, D.C., 1966.

[29] See especially "Dialect and Social Stratification," *American Anthropologist*, 1958.

[30] *Language in America*, 1970, p. 319. Other "regional" uses of German terms are discussed in works like E. B. Atwood, *The Regional Vocabulary of Texas*, 1962, pp. 93–94. Because of the Linguistic Atlas framework in which all these works have been produced, local distributions are stressed, and we have no comparisons of the different German communities in different parts of the United States. We can find out from Atwood that:

> *Clook* (Map 40), from German *die Kluche*, is often Anglicized to *cluck* or even *clucker*, but it shows its greatest frequency in the areas of greatest German concentration. (*p. 93*)

The collected works of the geographists do not inform us, however, whether even that one word of "German vocabulary" is also found in Grundy County, Illinois.

[31] *Sociolinguistic Patterns*, 1972, p. 309.

[32] "Aloofness from Spanish Influence in Texas English," *Word*, 1959. Sawyer also points out that the "Latins" simply did not learn local terms that have no bookish equivalent: *Christmas gift, snap beans, French harp.*

[33] William Edward Farrison, *The Phonology of the Illiterate Negro Dialect of Guilford County, North Carolina*, Ohio State University dissertation, 1936, documents the use of the term (in that pronunciation) among North Carolina Negroes. My own childhood experience is the source for Southern white use. Actually, I am certain that it was in use only in East Texas. It is

entirely possible that the general use is by Southern Blacks and that it was borrowed by whites only in that part of Texas. A priori, however, it seems highly likely that it would crop up among whites elsewhere.

[34] The use of the term *domain* in sociolinguistics is basically associated with the work of Joshua Fishman. It relates language usage to nonlinguistic circumstances, roughly the who, when, and where of usage. Thus, the Linguistic Atlas, which concentrates heavily upon the vocabulary of the farm and the kitchen, has given us a great deal of information about two *domains* of the vocabulary of those informants whom its selectional procedures have singled out.

[35] Although many linguists (even those who in recent times have worked most on child language) have ignored the peer-group factor, assuming that the child speaks a version of the language of its parents (never, as it happens, specifying whether that would mean one or both of its parents, and if only one, which one), there is clear evidence that the peer group is the more important factor. (The parents must, of course, be allowed a great deal of influence on children under three. Older informants, however, have always been used in dialect work.) For a convenient summary, see William Labov, *Sociolinguistic Patterns,* 1972, pp. 304–7. Acculturation is often a factor, but its patterns usually coincide with those of the peer group. A. Tabouret Kelley ("Sociological Factors of Language Maintenance and Shift," in Ferguson, Fishman, and das Gupta, 1968, p. 112) shows that in Dakar, where acculturation is to Wolof, when mother and father speak differently, "it is not the father or the mother who gives his or her language to the child, but the Wolof-speaking party."

[36] An interesting sidelight on the use of the term *Geechee* is that the term is used by the Portuguese-Creole-speaking Black residents of Cape Cod (recent immigrants from the Cape Verde islands). In their usage, it refers more specifically to behavioral and cultural patterns than to language. *Geechee* in that community refers to local cultural patterns, with the perhaps unfortunate but inevitable judgment that they represent a lack of "cultivation," or "refinement." Black Pride movements have, however, asserted positive attitudes, especially in recent times, and

have made terms like *soul, hard bop,* and *funky* terms of approval in relation both to jazz music and to a broader cultural tradition. Interestingly, one of the most prominent pianists in that jazz tradition is a native of Cape Cod—Horace Silver (born Silva).

[37] *Decreolization* has become, in creole studies, the conventional term to describe the merger of a creole variety of a given language (insofar as lexicon is concerned) with a more prestigious—often the standard—variety. This process is usually motivated by the superior standing (wealth, prestige, political power) of those who speak the standard language. For the Black American vernacular, the term was first used by William A. Stewart, in his 1967 and 1968 articles (see Bibliography).

[38] See the two articles by Stewart (1967 and 1968) and my *Black English* (1972). Further data are given in Chapters I, II, and IV.

[39] James Sledd, "Breaking, Umlaut, and the Southern Drawl," *Language,* 1966. See my "On the Beginnings of Black English in the New World," *Orbis,* 1972, for a rebuttal to some of Sledd's points.

[40] In spite of all the attention given to "Southern" phonology and its supposed effect on Black English, little or no attention has been given by linguists to such well-known (especially by folklorists and musicologists) forms as *Jedus,* 'Jesus' and *Norah,* 'Noah'. One would think that the latter, especially, as an example of "intrusive *r*" would have received special attention, since so many approaches to American dialectology have dealt with the articulation of *r*. Among the many obvious sources is the song "Noah" by the Peerless Four on Prestige/International LP 25008. Several different degrees of intervocalic retroflexion can be heard during this song.

[41] Soon after the Late Middle English period, Chaucer's time, the maritime use of some variety of English on an international scale must have begun. It is obviously not impossible that earlier English usages found their way into that trade variety. However, the relationship has hardly been looked into at all. Specialists in Early English have, in fact, refused even to consider the importance of contact or trade varieties.

⁴² An elaborate attempt has been made by William Labov, "Contraction, Deletion, and Inherent Variability of the English Copula," *Language,* 1969, to trace the Black English zero copula to phonological deletion processes. Although Labov draws no such conclusion, it has often been assumed that his article proves that the zero copula in Black English is a "spontaneous" development with no implications for historical relationships. Labov's rules seem unnecessarily elaborate, especially as they had to be amended to account for forms like *I'm is.* Furthermore, the Black English zero copula does not necessarily match the ordinary English present tense to which conventional historical treatments would relate it. There are rather frequent sentences like

> And I stayed in that hollow teeth [sic] until the storm over. (*Rich Amerson, Ethnic Folkways P471A*)

⁴³ On the unnecessary complexity of Labov's phonological rules, reducible to a much greater degree of simplicity by adopting a higher-level (syntactic) rule, see Philip A. Luelsdorff, *A Segmental Phonology of Black English,* Georgetown University dissertation, 1970.

⁴⁴ In this context, it makes little difference what theory of the origin of pidgin is adopted. From the point of view of ordinary English, Pidgin English does represent an extreme amount of restructuring (e.g., *He/she has been going* to *Him bina go*). It is quite likely, I believe, that Pidgin English history can be accounted for independently of that of ordinary English. If this is true, then ordinary English might just as well be considered the product of "restructuring." For the present purpose, however, it would be wasteful to quibble over such relationships.

⁴⁵ The purpose of, especially, Noam Chomsky, and his followers in dealing with linguistic universals has been insight into the complexity of the human mind, as indicated in the extremely complex ordering of languages. For their purposes, it has been very important to point out that all languages are more alike than different *as abstract systems.* Actually, such considerations are rather far removed from considerations of historical change and historical influence.

⁴⁶ Although modern theory becomes much more complex

than this, it is perhaps relevant in this context to point out sim-ply that all contact languages can make questions from state-ments (*John killed the bear* becomes *Did John kill the bear?*), can form passives (*The bear was killed by John*), and can negate any kind of structure (*John did not kill the bear*). In all kinds of human language, including the pidgins and contact varieties, very complex combinations of these operations are possible (*Did you know that the bear wasn't killed by John, or didn't you?*).

[47] The best researchers in this tradition have, however, been rooted firmly in historical documentation. Chomsky and Halle, *The Sound Pattern of English* (1968), the model for most such works, gives extensive attention to the works of the orthoepists.

[48] Students of Proto-Germanic, for example, have given an inordinate amount of attention to what seems to be a Germanic name, perhaps equivalent to the Hygelac of *Beowulf,* in Tacitus's *Germania,* a work that, although not fictional, subordinates the actual description of the Germanic people to a didactic purpose, which no serious reader could possibly miss.

[49] See note 35, and the works cited therein.

[50] A characteristic example is Elizabeth Closs Traugott, "Pid-ginization, Creolization, and the 'Naturalness' Hypothesis," Pa-pers of the IXth International Congress of Anthropological and Ethnological Sciences, 1973. Traugott, like a lot of others who have recently interested themselves in pidgin studies, overlooks a certain amount of data. She seems unaware, for example, that preverbal *been* marks past time in the Pidgin English of the West Coast of Africa as well as in Melanesian and other Pacific varieties of Pidgin English. For reasons like this, older works, like those of Gilbert D. Schneider (see Bibliography) remain inval-uable. Schneider, like others of his background, may be lacking in theoretical and methodological sophistication, but the many years he spent as a daily speaker of Pidgin English (what he calls "WesKos") in the Cameroons and Nigeria make for a depth of knowledge that can hardly be acquired in a brief period of field work or in a few interviews with a West African student at an American university.

[51] The collection by Williamson and Burke (see Bibliogra-phy) is a representative source of such attitudes.

⁵² See my *Black English,* Chapter IV, and Katz, *The Black West, passim.* Lorenzo Greene, *The Negro in Colonial New England,* 1942, is especially good on eighteenth-century relationships between Blacks and Indians of the Northeastern states.

⁵³ See Michael Silverstein, "Chinook Jargon: Language Contact and the Problem of Multi-Level Generative Systems," *Language,* 1972. Silverstein, however, like other theorists who have interested themselves in contact varieties in the past few years, seems to overlook the historical dimension. He apparently leans toward the assumption that Chinook Jargon is "re-created" by new generations of speakers of different languages (English, and some Northwestern Indian languages, for example) which come into contact.

⁵⁴ The connection is made in such works as John Leland, *Pidgin English Sing-Song,* 1900 (see pp. 2–3). The linguistics of such works is, of course, naïve in the extreme and a certain amount of Eurocentric condescension to Orientals is not lacking. On the other hand, once those objectionable attitudes are filtered out, a great deal of valuable historical material becomes available. Since virtually no one else recorded Pidgin English in earlier times, such sources are indispensable to the researcher with historical interests. On the precautions and methods necessary in the use of such sources, see William Stewart, "Sociopolitical Issues in the Linguistic Treatment of Negro Dialect," Report of the 20th Round Table, Georgetown University, 1970, and "Acculturative Processes and the Language of the American Negro," to appear in Gage (ed.), *Language in Its Social Setting.* As Stewart points out, liberal biases—those that reflect, for example, the liberal American ideal that all minority groups be treated equally and be assimilated perfectly into American mainstream society—can distort a descriptive and historical picture quite as much as racist biases. Stewart applies his reasoning primarily to the Black English vernacular, but it is obviously his intention to establish principles which can be applied to other situations.

⁵⁵ Charles C. Adams, *Boontling: An American Lingo,* University of Texas Press, 1971. See also Timothy Tyler, "Harping Boont in Boonville," *Time,* 1969. The book includes a dictionary of nearly one thousand words. Almost without exception, how-

ever, the entries consist of metaphorical reinterpretations of ordinary English words, like the examples given above. Tyler also asserts that some words (*wee, kimmie, tweed, deek*) were taken from Scotch-Irish dialect. Nothing about the Boont evidence, however, suggests actual transfer of Scotch-Irish dialects intact to the United States. Tyler also cites *gorm*, 'to eat', from French *gourmand* by "corruption."

[56] For one obvious historical example:

Still harping on my daughter
(*Hamlet*, Act II, Scene 2)

Such playful reinterpretation of word meanings is a commonplace occurrence, although perhaps not on the Boonville scale. One little girl of my acquaintance, for example, insisted on calling her brother's underwear "laconics," because her teacher had told the class to learn the word *laconic,* meaning 'short'.

[57] Examples below are influenced by, and in some cases taken directly from, Elizabeth Closs Traugott's *A History of English Syntax,* 1972. I have profited from a correspondence with Professor Traugott on these matters. We differ, however, in many points of view.

[58] The term, which is not an especially good one, characterizes a class of possessive relationships. Whereas both American English and British English would make:

He has tea at four.

into

Doesn't he have tea at four?

American English would make

He has five shillings.

into

Doesn't he have five shillings?

whereas the more characteristic British question would be

Hasn't he five shillings?

[59] The development of "do-support" belongs to Early Modern English. In many of Shakespeare's plays, for example, the older forms without *do* are used as questions:

Goes the king hence today?
(*Macbeth*, Act II, Scene 2)

[60] The two opposing theories of this development can be called *convergence* and *divergence*. For support of the convergence theory, see my "Black American English, Convergence or Divergence?" in Whitten and Szwed (eds.), *Afro-American Anthropology*, 1970. The implications of the convergence theory would be that "extreme" forms of Black English are traceable to West African language influence—which would have been stronger in the seventeenth and eighteenth centuries. The divergence theory, which is espoused by the geographists, would have it that these forms result from ecological considerations—which would mean that Black English vernacular was almost identical to ordinary English in the seventeenth and eighteenth centuries but has "deviated" in the nineteenth and twentieth. All documentary evidence supports the first conclusion.

[61] Robert Berdan, *Have/Got in the Speech of Anglo and Black Children*, Southwest Regional Laboratory Research and Development Professional Paper 22, 1973, summarizes:

The facts of Standard English seem best described by positing a rule of Got-Insertion. There is no evidence for such a rule in Black English. (*p. 14*)

[62] There is also the parallel evidence of convergence in other forms of behavior. See especially William R. Bascom, "Acculturation Among the Gullah Negroes," *American Anthropologist*, 1941.

[63] See *Black English*, Chapter V. Additional evidence for the conclusion presented there will be included in my "White through Black: The Neglected Side of New World Communication Patterns," to be published in the proceedings of the 1972 conference on creole languages and education held in Trinidad

and to be edited by Dennis Craig. Applied to the West Indies, this kind of statement is the merest commonplace, stated in such conventional sources as Frederic G. Cassidy's "The Pidgin Element in Jamaican Creole":

> The island-born whites became so creolized in their habits and speech [during the eighteenth century] that those not sent to England for education never did learn to speak proper British English. (Hymes [ed.], *Pidginization and Creolization of Languages*, p. 205)

Cassidy, a doctrinaire geographist, would, however, reject any such statement of Black English influence on Southern white English. His orientation apparently requires us to believe that in the eighteenth century the United States (or the colonies) were altogether different from the West Indian islands. There is, however, much historical evidence that the language situation was essentially the same—particularly insofar as the bringing together of many populations.

[64] See the many statements of Labov on how verbally superior (in the street vernacular) teen-agers are considered by their teachers to be deficient (e.g., *Language in the Inner City,* pp. 251–53).

[65] The kind of variation theory Labov himself has developed (see his 1969 article, Bibliography) would be more consistent with the interpretation that there was contextual variation in the use or "loss" of *r*—that, for example, postvocalic *r* was more likely to be given retroflex articulation in formal than in casual speech styles.

[66] *Sociolinguistic Patterns,* 1972, p. 145. Labov cites an unpublished manuscript, which I have not been able to see, by Richard Norman. The summary presented by Labov is, however, perfectly consistent with the theory of American English history which I had formulated before reading that summary.

[67] R. M. R. and Beatrice Hall, "Creole Conspiracies: Why Definite Answers Are Hard to Find" (unpublished), point out that *r*-lessness in the Southern states correlates strikingly with the presence of a large number of West African slaves, and that

those slaves would have brought a native-language phonology to the New World which would have made for *r*-lessness in words like *barn, bird,* etc.

[68] P. 227.

CHAPTER VI

[1] See comments on "substratum" and "adstratum" theories in Chapter I and elsewhere. In addition to overtranslation, there are such factors as *reverse carry-over*. Examples are easily seen in Puerto Rico. To avoid the problem of translating Spanish *mirar* or *buscar* by English *look at* or *look for,* Spanish speakers will often produce ambiguous English sentences like:

He is looking the house.

A student of mine once "solved" the problem by writing:

A few members will gather and look at for a house.

This phenomenon is, of course, often very like what is called *hypercorrection* in monolingual circumstances. It could be called *hyper-Anglicism*. On the other hand, in order to avoid the Anglicization of the Puerto Rican vocabulary practiced by those who replace (e.g.) *la monja* with *la sister,* certain others will avoid legitimate Spanish words like *cuestión*. Such reverse carry-over from the Anglicized vocabulary into the hyper-Hispanicized vocabulary is a much subtler influence than simple interference, but it is there.

[2] See definition and illustration of *diglossia* in Chapter IV.

[3] For these purposes, it is hardly necessary to enter into the vexed question of whether there is such a thing as "perfect" bilingualism. Studies like Sawyer's work on "aloofness" in Texas tend to show that even "Latin" speakers with no detectable accent (see Chapter IV) do not have the English words for simple, homey items, particularly those associated with the kitchen. For present purposes, it is adequate to consider a "perfect" bilingual as being one who could converse with speakers of his second language without their suspecting that he was not speaking his na-

tive language. It must be perfectly obvious that in any practical interaction, nonlinguistic factors would have an influence: personal appearance, dress, name, what the interlocutors knew beforehand as well as what they perceived during the conversation. Some attempts have been made to surmount these obstacles by using tape-recorded speech only. Whatever its use in experiments, such a device tells us little about sociolinguistic actuality.

[4] Washington Lloréns, "Lenguaje de Germanía en Puerto Rico," in *El Habla Popular de Puerto Rico,* Cuaderno No. III, 1968.

[5] Such pairs are conventionally called "false cognates" or "deceptive cognates." In the case of *fumar* and *fume,* there is rather little deception involved, since the semantics of the two words are so far apart. Other standard examples are Spanish *asistir,* 'attend', and English *assist,* Spanish *probar,* 'try', and English *prove.* The *gringo* in Spanish-speaking territory soon grows accustomed to "Mister, I cannot assist your class tomorrow" and "It may not work, but we can prove it." Amusingly, *probar* is closer to the older meaning of *prove* fossilized in the proverb "The exception proves the rule."

[6] There are many different grammatical analyses of expressions like *fill out, pick up, turn down,* etc. Virtually any change in linguistic theory is sure to engender a new analysis of them. Certainly they are quite unlike anything in Spanish or in the well-known Romance languages. For this reason, they cause endless troubles even to Puerto Ricans educated in the States. Some linguists consider them rather like the "separable prefixes" of German (*aufstehen,* 'to arise': *Ich stehe auf,* 'I arise'). Again, it will probably depend on one's orientation toward historical linguistics as to how much similarity one thinks there is. In *The System of English Grammar* (1971) Ralph B. and Dorothy Long consider that *pick* in the phrase *pick up my children* is a "predicator," *up* is "first complement," and *my children* is "second complement." Although this analysis ignores some permutational factors (*pick up the children* → *pick the children up* but not *pick up them* → *pick them up*), it seems adequate for most purposes in its compromise between traditional grammar and modern innovation.

[7] William R. Linneman and Harriet Fether, "Miami Beach Hotel Names," *Names* XXXIX (1964), pp. 196–200, describe the use of foreign-language features for glamour in Miami Beach.

[8] In the *fiestas patronales* of Loiza Aldea, widely regarded as the most "African" part of the island, temporary shacks from which food and drinks are sold often have the "names" or designations *come y calla* and *toma y dame* ('take and give me [money]'). As is usual in Afro-American studies, Puerto Ricanists are split on whether the Loiza area is an African survival or a Hispanic archaism. See the discussion below, and note 17.

[9] Listener reaction tests that show that respondents, even those from the Deep South, can distinguish Black from white speakers from tape-recorded evidence only, have been performed by Lambert and Tucker (*Social Forces*, 1969); Baratz, Shuy, and Wolfram (NIMH Report, unpublished, 1969); Baratz (*Child Development*, 1969); and James Bryden (University of Virginia dissertation, unpublished, 1968). For persistence in the older view, see the review of *Black English* by D'Eloia in the *Journal of English Linguistics*, 1973.

[10] The worst examples of such statements, as might be expected, are in the tourist literature. Such *Tourismo* publications as *¿Que Pasa in (sic) Puerto Rico?* are motivated, of course, by a desire to minimize any difficulty with the "language barrier."

[11] In a review of *Black English*, J. T. Sellers refers to the language system described as "an elaborate system of phonetic distortions and regional mispronunciations." Sellers, later in the same review, asserts:

> The mispronunciations, the poor vocabulary, the phonetic distortions are part of the stigma that America stamped on her black refugees from impoverished rural areas of the South and the neglected slums of the cities of the North. (*The Urban Review*, Vol. 6, No. 2)

If Sellers's ambiguous statement can be interpreted in terms of its actual wording, he seems actually to be suggesting that Black English is a Northern product ("stigma that America stamped on her black refugees from impoverished rural areas of the South"). This is a refreshing departure from the traditional misconception that Black English is entirely Southern in origin—if not one that can be taken with complete seriousness.

[12] See *Black English* (1972).

[13] Somewhat loosely, Papiamentu can be described as a "Spanish" Creole. This reflects the more immediate situation, in which Curaçao (and Aruba and Bonaire), being situated close to Venezuela, have been influenced linguistically by the South American country, and Papiamentu has borrowed much from Spanish. The earlier genetic relationship to a contact variety of Portuguese has, however, long been recognized. See T. Navarro Tomás, "Observaciones sobre el Papiamentu," *Nueva Revista de la Filología Española* VII (1951), and H. A. van Wijk, "Orígenes y Evolución del Papiamentu," *Neophilologus* XLII (1958).

[14] See Rose Nash, "The Emergence of a New Variety of English in Puerto Rico," forthcoming, and my own "Standard Average Foreign in Puerto Rican Spanish," in Atwood and Hill (eds.), *Studies in Language, Literature, and Culture of the Middle Ages and Later,* University of Texas Press, 1969.

[15] See any one of the standard histories of the English language, like that of Albert C. Baugh (1933). Such histories tend to minimize the effect of French on any part of English except the vocabulary, as they try to minimize the earlier influence of the Old Norse of the Viking invaders. It is rather obvious, however, that there was a great deal of influence from each of the languages of the successful invaders of Anglo-Saxon England. There are, in fact, striking resemblances to the Puerto Rican language contact situation, especially in the Norman French-Old English contact beginning in 1066. One hundred and fifty years after the battle of Hastings (c. 1216), a tremendous amount of influence from French was felt in English. The presence of Americans in Puerto Rico has, by contrast, been limited to a 77-year period (1898–1975).

[16] For purposes of comparison, it should be remembered that Anglo-Saxon England before the Viking and Norman conquests was hardly unified. The traditional (although oversimplified) division has been into the seven kingdoms of the "heptarchy."

Language historians, also, have stressed the great dialect differences in Old English, frequently asserting that there was a limited amount of mutual intelligibility.

[17] One might note that, whereas Papiamentu speakers may vary between

Mi ta pensá

and

Mi ta pensando, 'I am/was thinking'

depending upon the amount of Hispanic influence they have experienced, some Puerto Rican speakers say, *Yo ta pensando.*

In the spiritualist meetings, largely attended by Black Puerto Ricans and poorer whites, wherein older, voodoolike religious practices survive, most Puerto Ricans believe that a much more "nonstandard" variety of Spanish is used. One informant, a close acquaintance of mine, has told me that she believes *Yo ta pensá* might be heard in such meetings. She totally rejects, however, *Me/Mi ta pensá.* Unfortunately, I am unable to achieve access to the *espiritismo* meetings and must depend upon second-hand reports.

The study of Creole influence on Spanish varieties of the New World received a tremendous boost from the discovery of Palenquero in Colombia (Aquilas Escalante and Derek Bickerton, "Palenquero: A Spanish-Based Creole of Northern Colombia," *Lingua,* 1970). The suggestion of a pan-Caribbean Spanish Creole had been made as early as 1949 (Max Leopold Wagner, *Lingue e Dialetti dell' American Spagnola*). Germán de Granda ("Cimarronismos, Palenques, y Hablas 'Criollas' en Hispano America," Instituto Caro y Cuervo, Bogotá, 1970) and Ricardo Otheguy ("Linguistic Arguments in the Determination of Creole Typology: The Case of 'Habla Bozal Antillana'," in C.-J.N. Bailey and Roger W. Shuy [eds.], *New Ways of Analyzing Variability in English,* Georgetown University Press, 1973) have given special attention to Cuba, where large-scale African survivals are clearer. The folklorist Lydia Cabrera has recorded religious texts from Cuban Negroes which are especially useful sources for such study.

[18] This is the point of view of the Spanish dialectologist Tomás Navarro Tomás, whose *El Español en Puerto Rico* (1948) has been one of the most influential books in the field of New World Spanish dialectology.

[19] See Manuel Álvarez Nazario, *El Elemento Afronegroïde en el Español de Puerto Rico* (1961). The newest work by Álvarez Nazario, *La Herencia Lingüística de Canarias en Puerto Rico,* stresses the resemblances between Puerto Rican Spanish and that of the Canary Islands. He further asserts that the emigrant population from the Canary Islands became the dominant one in the Puerto Rican population. However that may be, the Canary Islands are by their very geographic nature prime candidates for involvement in the maritime language contact that is basic to the Creoles. (See Chapter I, and the references there.)

[20] For *chévere,* see Álvarez Nazario's 1961 book. For *okay,* see David Dalby, "The African Element in Black American English," in Kochman (ed.), *Rappin' and Stylin' Out* (1972).

[21] For Trinidad, see Maureen Warner, "Trinidad Yoruba— Notes on Survival," *Caribbean Quarterly,* Vol. 17 (June 1971), pp. 40–49.

[22] The monogenesis theory of Creole origins, which hypothesizes a common origin for both of these and French Creole, has perhaps its strongest statement in the article by Jan Voorhoeve in *Language in Society,* 1973.

[23] This statement is that of Richard Wood, *Neophilologus,* 1972. For the earlier Portuguese affiliations, see the sources cited in note 17, above.

[24] Derek Bickerton and Aquilas Escalante, ("Palenquero: A Spanish-Based Creole of Northern Colombia," *Lingua* 24 [1970], pp. 254–67) make this an important characteristic of Palenquero.

[25] José Perez Marís and D. Luis Cueto y Gonzalez, *Historia de la Insurreción de Lares,* Barcelona, 1872.

[26] P. 75. This passage, in its overall context, makes it perfectly clear that the agitators (from the point of view of the Spanish

authors) appealed specifically to collections of Blacks (*negradas*).

[27] See Navarro Tomás (*op. cit.*)

[28] On African elements in that culture, see especially Ricardo Alegría, *La Fiesta de Santiago Apóstol en Loiza Aldea,* Madrid, 1954. For Indian elements, especially in the interior, see Pedro C. Escabí (ed.), *Morovis: Vista Parcial del Folklore de Puerto Rico,* Universidad de Puerto Rico, Centro de Investigaciones Sociales, n.d. Unfortunately, comparisons with the folk cultures of the surrounding islands are rare. My own "How Not to Classify the Folk Tales of the Antilles," *Caribbean Studies,* 1964, is an attempt to make a beginning in such a comparison.

[29] The most extreme statement about the influence of English on Puerto Rican Spanish is Germán de Granda's *Transculturación e Interferencia Lingüística en el Puerto Rico Contemporáneo (1898–1968),* Bogotá, 1972. An attempted refutation is in Paulino Pérez Sala, *Interferencia Lingüística del Inglés en el Español Hablado en Puerto Rico,* San Juan, 1973.

[30] These sentences are taken from Wolfram, Shiels, and Fasold, *Overlapping Influence in the English of Second Generation Puerto Rican Teenagers in Harlem,* Final Report, Office of Education Grant No. 3-70-033 (508), 1971. It is, however, quite easy to collect similar data from many sources.

[31] These are also taken from Wolfram, Shiels, and Fasold, *op. cit.*

[32] These sentences are from Wolfram, Shiels, and Fasold. The first report of such sentences by Puerto Rican teen-agers in New York City was made, however, by Stuart Silverman (*The Effects of Peer Group Membership on Puerto Rican English,* Ferkauf Graduate School of Yeshiva University dissertation, 1971) which preceded and seemingly influenced the Wolfram, Shiels, and Fasold work.

[33] This point is made both by Silverman and by Wolfram, Shiels, and Fasold.

[34] On hypercorrection, see above, Chapter V.

[35] That is, tense is marked once or more in a string of two or more verbs. It is not necessarily the first verb that is so marked. An example is:

And so I comin' down an' she out there
blabbin' her mouth told my sister I
playin' hookey from school.

[36] From Wolfram, Shiels, and Fasold.

[37] Collected independently at the Urban Language Study of the District of Columbia in 1966–67.

[38] The San Juan *Star*, November 3, 1973, p. 1.

[39] Among the Arawak words taken into American English, most of them in a very early period, are *barbecue, cacique, cannibal, canoe*. It is interesting that in Puerto Rico the American English treatment of the first as an acronym (*Bar B Q*) is widespread. Although there have been other suggested etymologies for *barbecue* (e.g., French *barbe à queue,* "head to tail"), the OED's attribution to a Carib Indian source is undoubtedly the correct one.

[40] In the play *La Juega de Gallos o el Negro Bozal* (1859), discussed above in connection with the speech of the *Negro bozal* José, there is a character named Seño [Señor] Epifanio who is halfway between the slaves and the Spanish grandees in rank (he takes care of the fighting cocks that belong to one of the latter, but seems to be free) and who speaks with the phonological characteristics that have become (and perhaps already were in the nineteenth century) stereotypical of "Puerto Rican dialect." Historical treatments have never taken such attestations into account, preferring to look for origins in the "regional" dialects of Spain or—much more rarely—in Africanisms. The American English influence on Puerto Rican Spanish has been emphasized, argued about, and both overstated and understated. An excellent example of the overstatement is the tracing of *zafacon*, 'garbage can', to American English *safety can*. The major problem here is that there is no American English term *safety can*.

CHAPTER VII

[1] Albert C. Baugh's *History of the English Language*, 1933, is a convenient source for a treatment of English as "a world language." Virtually every history of the English language (see Bibliography) has such a chapter, conventionally placed toward

the end. In *Language in America* (1970) Charlton Laird has a chapter entitled "American English Abroad" which deals with Americanisms reexported to England, American English loan words in some foreign languages, and (briefly) Pidgin English. Like others, Laird speculates that English "is spreading throughout the world because it is a good language with a simple grammar and a vast and highly flexible vocabulary." Although he does say a little about the concomitant advance of "American culture," he ignores lingua franca considerations. The position taken here is that sociolinguistic considerations have to be of primary importance in any such spread, since linguistic "goodness" and "simplicity" are purely relative terms.

[2] This term is used by Eric Partridge and John W. Clark, *British and American English Since 1900* (1951), p. 268. This book, which I discovered when the present work was all but complete, has a number of interesting insights, although it is rather lacking in documentation. It is an interesting corrective to the establishment point of view reflected by Laird, Marckwardt, and others quoted herein.

[3] The historical development of Liberian Pidgin English was clearly related to that of Sierra Leone Krio (or the "Taki Taki patois"), although expert opinion remains divided in both cases. Some scholars (like Jack Berry, "English Loanwords and Adaptations in Sierra Leone Krio," *Creole Language Studies* II, 1961) have assumed a nineteenth-century origin, related to "repatriation," for Krio. More recent work, especially by Hancock (see Bibliography), however, casts doubt on both the lateness of the origin and the separateness of the West African English varieties.

[4] See Ian F. Hancock's "Some Aspects of English in Liberia," *Liberian Studies Journal* III (1970–71), 207–13.

[5] The well-known Black American *zoot suit* is obviously related.

[6] A statement of this type has been regularly attributed to Black boxers, the first of whom may have been Joe Louis (before his second fight with Billy Conn).

[7] *Chunk*, 'throw', is a well-known Americanism, although possibly related to the more British *chuck*. The OED calls it "U.S. colloquial" and relates it to the noun *chunck*, 'a thick, more or

less cuboidal lump', with entries dating from 1835. The OED cites, although it apparently does not consider to be related, American Indian *chunk, chunky,* a game involving throwing, of which there are attestations as early as 1773. The nasalization of the vowel of *chunk* (addition of the nasal consonant /n/) is usually considered as such a commonplace phonological development that it does not need explanation, although in principle all changes need some explanation. The *Dictionary of Americanisms* follows the OED in defining the word as 'to throw at or pelt with, or as with, chunks of wood'. The earliest citations (1835 and 1841) do not, however, suggest the use of chunks of wood more than any other kind of missile for throwing.

[8] The African source of this word, widely used in the Southern United States (and, in compounds like *tote road,* in the North) was shown by Lorenzo Dow Turner, *Africanisms in the Gullah Dialect,* 1949. The Liberian form could have been borrowed directly from a West African language, or it could have been reimported by repatriated ex-slaves. It is likely that the two processes reinforced each other. The same could be said about most of the other terms under discussion here.

[9] On the background of this term, see Paul Christophersen's important article "A Note on the Words *dash* and *ju-ju* in West African English," *English Studies,* 1959.

[10] See works by Gilbert D. Schneider, by David Smith and his collaborators (both in Bibliography), and William Welmers and Warren d'Azevedo, *Some Terms from Liberian Speech,* 2nd ed., U.S. Peace Corps in Liberia, Monrovia, 1970.

[11] The vowel nucleus, characteristic of Barundi realization of English /ow/, can be fairly well represented by /ew/.

[12] Actually, my exposure to the etymon probably came from a childhood experience with a movie serial about Zungu, the white man-ape (a kind of variation of the theme of Tarzan). The name had been forgotten, however, until I encountered the Swahili word.

[13] See definition of *diglossia* and of the terms *H language* and *L language* above, p. 289. In *How to Learn a Foreign Language* (New York, 1955) Ed Cornelius gives some expert counseling to Americans who want to continue to swim against

this linguistic tide. One subchapter, picturesquely entitled "You Stink," deals with a favorite ploy—insisting "I can't understand you," so as to be able to complete the desired shift to English. A subtler ploy described in another subchapter is "You Speak Beautifully"—an often insincere compliment that helps to block further improvement in the target language.

[14] *The New Yorker,* November 29, 1947, p. 114.

[15] *The New Yorker,* January 10, 1948.

[16] *The New Yorker,* January 8, 1949, p. 45.

[17] See Chapter I of *Black English* (1972) and Section II of the Bibliography of that work.

[18] The Black English basilect of very young children, like certain Creole languages and certain West African languages, also does not have this pronoun gender feature.

[19] This, again, is a feature shared with languages like Haitian Creole and certain West African languages. Puerto Rican Spanish, which has a certain amount of influence from West African languages (see Álvarez Nazario, Bibliography), also permits the use of *hombre* as a term of address between women.

[20] *Basic Tagalog for Foreigners and Non-Tagalogs,* Manila. First printed in 1956, this book had new editions in 1957, 1959, and 1964.

[21] P. 23. A former managing editor of *Caribbean Studies,* a nonnative speaker of English, objected to my designation of this sentence as "odd English" on the grounds that it (i.e., *guilders*) was Dutch, not Old English. Of course, in a mixed-language setting I would have been much better advised to use the adjective *strange.* Touchiness about what she conceived as criticism of the English of a foreigner may have also been a motivating factor in the editor's objections. Such situations arise frequently in any international context.

[22] *Ibid.,* p. 20.

[23] This kind of influence has long been recognized in the linguistic literature. See, for example, Kenneth Pike, *Phonemics,* 1947, p. 32.

[24] False cognates are words with common historical origins that have developed different semantic associations in different languages. A good example is Spanish *traducir,* 'translate', com-

pared to English *traduce,* 'falsify, misrepresent, pervert'. Both derive, ultimately, from Latin *trans,* 'around', and *ducere,* 'lead'. The Spanish word has developed metaphorically and has been restricted to a linguistic context; the English word has undergone pejoration without such restriction. Another good example is Spanish *molestar,* which means 'bother, annoy', and English *molest,* which tends to have a sexual connotation. There is a standing joke about the South American student who wrote a letter thanking the hosts of his stay in the United States and concluded, "I hope I did not molest your mother and sisters too much."

[25] Lists of false cognates for French, Spanish, German, and some of the other well-known European languages are easily available. Popular works on language like Mario Pei's *The Story of Language* are now somewhat more likely to contain information of this type than are more recent technical linguistic works. Linguists tend to deprecate popular use of such works, but not to provide viable alternatives for laymen in need of practical linguistic advice. The field of English as a second (or foreign) language, which is especially subject to fads, has all but eliminated lists of false (or "deceptive") cognates in the past few years. They remain, however, real problems for teachers and for learners of foreign languages.

[26] The OED lists several examples of *assist,* 'be present', mainly in the sixteenth and seventeenth centuries. Two nineteenth-century entries in that sense are, however, in an obviously archaizing stylistic context. The last two (1854 and 1873) specifically evoke French *asister,* which retains much the same meaning as Spanish *asistir.* In spite of the fact that a kind of lunatic fringe of linguists who apply "language universals" to theories of linguistic change might think so, there seems to be no sensible reason to believe that a speaker of French or Spanish who uses *assist* in English in the sense of the misleading cognate in his own language has been able, in some mysterious way, to utilize Early English patterns.

[27] Lewis Herman and Marguerite Shalett Herman, *Foreign Dialects: A Manual for Actors, Directors, and Writers,* New York, Theatre Arts Books, 1943. See William A. Stewart's praise of

some of the general statements (although not of many of the specific linguistic details) in *American Dialects: A Manual for Actors, Directors, and Writers,* New York, Theatre Arts Books, 1947. Stewart's remarks occur in his review of Wolfram and Clark, *Black-White Speech Differences, Florida FL Reporter,* 1972.

²⁸ In their "Spanish Monolog" (p. 244) Herman and Herman include the sentences *I don't be want to see you no more* and *Because I don't be see you no more!* Although the double negatives can easily be explained in terms of Spanish, *don't be want* and *don't be see* are quite unlike Spanish interference patterns. Lithuanian, Yugoslav, Finnish, and Hungarian "dialects" are also represented in the book, along with about twenty others.

²⁹ New York, Philosophical Library, 1968. A recent article discussing this tradition was Nelson Brooks, "Language Learning: The New Approach," *Florida FL Reporter,* 1967.

³⁰ P. 132, quoting from Georges J. Joyaux, "Foreign Languages and the Humanities," *The Modern Language Journal,* Vol. XLIX, No. 2 (February 1965), p. 102.

³¹ Oliva, "Modern Trends in Foreign Languages," pp. 328–38.

³² *Ibid.,* p. 330.

³³ *Ibid.,* p. 331.

³⁴ Contrastive analysis and its application to language teaching is predicated on the assumption that a speaker is likely to have trouble with those sounds, words, or structures in the "target" language that are not matched in his own. Thus, the speaker of an intonational language like English, when trying to learn Chinese, will have perhaps most trouble of all with the lexical tones. Spanish speakers, for whom the one preposition *en* will do most of the work of English *in* and *on,* have a great deal of trouble with these English words. English speakers, on the other hand, tend to confuse Spanish *para* and *por,* both of which can usually be fairly well rendered by English *for.*

³⁵ Oliva, *op. cit.,* p. 331.

³⁶ James W. Dodge, editor, *Other Words, Other Worlds: Language-in-Culture,* 1972. The first section, "On Teaching Another Language as Part of Another Culture," is by J. L. Dillard,

Mary Rita Miller, and William A. Stewart. In that section, somewhat more than in Section II ("Sociocultural Aspects of Foreign Language Study"), much is made of informal culture (kinesics, body language, timing, interpersonal awareness, unspoken assumptions) rather than of some academy-approved set of masterpieces.

[37] In this context (as argued in Chapter I), a "natural" language could be Sabir (the Mediterranean Lingua Franca) or any pidgin. Computer languages, however, are not such languages; and it is probably inappropriate to place Esperanto in the same category.

[38] *Op. cit.,* p. 329.

[39] Unfortunately, most programs set up for educating students on variation in American English start with dialect geography and never really get around to the social types of variation, although the latter are frequently mentioned in the syllabus. An example of such a program is outlined in R. W. Shuy, "Teacher Training and Urban Language Problems," in Fasold and Shuy (eds.), *Teaching Standard English in the Inner City,* Washington, D.C., 1970.

[40] It is noteworthy that histories of the English language (see Bibliography for some examples), to which American English is usually appended as a kind of minor afterthought, are heavily grounded in the reconstructive tradition. This is understandable and in a way laudable. There is a lot of important intellectual content to the reconstruction of Proto-Indo-European and other hypothetical proto-languages. There is, however, the unfortunate concomitant result that such well-known varieties as Australian English and American English are hardly mentioned at all, so that the history of the English language gives much more attention to a few million Anglo-Saxons than it does to over two hundred million contemporary American speakers of the language. And of course a few hundred million foreign speakers never get mentioned at all. The approach also tends to produce disproportion in that extensive attention is given to "historical" facts, which are only hypothetical, and very little to events within recent historical time, which are extensively documented and thoroughly studied by historians. As indicated in Chapters I and II,

I feel that such emphases have been especially unfortunate where the evaluation of the effects of migration and the processes involved therein are concerned.

[41] According to the Venerable Bede (*Historia Ecclestica Gentis Anglorum*), the Anglos, Saxons, and Jutes crossed the English Channel at the invitation of the Romanized Celts, who were unable to cope with the Picts and other "wild" tribes, in 449 A.D. Bede's account was written in 731 A.D., nearly three hundred years after the fact. It could have represented nothing more reliable than oral tradition. Furthermore, as has been frequently pointed out, the names of the Germanic leaders (Hengst and Horsa) suggest mythological—or at least legendary—sources as much as they do more reliable historical traditions. *Faute de mieux,* it has been the practice of historians of Early English to accept this statement—in general terms, if not as a matter of precise detail. It should, however, be borne in mind that such information is not at all comparable to the historically documented accounts we have of the European migrations to the North American continent. Furthermore, extensive written records from the Germanic migrants to England are not available for some three centuries after their supposed arrival in the British Isles. Records of the American immigrants, on the other hand, are available—from both sides of the Atlantic—in great detail and from fully contemporary sources. It would, thus, seem reasonable to form our notions of the Anglo-Saxon-Jute immigration from what we know about the North American immigration by Europeans, not vice versa. The opposite has, unfortunately, been the practice in language histories. That procedure is sometimes even dignified with the high-flown title of Science.

BIBLIOGRAPHY

A Language in Common. The Times Literary Supplement No. 3,154 (Friday, August 10, 1962).

Aarons, Alfred C., Barbara Y. Gordon, and William A. Stewart (eds.). *Linguistic-Cultural Differences and American Education.* Miami, 1969.

Abercrombie, David. *Problems and Principles: Studies in the Teaching of English as a Second Language.* London, 1955.

Adams, Rev. James, S.R.E.S. *The Pronunciation of the English Language Vindicated from Imputed Anomaly and Caprice.* Edinburgh, 1799.

Adams, Ramon F. *Western Words, A Dictionary of the American West.* University of Oklahoma Press, 1968.

Alegría, Ricardo. *La Fiesta de Santiago Apóstol en Loiza Aldea.* Madrid, 1954.

Algeo, John. *Problems in the Origins and Development of the English Language.* New York, 1972.

Allen, Harold B. and Gary Underwood (eds.). *Readings in American Dialectology.* New York, 1971.

Álvarez Nazario, Manuel. *El Elemento Afronegroïde en el Español de Puerto Rico.* San Juan de Puerto Rico, 1961.
——. *La Herencia Lingüistica de Canarias en Puerto Rico.* San Juan de Puerto Rico, 1972.

Amerson, Rich. "Texas Sandstorm," in *Negro Folk Music of Alabama*. Recorded by Harold Courlander. Ethnic Folkways Record P471A.

Andrews, Charles M. *The Fathers of New England, A Chronicle of the Puritan Commonwealth*. The Chronicles of America, Vol. 6, 1919.

Armstrong, Virginia. *I Have Spoken; American History Through the Voices of Indians*. New York, 1971.

Asbury, Herbert. *The Barbary Coast*. New York, 1933.

Aspillera, Paraluman S. *Basic Tagalog for Foreigners and Non-Tagalogs*. Manila, 1956.

Atkins, John. *A Voyage to Guinea, Brasil, and the West Indies*. London, 1737.

Atwood, E. Bagby. "The Methods of American Dialectology." *Zeitschrift für Mundartforschung*, 1963.

———. *The Regional Vocabulary of Texas*. Texas University Press, 1962.

———. *A Survey of Verb Forms in the Eastern United States*. Ann Arbor, Michigan, 1953.

Bach, Emmon, and Robert T. Harms (eds.). *Universals in Linguistic Theory*. New York, 1968.

Bailey, Charles-James N. Review of Dillard, *Black English: Its History and Usage in the United States. Foundations of Language* 11 (1971), pp. 299–309.

Baker, Sydney J. *The Australian Language*. Sydney, 1966.

Baratz, Joan C. "A Bidialectal Task for Determining Language Proficiency in Economically Disadvantaged Children." *Child Development* 40 (September 1969), pp. 889–901.

———. Roger W. Shuy, and Walter Wolfram. *Sociolinguistic Factors in Speech Identification*. Final Report, NIMH Grant No. 15048, 1969.

Barrere, Albert, and Charles G. Leland. *A Dictionary of Slang, Jargon, and Cant*. London, 1889.

Bascom, William R. "Acculturation Among the Gullah Negroes." *American Anthropologist* 43 (1941), pp. 43–50.

Baugh, Albert C. *A History of the English Language.* New York, 1935.

Beadle, John H. *Western Wilds and the Men Who Redeem Them.* Philadelphia, 1878.

Beadle, Samuel Alfred. *Adam Shuffler.* 1890.

Beck, Robert ("Iceberg Slim"). *Pimp: The Story of My Life.* Los Angeles, 1967.

———. *Trick Baby.* Los Angeles, 1968.

Beecher, Lyman, and Joseph Harvey. *Memoirs of Obookiah, A Native of Owyhee and a Member of the Foreign Mission School, Who Died at Cornwall, Conn., February 17, 1818, Aged 26 Years.* New Haven, Office of the Religious Intelligencer, 1818.

Beers, Paul B. *The Pennsylvania Sampler.* Harrisburg, 1970.

Bender, Harold H. *The Home of the Indo-Europeans.* Princeton University Press, 1922.

Bense, J. F. *Dictionary of the Low Dutch Element in the English Vocabulary.* The Hague, 1939.

Berdan, Robert. *Have/Got in the Speech of Anglo and Black Children.* Southwest Regional Laboratory Research and Development Paper 22, 1973.

Bernard, J. R. L.-B. "On the Uniformity of Spoken Australian English." *Orbis* 18 (1969), pp. 62–73.

Berry, Jack. "English Loanwords and Adaptations in Sierra Leone Krio," in R. B. LePage (ed.), *Creole Language Studies II.* London, 1961.

Beyer, Richard Lawrence. "Robert Hunter, Royal Governor of New York: A Study in Colonial Administration." Iowa University Studies in the Social Sciences X, 1932.

Bickerton, Derek, and Aquilas Escalante. "Palenquero: A Spanish-Based Creole of Northern Colombia." *Lingua* 24 (1970), pp. 254–67.

Blanc, Haim. *Communal Dialects of Baghdad Arabic.* Harvard Middle Eastern Monographs, No. 10. Cambridge: Harvard University Press, 1954.

————. "The Israeli Koiné as an Emergent National Standard," in Fishman, Ferguson, and das Gupta (eds.), *Language Problems of Developing Nations*, New York, 1968.

Blanco, Tomas. *Anglocomodismos en el Vernáculo Puertorriqueño*. Havana, Sociedad Economica de Amigos del Pais I. 1955.

Bloomfield, Leonard. *Language*. New York, 1933.

Bolton, Herbert and Mary Ross. *The Debatable Land. A Sketch of the Anglo-Spanish Contest for the Georgia Country*. Berkeley, California, 1925.

Bossu, Jean-Bernard. *Travels in the Interior of North America*. Translated by Seymour Feiler. University of Oklahoma Press, 1925.

Boucicault, Dion. *The Octoroon; or, Life in Louisiana*. 1861.

Bourke, John G. *On the Border with Crook*. New York, 1892.

Bowles, Samuel. *Our New West*. Hartford, 1869.

Bradbury, John. *Travels in the Interior of America*. London, 1817.

Bradford, William. *History of Plymouth Plantation*. Boston, 1896.

Brooks, Nelson. "Language Learning: The New Approach." *Florida Foreign Language Reporter*, 1967.

Browne, J. Ross. *Adventures in the Apache Country*. New York, 1854.

Bryant, Margaret. *The English Language and Its History*. New York, 1962.

Bryden, James. *An Acoustic and Social Dialect Analysis of Perceptual Variables in Listener Identification and Rating of Negro Speakers*. U.S. Office of Education, Final Report, Project No. 7-C-003.

Burton, Sir Richard Francis. *Wanderings in West Africa*. London, 1863.

————. *The Look of the West*. London, 1860.

Caballero, Ramon C. F. *La Juega de Gallos o El Negro Bozal: Comedia en dos actos y en prosa*. Ponce, Puerto Rico, 1852.

Cabrera, Lydia. *Anago: Vocabulario Lucumí (el Yoruba que se habla en Cuba)*. Havana, 1957.

———. *La Sociedad Secreta Abakua, Narrada por Viejos Adeptos*. Havana, 1959.

———. *El Monte, Igbo, Finda, Ewe, Orishi, Vititi, Nfinda*. Miami, 1968.

———. "Ritual y Símbolos de la Iniciacion en la Sociedad Secreta Abakua." *Journal de la Societé des Americanistes* LVIII (1969), pp. 139–71.

Campbell, Duncan. *Nova Scotia in Its Historical, Mercantile, and Industrial Relations*. Montreal, 1873.

Campbell, E. C. "Down Among the Red Men," *Kansas State Historical Society Review* XVII, 1928.

Carawan, Candie, and Guy Carawan. *Ain't You Got a Right to the Tree of Life?* New York, 1967.

Cassidy, Frederic G. *Jamaica Talk: Three Hundred Years of the English Language in Jamaica*. London, 1961.

———, and David DeCamp. "Names for an Albino Among Jamaican Negroes." *Names* 14 (September 1966), pp. 129–33.

———. "Tracing the Pidgin Element in Jamaican Creole (with notes on method and the nature of pidgin vocabularies)," in Dell Hymes (ed.), *Pidginization and Creolization of Languages*. Cambridge University Press, 1971.

———, and R. B. LePage (eds.). *Dictionary of Jamaican English*. Cambridge University Press, 1967.

Catlin, George. *Illustrations of the Manners, Customs, and Conditions of the North American Indians*. London, 1856.

———. *Life Among the Indians*. London, 1874.

Cebollero, Pedro. *A School Language Policy for Puerto Rico*. San Juan, 1945.

Chomsky, A. Noam. *Cartesian Linguistics*. New York, 1966.

———, and Morris Halle. *The Sound Pattern of English*. New York, 1968.

Christophersen, Paul. "Some Special West African English Words." *English Studies* 34 (1953), pp. 282–91.

———. "A Note on the Words *dash* and *ju-ju* in West African English." *English Studies* 39 (1959), pp. 115–18.

Clapin, Sylvia. *A New Dictionary of Americanisms*. New York, n.d.

Clark, Joseph G. *Lights and Shadows in Sailor Life*. Boston, 1847.

Clark, Virginia P., Paul A. Eschholz, and Alfred R. Rosa (eds.). *Language: Introductory Readings*. New York, 1972.

Clarkson, John. *Journal,* August 6, 1791 through March 18, 1792. Howard University Library manuscript.

Claudel, Calvin A. "The Changing Aspects of Teaching Spanish," in Joseph S. Roucek (ed.), *The Study of Foreign Languages*. New York, 1968.

Coleman, William Macon. *The History of the Primitive Yankees, or the Pilgrim Fathers in England and Holland*. Washington, D.C., 1881.

Coleridge, Henry N. *Six Months in the West Indies in 1825*. London, 1826.

Cook, James. *Fifty Years on the Old Frontier*. Norman, Oklahoma, 1954.

Cornelius, Ed. *How to Learn a Foreign Language*. New York, 1955.

Craigie, William A. and James R. Hulbert (eds.). *A Dictionary of American English on Historical Principles*. University of Chicago Press, 1938–44.

Crane, Verner W. *The Southern Frontier, 1670–1732*. Philadelphia, 1929.

Cremony, John C. *Life Among the Apaches*. San Francisco, 1968.

Creswell, Nicholas. *The Journal of Nicholas Creswell, 1774–77*. London, 1924.

Crèvecoeur, Michel Guillaume Jean de. *Letters from an American Farmer*. London, 1782.

Crofutt, George A. *Transcontinental Tourist Guide*. 1871.

Crow, Hugh. *Memoirs of the Late Hugh Crow of Liverpool.* Frank Cass and Co., Ltd., 1970.

Dalby, David. *Black Through White: Patterns of Communication in Africa and the New World.* Hans Wolff Memorial Lecture. Bloomington, Indiana, 1969.

————. "The African Element in Black American English," in Thomas Kochman (ed.), *Rappin' and Stylin' Out.* University of Illinois Press, 1972.

Dana, Richard Henry. *Two Years Before the Mast.* New York, 1840.

Danker, Donald F. (ed.), *Mollie: The Journal of Mollie Dorsey Sanford in Nebraska and Colorado Territories, 1857–1866.* University of Nebraska Press, 1959.

Davis, A. L. (ed.). *Culture, Class, and Language Variety. A Resource Book for Teachers.* Urbana, Illinois, 1972.

Davis, John. *Travels of Four Years and a Half in the United States of America During 1798, 1799, 1800, 1801, and 1802.* New York, 1809.

DeCamp, David. "African Day-Names in Jamaica." *Language* 43 (1967), pp. 139–47.

D'Eloia, Sarah G. "Issues in the Analysis of Nonstandard Negro English: A Review of J. L. Dillard's *Black English.*" *Journal of English Linguistics* 7 (1973), pp. 87–106.

de Goeje, C. H. *Verslag der Toemoekhoemakexpeditie (Tumuchumachexpeditie).* Leiden, 1908.

de Granda, Germán. "Cimarronismos, Palenques, y Hablas 'Criollas' en Hispano America." Instituto Caro y Cuervo, Bogotá, 1970.

————. *Transculturación e Interferencia Lingüistica en el Puerto Rico Contemporáneo. (1898–1968).* Bogotá, 1972.

————. "Portuguésismos Léxicos en la 'Lengua Congo' de Cuba." *Boletín de Filología* XXII (1973), pp. 235–50.

————. "Papiamentu en Hispano America." Institute Caro y Cuervo, Bogotá, 1973.

————. "Estado Actual y Perspectivas de la Investigacion

sobre Hablas Criollas en Hispanoamerica." *Anuario de Letras* X (1972), pp. 5–27.

———. "De la Matrice Africaine de la 'Langue Congo' de Cuba." Centre de Hautes Etudes Afro-Ibero-Americaines, Université de Dakar, 1973.

Delattre, Genevieve. "The Changing Aspects of Teaching French," in Joseph S. Roucek (ed.), *The Study of Foreign Languages*. New York, 1968.

Dick, Everett N., *The Dixie Frontier*. New York, 1948.

———. *Vanguards of the Frontier*. 1941.

Dickinson, Jonathan. *Jonathan Dickinson's Journal; or, God's Protecting Providence, Being the Narrative of a Journey from Port Royal in Jamaica to Philadelphia between August 23, 1696, and April 1, 1697. New Haven, 1944.*

Dictionary of Canadianisms on Historical Principles, Toronto, 1967.

Dike, K. O. *Trade and Politics in the Niger Delta*. Oxford, 1956.

Dillard, J. L. "Principles in the History of American English: Paradox, Virginity, and Cafeteria." *Florida FL Reporter*, 1970.

———. "Creole English and Creole Portuguese: The Early Records." *Journal of African Languages*. Forthcoming.

———. Review of Courtney Cazden, Vera P. John, and Dell Hymes (eds.), *Functions of Language in the Classroom*. *Science*, May 11, 1973.

———. "American Negro Dialects: Convergence or Divergence?" *Florida FL Reporter*, 1968. Reprinted in Whitten and Szwed (eds.), *Afro-American Anthropology: Contemporary Perspectives*. New York, 1970.

———. "The History of Black English in Nova Scotia—A First Step." *African Language Review*, 1973.

———. "Lay My Isogloss Bundle Down: The Contribution of Black English to American Dialectology." *Linguistics* 119 (January 1974), pp. 5–14.

————. "On the Beginnings of Black English in the New World." *Orbis* XXI (1972), pp. 523–36.

————. "White Through Black: The Neglected Side of New World Communication Patterns." In Dennis Craig (ed.), *Proceedings of the Trinidad Conference on Creole Languages and Education.* Forthcoming.

————. "Standard Average Foreign in Puerto Rican Spanish," in E. Bagby Atwood and Archibald A. Hill (eds.), *Studies in Language, Literature, and Culture of the Middle Ages and Later.* University of Texas Press, 1969. Reprinted (under the title "Standard Average Foreign in Puerto Rico") in Richard W. Bailey and Jay L. Robinson (eds.), *Varieties of Present Day English.* New York, 1973.

————. "How Not to Classify the Folk Tales of the Antilles." *Caribbean Studies* 3 (1964), pp. 30–34.

————. "Creole Studies and American Dialectology." *Caribbean Studies* 4 (January 1973), pp. 76–91.

————, Mary Rita Miller, and William A. Stewart. "On Teaching Another Language as Part of Another Culture," in James W. Dodge (ed.), *Other Words, Other Worlds: Language-in-Culture.* Montpelier, Vermont, 1972.

————, and Charles Gilman. "Bamileke Phonological Interference on the Learning of English." *Cameroon Review of Education* 4 (1965).

Dollard, John. *Class and Caste in a Southern Town.* New Haven, 1937.

Dorson, Richard M. *Negro Folk Tales from Pine Bluff, Arkansas, and Calvin, Michigan.* Indiana University Folklore Series No. 23, Bloomington, 1958.

————. *Negro Folk Tales in Michigan.* Cambridge, Massachusetts, 1956.

Drechsel, Emanuel J. "An Essay on Pidginization and Creolization of American Indian Languages." *International Journal of the Sociology of Language.* Forthcoming.

Dresel, Gustav. *Houston Journal.* Translated from German by Max Freund. Texas University Press, 1954.

Drotning, Philip T. *Black Heroes in Our Nation's History.* New York, 1969.

Dulles, Foster Rhea. *The Old China Trade.* Boston, 1930.

Dundes, Alan (ed.). *Mother Wit from the Laughing Barrel. Readings in the Interpretation of Afro-American Folklore.* Englewood Cliffs, New Jersey, 1973.

Dunn, Milton, "History of Nachitoches." *The Louisiana Historical Quarterly* III (1920): 26–56.

Durham, Philip L., and Everett L. Jones. *The Negro Cowboys.* New York, 1965.

Earle, Alice Morse. *Child-Life in Colonial Days.* New York, 1899.

Ellis, William. *A Narrative of a Tour Through Hawaii, or Owhyhee; with Remarks on the History, Traditions, Manners, Customs, and Language of the Inhabitants of the Sandwich Islands.* Honolulu, 1917.

Elworthy, Frederic Thomas. *The Dialect of West Somerset.* Kraus Reprint. Ltd., 1965.

Escabi, Pedro C. (ed.). *Morovis: Vista Parcial del Folklore de Puerto Rico.* Universidad de Puerto Rico, Centro de Investigaciones Sociales, n.d.

Escalante, Aquilas. "Notas sobre el Palenque de San Basilio, una Comunidad Negro en Colombia." *Divulgaciones Etnologicas* 3 (1954), pp. 207–359.

Falconbridge, Anna Maria. *Two Voyages to Sierra Leone.* London, 1794.

Falconer, William. *The Mariner's Dictionary,* 1805.

Farrison, William Edward. *The Phonology of the Illiterate Negro Dialect of Guilford County, North Carolina.* Ohio State University dissertation, 1936.

Fasold, Ralph and Roger W. Shuy (eds.). *Teaching Standard English in the Inner City.* Washington, D.C., 1970.

Feinsilver, Lillian Mermin. *The Taste of Yiddish.* New York, 1970.

Ferguson, Charles. "Diglossia." *Word* 15 (1959), pp. 325–40.

334

————, Joshua Fishman, and J. das Gupta (eds.), *Language Problems of Developing Nations*. New York, 1968.

Ferguson, William. *America by River and Rail*. London, 1856.

Fisher, Ruth. *Extracts from the Records of the African Companies*. Washington, D.C., 1924.

Fisher, Sydney G. *The Quaker Colonies, A Chronicle of the Proprietors of the Delaware*. New Haven, 1919.

Fishman, Joshua A. (ed.). *Readings in the Sociology of Language*. The Hague, 1968.

————. "The Breadth and Depth of English in the United States," in Aarons, Gordon, and Stewart (eds.), *Linguistic-Cultural Differences and American Education (The Florida FL Reporter*, Vol. 7, No. 1, Spring/Summer 1969).

————. *Language Loyalty in the United States*. The Hague 1966.

————. "Language Maintenance and Language Shift as Fields of Inquiry." *Linguistics* 9 (1964), pp. 32–70.

————. "Who Speaks What Language to Whom and When?" *La Linguistique* 2 (1965), pp. 67–88.

————, R. L. Cooper, Roxana Ma, et al. (eds.). *Bilingualism in the Barrio*. Final Report to DHEW under contract no. OEC-1-7-061817-0297, New York.

Flick, Alexander C. (ed.). *History of the State of New York*. 10 vols. Columbia University Press, 1933.

Forbes, Jack D. *Mexican-Americans, A Handbook for Educators*. 1966.

Foreman, Grant. "Notes from the Indian Advocate." *Chronicles of Oklahoma* 14 (1926), pp. 76–79.

Fortier, Alcée. "The Acadians of Louisiana and their Dialect." *Publications of the Modern Language Association* VI (1891), pp. 1–33.

Frake, Charles O. "Lexical Origins and Semantic Structures in Philippine Creole Spanish." in Dell Hymes (ed.), *Pidginization and Creolization of Languages*, Cambridge University Press, 1971.

Francis, W. Nelson. "Some Dialectal Verb Forms in England." *Orbis.* 1961.

————. *The English Language, An Introduction.* New York, 1963.

Frank, Helena. *Yiddish Tales.* The Jewish Publication Society. Philadelphia, 1912.

Franklin, Benjamin. "Information to Those Who Would Remove to America," in *Writings* (ed. Smythe), Vol. VIII.

Frazier, E. Franklin, *Black Bourgeoisie: The Rise of a New Middle Class.* New York, 1957.

Fyfe, Christopher. *History of Sierra Leone.* Freetown, 1962.

Garrell, Julia Kathryn. *Green Flag Over Texas.* Dallas, 1939.

Garvin, Paul. "The Standard Language Problem: Concepts and Methods." *Anthropological Linguistics* 1 (1959), pp. 28–31.

Giddings, Joshua R. *The Exiles of Florida.* Columbus, Ohio, 1858.

Goilo, E. R. *Papiamentu Textbook,* Aruba, 1962.

Gonzales, Ambrose. *The Black Border.* Columbia, South Carolina, 1964.

Goveia, Elsa V. *Slave Society in the British Leeward Islands at the End of the Eighteenth Century.* Yale University Press, 1965.

Graham, Stephen. "The American Language," in *With Poor Immigrants to America.* New York, 1914.

Granville, Stuart. *Forty Years on the Frontier* (edited by Paul C. Phillips). Cleveland, 1925.

Granville, Wilfred. *A Dictionary of Sailors' Slang.* London, 1962.

Greaves, Ida C. *The Negro in Canada.* McGill Economic Studies, 1930.

Green, Lawrence G. *Islands Time Forgot.* London, 1962.

Greenberg, Joseph. *Universals of Language.* Cambridge, Massachusetts, 1963.

Greene, Lorenzo J. "Slave Holding New England and Its

Awakening." *Journal of Negro History* XII (1942), pp. 492–533.

———. *The Negro in Colonial New England 1620–1776.* Columbia University Studies in History, Economics, and Public Law No. 494, 1942.

Greenough, James B., and George L. Kittredge. *Words and Their Ways in English Speech.* New York, 1920.

Gregg, Josiah. *The Commerce of the Prairies.* 1844.

Grose, Francis. *A Classical Dictionary of the Vulgar Tongue.* London, 1785.

Gumperz, John. "Dialect and Social Stratification in a North Indian Village." *American Anthropologist* 60 (1958), pp. 668–92.

———. "Phonological Differences in Three Hindi Dialects." *Language* 34 (1958), pp. 212–24.

———. "Speech Variation and the Study of Indian Civilization." *American Anthropologist* 63 (1961), pp. 976–88.

Haliburton, Thomas Chandler (pseudonym Sam Slick). *The Clockmaker; or, the Sayings and Doings of Sam Slick of Slickville.* Philadelphia, 1840.

Hall, R. M. R., and Beatrice Hall. "Creole Conspiracies and Convergences: Why Definitive Answers are Hard to Find," in J. L. Dillard (ed.), *Current Trends in the Study of Black English in the New World.* The Hague, forthcoming.

Hall, Robert A., Jr. *Pidgin and Creole Languages.* Cornell University Press, 1966.

———. *Hands Off Pidgin English!* New South Wales, Pacific Publications, 1955.

———. *Melanesian Pidgin English: Grammar, Texts.* Baltimore, Waverly Press, 1943.

———. "Pidgin English and Linguistic Change." *Lingua* 3 (1953), pp. 138–46.

———. "How We Noun-incorporate in English." *American Speech* 31 (1956), pp. 83–88.

———. "The Life-cycle of Pidgin Languages." *Lingua* 11 (1962), pp. 151–56.

Hamilton, Alexander. *Hamilton's Itinerarium, Being a Narrative of a Journey from Annapolis, Maryland . . . from May to September, 1744.* St. Louis, Missouri, 1907.

Hamilton, Thomas. *Men and Manners in America.* Philadelphia. 1833.

Hancock, Ian F. "Lexical Expansion Outside a Closed System." *Journal of African Languages* XII (1973).

———. "A Domestic Origin for the English-Derived Atlantic Creoles." *Florida FL Reporter,* 1972.

———. *A Study of the Sources and Development of the Lexicon of Sierra Leone Krio,* University of London dissertation, 1970.

———. "Nautical Sources of Krio Vocabulary." *International Journal of the Sociology of Language.* Forthcoming.

———. "Malacca Creole Portuguese," in Dennis Craig (ed.), *Proceedings of the Conference on Creole Languages and Educational Development.* Forthcoming.

———. "Some Aspects of English in Liberia." *Liberian Studies Journal* III (1970–71), pp. 207–13.

Handler, Jerome S., and Charlotte J. Frisbie. "Aspects of Slave Life in Barbados: Music and Its Cultural Aspects." *Caribbean Studies* II (1972), pp. 5–46.

Hansen, Marcus Lee. *The Atlantic Migration 1607–1860; A History of the Continuing Settlement of the United States.* Harvard University Press, 1940.

———. *The Immigrant in American History.* Harvard University Press, 1940.

Harrison, J. W. "Negro English." *Anglia,* 1884.

Haskins, Jim, and Hugh F. Butts. *The Psychology of Black Language.* New York, 1973.

Haugen, Einar. *Bilingualism in the Americas: A Bibliography and Research Guide.* University of Alabama, 1956.

———. "Language Contact," in *Proceedings of the Eighth International Congress of Linguists.* Oslo, 1958.

———. *The Norwegian Language in America: A Study of Bilingual Behavior.* University of Pennsylvania Press, 1953.

Hayward, Jane Screven. *Brown Jackets.* Columbia, South Carolina, 1923.

Herlein, J. D. *Beschryvinge van de Volksplantingne Zuriname.* Leeuwarden, 1718.

Herman, Lewis, and Marguerite Shalett Herman. *Foreign Dialects: A Manual for Actors, Directors, and Writers.* New York, 1943.

———. *American Dialects for Actors, Directors, and Writers.* New York, 1947.

Hernandez, William J., and Henry S. Johnson. *Educating the Mexican American.* Valley Forge, Pennsylvania, 1971.

Herskovits, Melville J. *The Myth of the Negro Past.* Boston, 1942.

———, and Frances Herskovits. *Suriname Folk-Lore.* Columbia University Contributions to Anthropology, 27, 1936.

Hills, E. C. "Linguistic Substrata of American English." *American Speech* 4 (1929), pp. 431–33.

Hitchcock, Ethan Allen. *A Traveller in Indian Territory.* Cedar Rapids, Iowa, 1930.

Hobart, Benjamin. *A History of the Town of Abingdon, Plymouth County, Massachusetts.* Boston, 1866.

Hockett, Charles F. *A Course in Modern Linguistics.* New York, 1958.

Hoenigswald, Henry M. *Language Change and Linguistic Reconstruction.* University of Chicago Press, 1960.

Horsmanden, Daniel P. *The New York Conspiracy, or a History of the Negro Plot, with the Journal of the Proceedings against the Conspirators at New-York in the Years 1741–2.* New York, 1744.

Hubbard, Claude. "The Language of Ruxton's Mountain Men." *American Speech,* 1968.

Hulbert, Archer B. *Frontiers, the Genius of American Nationality.* Boston, 1929.

Hymes, Dell (ed.). *Pidginization and Creolization of Languages.* Cambridge University Press, 1971.

Ingraham, Joseph Holt. *The Southwest by a Yankee.* New York, 1835.

Jackson, Kenneth. *Language and History in Early Britain.* University of Edinburgh Press, 1953.

James, G. L. *Shall I Try Australia?* London, 1892.

Janson, Charles William. *Stranger in America.* London, 1807.

Jespersen, Otto. *Mankind, Nation and Individual from a Linguistic Point of View.* Bloomington, Indiana, 1964.

Jones, E. C. "Mid-nineteenth Century Evidences of a Sierra Leone Patois." *Sierra Leone Language Review* I (1962), pp. 19–26.

Jones, Morgan E. *A Phonological Study of English as Spoken by Puerto Ricans Contrasted with Puerto Rican Spanish and American English.* University of Michigan dissertation, 1962.

Joyaux, Georges J. "Foreign Languages and the Humanities." *The Modern Language Journal* XLIX (February 1965).

Kahane, Henri, Renee Kahane, and A. Tietze. *The Lingua Franca in the Levant, Turkish Nautical Terms of Italian and Greek Origin.* Urbana, Illinois, 1958.

Katz, William Loren. *The Black West.* Garden City, N.Y. 1971.

Kelley, A. Tabouret. "Sociological Factors of Language Maintenance and Shift," in Charles A. Ferguson, Joshua A. Fishman, and J. das Gupta (eds.), *Language Problems of Developing Nations.* New York, 1968.

Kendall, George Wilkins. *Narrative of the Texan Santa Fé Expedition.* New York, 1846.

King, Robert D. *Historical Linguistic and Generative Grammar.* Englewood Cliffs, New Jersey, 1969.

Krapp, George Philip. *The English Language in America.* New York, 1925.

Kurath, Hans. "The Origin of Dialectal Differences in Spoken

American English." *Modern Philology* XXV (1928), pp. 385–95.

———. "The Linguistic Atlas of the United States and Canada," in D. B. Fry and Daniel Jones (eds.), *Proceedings of the Second International Conference of Phonetic Sciences*. 1936.

———. "Some Aspects of Atlantic Seaboard English Considered in Connection with British English." *Communications et Rapports, Troisième Partie*. Louvain, 1965.

———, "The Investigation of Urban Speech." Publications of the American Dialect Society 49 (April 1968), pp. 1–7.

———. "Dialect Areas, Settlement Areas, and Cultural Areas in the United States," in C. F. Ware (ed.), *The Cultural Approach to History*, New York.

———. "Linguistic Regionalism," in Merrill Jenson (ed.), *Regionalism in America*. University of Wisconsin Press, 1952.

———. "English Sources of Some American Regional Words and Verb Forms." *American Speech*, 1969, pp. 60–68

Labov, William. *The Social Stratification of English in New York City*, Washington, D.C., 1966.

———. "Contraction, Deletion, and Inherent Variability of the English Copula." *Language* 45 (1969), pp. 715–62.

———. "The Social Motivation of a Sound Change." *Word* 19 (1963), pp. 273–309.

———. "On the Mechanism of Linguistic Change," in C. W. Kreidler (ed.), *Report of the Sixteenth Annual Round Table Meeting Linguistics and Language Studies*. Georgetown University Press, 1965.

———. *Language in the Inner City*. University of Pennsylvania Press, 1972.

———. *Sociolinguistic Patterns*. University of Pennsylvania Press, 1972.

———. "The Linguistic Consequences of Being a Lame." *Language in Society* 2 (1973), pp. 81–116.

———. "Academic Ignorance and Black Intelligence." *Atlantic Monthly* 229 (June 1972), pp. 59–67.

———, Paul Cohen, Clarence Robins, and John Lewis. *A Study of the Non-Standard English of Negro and Puerto Rican Speakers in New York City.* U.S. Office of Education, Cooperative Research Project No. 3288, Final Report, 1968.

Laird, Charlton. *Language in America.* New York, 1970.

Layton, C. W. T. *Dictionary of Nautical Words and Terms.* Glasgow, 1955.

Leckie, William H. *The Buffalo Soldiers.* University of Oklahoma Press, 1967.

Leechman, Douglas, and Robert A. Hall, Jr. "American Indian Pidgin English: Attestations and Grammatical Peculiarities." *American Speech* 30 (1955), pp. 163–71.

Lehmann, W. P. *Descriptive Linguistics, An Introduction.* New York, 1972.

———. *Historical Linguistics, An Introduction.* New York, 1962.

———. *Proto-Indo-European Phonology.* University of Texas Press, 1952.

Leland, John. *Pidgin English Sing-Song.* London, 1900.

Lentzner, Karl. *Worterbuch der Englischen Volkssprache in Australien und einiger Englische Mischsprachen.* Halle-Leipzig, 1892.

Leonard, John William. *History of the City of New York.* New York, 1910.

Leopold, Werner F. "The Decline of German Dialects." *Word* 15 (1959), pp. 130–53.

LePage, Robert B. (ed.). *Proceedings of the Conference on Creole Language Studies* (Creole Language Studies II). London, 1961.

———, and David DeCamp. *Jamaican Creole* (Creole Language Studies I). London, 1960.

"Letters of Rev. Jonathan Boucher." *Maryland Historical Magazine* X (1916) , pp. 15–36.

Levitt, John, and Joan Levitt. *The Spell of Words.* London, 1959.

Lifson, David S. *The Yiddish Press—An Americanizing Agency.* New York, 1969.

Lindquist, Gustavus E. *The Red Man in the United States.* New York, 1923.

Lomax, Alan. *The Rainbow Sign.* New York, 1959.

Lopes, David. *A Extensão do Português na Oriente.* Lisbon, 1936.

Luelsdorff, Philip A. *A Segmental Phonology of Black English.* Georgetown University dissertation, 1970.

Mackay, Alex. *The Western World, or Travels in the United States in 1846–7.* London, 1850.

Malmstrom, Jean, and Annabel Ashley. *Dialects—USA.* Champaign, Illinois, 1963.

Marckwardt, Albert H. *American English.* New York, 1958.

Marcy, Colonel R. B. *Thirty Years of Army Life on the Border.* New York, 1866.

Markman, Alan M., and Erwin R. Steinberg. *English Then and Now: Readings and Exercises.* New York, 1970.

Marly; or the Life of a Planter in Jamaica. Glasgow, 1828.

Mason, Julian. "The Etymology of *Buckaroo.*" *American Speech* XXV (1960), pp. 51–55.

Mathews, Mitford M. (ed.). *A Dictionary of Americanisms on Historical Principles.* University of Chicago Press, 1951.

———. *Some Sources of Southernisms.* University of Alabama Press, 1948.

———. *The Beginnings of American English.* University of Chicago Press, 1931.

Matthews, W. "Sailors' Pronunciation in the Second Half of the Seventeenth Century." *Anglia* 1935.

———. "Sailors' Pronunciation, 1770–1783." *Anglia*, 1937.

Maynarde, Thomas (ed.). *Sir Francis Drake: His Voyages 1595.* Hakluyt Society, 1849.

McCulloch, Walter P. *Woods Words: A Comprehensive Dic-*

tionary of Logging Terms. The Oregon Historical Society and the Champoeg Press, 1958.

McDavid, Raven I., Jr. "Historical, Regional, and Social Variation." *Journal of English Linguistics* 1 (1967), pp. 24–40.

———. "The Position of the Charleston Dialect." *Publications of the American Dialect Society,* 1955.

———. "Addendum" to McDavid and McDavid, 1951, in Walter Wolfram and Nona R. Clarke (eds.), *Black-White Speech Relationships,* Washington, D.C., 1971.

———, and Virginia Glenn McDavid. "The Relationship of the Speech of American Negroes to the Speech of Whites." *American Speech* 26 (1951), pp. 3–17.

———, and Raymond K. O'Cain. "Sociolinguistics and Linguistic Geography." *Kansas Journal of Sociology* 9 (1973), pp. 137–56.

McLaughlin, John C. *Aspects of the History of English.* New York, 1970.

McReynolds, Edwin C. *The Seminoles.* Norman, Oklahoma, 1957.

Mead, Margaret. *New Lives for Old: Cultural Transformation—Manus 1928–1953.* New York, 1966.

Mencken, Henry Louis. *The American Language.* New York, 1919. Second Edition, 1921. Third Edition, 1923. Fourth Edition, 1936. Supplement One, 1945. Supplement Two, 1948.

Meredith, Mamie. "Longfellow's Excelsior Done Into Pidgin English." *American Speech* IV (1929), pp. 148–51.

Miller, Mary Rita. "Attestations of American Indian Pidgin English in Fiction and Non-Fiction." *American Speech* (May) 1967, pp. 142–47.

Mitchell, A. G. *The Pronunciation of English in Australia.* Sydney, 1946.

Molloy, Robert. *Charleston: A Gracious Heritage.*

Morgan, Raleigh, Jr. "Structural Sketch of St. Martin Creole." *Anthropological Linguistics* 1 (1959), pp. 20–24.

―――. "The Lexicon of Saint Martin Creole." *Anthropological Linguistics* 2 (1960), pp. 7–29.

Morrison, Samuel Eliot. *The Maritime History of Massachusetts,* Boston, 1961.

Murray, J. A. H., et al. (eds.). *Oxford English Dictionary.* Oxford University Press, 1884–1928, 1933.

"My Name Is Norval." Quoted in Samuel Bowles, *Our New West.* Hartford, 1869, pp. 37–38.

Nash, Rose. "The Emergence of a New Variety of English in Puerto Rico." Manuscript.

―――. *Readings in Spanish and English Contrastive Linguistics.* Hato Rey, Puerto Rico, 1973.

Nathan, Hans. *Dan Emmett and the Rise of Early Negro Minstrelsy.* University of Oklahoma Press, 1962.

Navarro Tomás, Tomás. "Observaciones sobre el Papiamentu." *Nueva Revista de la Filología Española* VII (1951).

―――. *El Español en Puerto Rico.* Río Piedras, Puerto Rico, 1948.

Nee, Victor G., and DeBary Nee. *Longtime Californ': A Documentary Study of an American Chinatown.* New York, 1972.

Nida, Eugene, and Harold Fehdereau. "Indigenous Pidgins and Koinés." *International Journal of American Linguistics* 37 (1971).

Norton, A. Banning. *History of Knox County, Ohio.* Columbus, 1862.

Norton, Thomas. *New England Canaan.* 1632.

O'Hara, John. *From the Terrace.* New York, 1958.

Oliva, Peter F. "Modern Trends in Foreign Languages," in Joseph S. Roucek (ed.), *The Study of Foreign Languages.* New York, 1968.

Orbeck, Anders. *Early New England Pronunciation.* Ann Arbor, Michigan, 1927.

Osgood, Cornelius (ed.). *Linguistic Structures of Native America.* New York, 1946.

Otheguy, Ricardo. "Linguistic Arguments in the Determination of Creole Typology: The Case of 'Habla Bozal Antillana,' " in C.-J. N. Bailey and Roger W. Shuy (eds.), *New Ways of Analyzing Variability in English,* Georgetown University Press, 1973.

Ottley, Roy, and William J. Weatherby. *The Negro in New York, An Informal Social History.* New York, 1967.

Owen, W. F. W. *Voyages to Explore the Shores of Africa, Arabia, and Madagascar.* New York, 1833.

Partridge, Eric. *A Dictionary of Slang and Unconventional Usage.* 6th Ed., New York, 1967.

——, and John W. Clark, *British and American English Since 1900.* London, 1951.

Paullin, Charles, and John K. Wright. *Atlas of the Historical Geography of the United States.* Washington, D.C., 1932.

Payzant, Henry Young. *People: A Story of the People of Nova Scotia.* Bridgewater, Nova Scotia, 1935.

Pedersen, Lee, Raven I. McDavid, Jr., William Foster, and Charles E. Billard (eds.), *A Manual for Dialect Research in the Southern States.* Atlanta, 1972.

Peerless Four. "Noah," on *The Eastern Shores.* Prestige/International LP 25008.

Pei, Mario. *The Story of Language.* Philadelphia, 1949.

Pérez Moris, José, and D. Luis Cueto y Gonzalez, *Historia de la Insurrección de Lares,* Barcelona, 1872.

Pérez Sala, Paulino. *Interferencia Lingüistica del Inglés en el Español Hablado en Puerto Rico.* San Juan, 1973.

Perry, Bliss. *The American Spirit in Education, A Chronicle of Great Interpreters. Chronicles of America Series,* Volume 34, 1918.

Peters, Robert A. *A Linguistic History of English.* Boston, 1968.

Pickford, Glenna Ruth. "American Linguistic Geography: A Sociological Appraisal." *Word* 12 (1956), pp. 211–29.

Plooij, D., D.D. *The Pilgrim Fathers from a Dutch Point of View.* New York, 1952.

Pop, Sever. *La Dialectologie. Aperçu Historique et Methods de Enquêtes Linguistiques.* Louvain, 1950.

Poquelin, Jean Baptiste (pseudonym Molière). *Le Bourgeois Gentilhomme,* 1665.

Porter, Kenneth Wiggins. *The Negro on the American Frontier.* New York, 1970.

———. "Relations Between Negroes and Indians Within the Present Limits of the United States." *Journal of Negro History* 17 (1932), pp. 287–367.

———. "Abraham." *Phylon* 2 (1941), pp. 107–16.

———. "Florida Slaves and Free Negroes in the Seminole War, 1835–1842." *Journal of Negro History* 28 (1943), pp. 390–421.

———. "Three Fighters for Freedom." *Journal of Negro History* 28 (1943), pp. 51–72.

———. "Notes on Seminole Negroes in the Bahamas." *Florida Historical Quarterly* 24 (1945), pp. 56–60.

———. "John Caesar: Seminole Negro Partisan." *Journal of Negro History* 31 (1946), pp. 190–207.

———. "Negroes and Indians on the Texas Frontier, 1831–1876." *Journal of Negro History* 41 (1956), pp. 185–214, 285–310.

Price, Richard. "Avenging Spirits and the Structure of Saramaka Lineages." in *Bijdragen tot de Taal-, Land-, en Volkenkunde,* 1973.

———. *Maroon Societies: Rebel Slave Communities in the United States.* Garden City, New York, 1973.

Prince, J. Dyneley. "An Ancient New Jersey Indian Jargon." *American Anthropologist* 14 (1912), pp. 508–24.

———. "Jersey Dutch." *Dialect Notes* III (1910), pp. 459–69.

Puckett, Newbell Niles. *Folk Beliefs of the Southern Negro.* Chapel Hill, North Carolina, 1926.

Putnam, George N., and Edna O'Hern. "The Status Significance of an Isolated Urban Dialect." *Language* 34 (1955).

Pyles, Thomas. *Words and Ways in American English.* New York, 1952.

————. *The Origins and Development of the English Language*. New York, 1964.

Rawick, George P. (ed.). *The American Slave: A Composite Autobiography*. 19 Vols. Contributions in Afro-American Studies, 1972.

Ray, Punya Sloka. *Language Standardization*. The Hague, 1963.

Read, Allen Walker. "British Recognition of American Speech in the Eighteenth Century." *Dialect Notes* 6 (1933), pp. 313–34.

————. "Assimilation of the Speech of British Immigrants in Colonial America." *Journal of English and Germanic Philology* 37 (1938), pp. 70–79.

————. "English of Indians, 1705–1745." *American Speech* 16 (1941), pp. 72–74.

Read, Kenneth E. *The High Valley*. New York, 1965.

Read, William A. *Louisiana French*. Louisiana State University Press, 1963.

Reed, Carroll E. *Dialects of American English*. Cleveland, 1967.

Reinecke, John. *Language and Dialect in Hawaii*. University of Hawaii Press, 1969.

Reinstein, S. and J. Hoffman. "Dialect Interaction Between Black and Puerto Rican Children in New York City: Implications for Language Arts." *Elementary English* 49 (1972), pp. 190–96.

Rens, L. L. E. *The Historical and Social Background of Surinam Negro-English*. Amsterdam, 1953.

Richardson, A. D. *Beyond the Mississippi*. Hartford, 1865.

Robertson, Stuart F., and Frederic G. Cassidy. *The Development of Modern English*. 2nd Edition. Englewood Cliffs, New Jersey, 1954.

Ross, A., and A. Moverley. *The Pitcairnese Language*. London, 1964.

Rosten, Leo. *The Joys of Yiddish*. New York, 1968.

Roucek, Joseph S. *The Study of Foreign Languages.* New York, 1968.

Rowe, J. R. "Archaeological Dating and Cultural Process." *Southwestern Journal of Anthropology* 15 (1959), pp. 317–24.

Rusling, Brigadier General James F. *Across America; or, the Great West and the Pacific Coast.* New York, 1875.

Salmora, Julian. *La Raza: Forgotten Americans.* South Bend, 1966.

Sawyer, Janet B. "Aloofness from Spanish Influence in Texas English." *Word* 15 (1959), pp. 270–81.

Schneider, Gilbert D. *Dey Don Klin; Rida Nomba Fo.* Mimeographed, 1964.

———. *First Steps in Wes-Kos.* Hartford, 1963.

———. *Wes-Kos Proverbs, Idioms, Names.* Mimeographed, 1965.

———. *West African Pidgin English.* Hartford Seminary Foundation dissertation, 1966.

———. *West African Pidgin English: An Historical Overview.* Ohio University: Papers in International Studies, No. 8 (1967).

Schuchardt, Hugo. "Die Lingua Franca." *Zeitschrift für Romanische Philologie* XXXIII (1909), pp. 441–61.

———. *Die Sprache der Saramakkaneger in Surinam.* Amsterdam, 1914.

Schur, Norman. *British Self-Taught, with Comments in American.* New York, 1973.

Scott, Charles T., and J. L. Erickson. *Readings for the History of the English Language.* Boston, 1968.

Shakespeare, William. *The Life of Henry the Fifth.* In Helge Kökeritz (ed.), facsimile edition, *Mr. William Shakespeare's Comedies, Histories, & Tragedies.* Yale University Press, 1954.

Sheard, J. A. *The Words of English.* New York, 1966.

Sheldon, E. S. "What is a Dialect?" *Dialect Notes* I (1892), p. 293.

Sheldon, George. *A History of Deerfield, Massachusetts*. Deerfield, 1895–6.

Shuy, Roger W. *Discovering American Dialects*. National Council of Teachers of English, 1967.

——. *The Northern-Midland Dialect Boundary in Illinois*. Publications of the American Dialect Society, No. 38 (1962).

Silverman, Stuart H. *The Effects of Peer Group Membership on Puerto Rican English*. Ferkauf Graduate School of Yeshiva University dissertation, 1971.

Silverstein, Michael. "Dynamics of Recent Linguistic Contact." In I. Goddard (ed.), *Handbook of North American Indians*, Vol. XVI: Languages. Forthcoming.

——. "Chinook Jargon: Language Contact and the Problem of Multi-Level Generative Systems." *Language* 48 (1972), pp. 378–406, 596–625.

Sledd, James. "Breaking, Umlaut, and the Southern Drawl." *Language* 42 (1966), pp. 18–41.

Sloson, Edwin F. *The American Spirit in Education*. Chronicles of America Series, Vol. 33 (1918).

Smith, David, and Roger W. Shuy (eds.), *Sociolinguistics in Cross-cultural Analysis*. Washington, D.C., 1972.

Smith, William. *A New Voyage to Guinea*. London, 1744.

Smyth, J. F. D. *A Tour of the United States of America*. London, 1784.

Sommerfelt, Alf. "The Origin of Language: Theses and Hypotheses." *Journal of World History* 1 (1954), pp. 885–902.

Spencer, J. *The English Language in West Africa*. London, 1971.

——. *Language in Africa. Papers of the Leverhulme Conference on Universities and the Language Problems of Tropical Africa*. Cambridge University Press, 1963.

Spicer, Edward H. *Cycles of Conquest; the Impact of Spain, Mexico, and the United States on Indians of the Southwest*. University of Arizona Press, 1962.

Springer, Otto. "The Study of Pennsylvania German Dialect." *Journal of English and Germanic Philology* XLII (1943), pp. 1–39.

Stearns, Marshall. *The Story of Jazz.* New York, 1956.

———, and Jean Stearns. *Jazz Dance: A History of Dancing to Jazz, from Its African Origins to the Present.* New York, 1968.

Stevick, Robert D. *English and Its History. The Evolution of a Language.* Boston, 1968.

Stewart, William A. "Creole Languages in the Caribbean." In F. A. Rice (ed.), *Study of the Role of Second Languages in Asia, Africa, and Latin America.* Washington, D.C. 1962.

———. "The Functional Distribution of French and Creole in Haiti." Georgetown University Monograph Series on Languages and Linguistics No. 15 (1962).

———. "Sociolinguistic Factors in the History of American Negro Dialects." *Florida FL Reporter,* 1967.

———. "Continuity and Change in American Negro Dialects." *Florida FL Reporter,* 1968.

———. "Sociopolitical Issues in the Linguistic Treatment of Negro Dialect." Report of the 20th Round Table, Georgetown University, 1970.

———. "Acculturative Processes and the Language of the American Negro," in W. Gage (ed.), *Language in Its Social Setting.* Washington, D.C., forthcoming.

———. "A Sociolinguistic Typology for Describing National Multilingualism," in Joshua A. Fishman (ed.), *Readings in the Sociology of Language.* The Hague, 1968.

Stokes, I. N. Phelps. *The Iconography of Manhattan Island.* 6 Vols. New York, 1915–28.

Stowe, Harriet Beecher. "Sojourner Truth: The Libyan Sibyl." *Atlantic Monthly,* 1863, pp. 473–81.

Struble, George C. "The English of the Pennsylvania Germans." *American Speech* X (1935), pp. 163–72.

Stuart, Granville. *Montana As It Is.* New York, 1865.

Sturtevant, Edgar. *Linguistic Change.* University of Chicago Press, 1917.

———. *Introduction to Linguistic Science.* New Haven, 1949.

Sullivan, James Patrick. *Interference, Integration, and Shift: The Genesis of Anglo-Irish.* Ferkauf Graduate School, Yeshiva University, dissertation, 1974.

Szass, Ferenc M. "The New York Slave Revolt of 1741: A Re-Examination." *New York History* XLXIII (1967).

Tate, Charles Montgomery. *Chinook as Spoken by the Indians of Washington Territory, British Columbia, and Alaska.* Victoria, 1889.

Taylor, Douglas McRae. "New Languages for Old in the West Indies." *Comparative Studies in Society and History* 3 (1961), pp. 155–61.

———. "Language Shift or Changing Relationship?" *International Journal of American Linguistics* 26 (1960), pp. 155–61.

———. "Language Contacts in the West Indies." *Word* 12 (1956), pp. 391–414.

———. Review of *Spanish Contact Vernaculars in the Philippine Islands,* by Keith Whinnom. *Word* 13 (1957), pp. 489–99.

———. "The Origin of West Indian Creole Languages: Evidence from Grammatical Categories." *American Anthropologist* 65 (1963), pp. 800–14.

———. Review of *Jamaican Creole,* by Robert B. LePage and David DeCamp. *Language* 39 (1963), pp. 316–22.

The Religious Intelligencer. New Haven, Connecticut, 1821.

Thomas, Charles K. "Recent Discussion of Standardization in American Pronunciation." *Quarterly Journal of Speech* XII (1927), pp. 442–57.

Thompson, Robert W. "A Note on Some Possible Affinities Between the Creole Dialects of the Old World and the New." In LePage (ed.), *Creole Studies II,* 1961.

Thornbrough, Emma Lou. *The Negro in Indiana.* Indiana Historical Bureau, 1957.

Thorpe, Thomas Bangs. *The Hive of the "Beehunter."* New York, 1854.

Thurman, Sue Bailey. *Pioneers of Negro Origin in California.* San Francisco, 1952.

Tinker, Edward Larocque. "Creole Comes to Philadelphia." *American Antiquarian Society Proceedings* 67 (1957), pp. 50–76.

―――. *Gombo: The Creole Dialect of Louisiana. Together with a Bibliography.* Worcester, Massachusetts, 1936.

―――. "Louisiana Gombo." *The Yale Review,* New Series, XXI (1932), pp. 566–79.

Tocqueville, Alexis de. *Democracy in America.* 1835.

Tovar, Ant. "Linguistics and Prehistory." *Word* X (1954), pp. 333–50.

Traugott, Elizabeth Closs. "Pidginization, Creolization, and the 'Naturalness' Hypothesis." Papers of the IXth International Congress of the Anthropological and Ethnological Sciences. 1973.

―――. *A History of English Syntax.* New York, 1972.

―――. "Principles in the History of American English—A Reply." *Florida FL Reporter,* 1972.

Tucker, G. Richard and Wallace A. Lambert. "White and Negro Listeners' Reactions to Various American-English Dialects." *Social Forces* 47 (June 1969), pp. 463–68.

Tucker, Gilbert M. *American English.* New York, 1921.

Turner, Frederick Jackson. *Rise of the New West* in *The American Nation: A History.* 1906.

Turner, G. W. *The English Language in Australia and New Zealand.* London, 1966.

Turner, Lorenzo Dow. *Africanisms in the Gullah Dialect.* University of Chicago Press, 1949.

Underwood, Gary N. "Vocabulary Change in the Upper Midwest." *Publications of the American Dialect Society* 49 (1968), pp. 8–28.

Valkhoff, Marius. *Studies in Portuguese and Creole.* Witwatersrand University Press, 1966.

353

————. "Contributions to the Study of Creole," *African Studies* 19 (1960), pp. 77–87.

Van Wijk, H. A. "Origenes y Evolución del Papiamentu." *Neophilologus* XLII (1958).

Vendryes, J. *Le Langage*. Paris, 1923.

Viereck, Wolfgang. "The Growth of Dialectology." *Journal of English Linguistics* 7 (March 1973), pp. 69–86.

Vogel, Virgil L. *American Indian Medicine*. Norman, Oklahoma, 1970.

Voorhoeve, Jan. "Historical and Linguistic Evidence in Favor of the Relexification Theory in the Formation of Creoles." *Language in Society* II (1973), pp. 133–46.

Wade, Richard C. *The Urban Frontier*. University of Chicago Press, 1959.

Wagner, Max Leopold. *Lingue e Dialette dell'America Spagnole*. Florence, 1949.

"War Bow—Poet—Philosopher and Farmer." *Chronicles of Oklahoma* XV (1937), pp. 223–24.

Warner, Maureen. "Trinidad Yoruba—Notes on Survivals." *Caribbean Quarterly* 17 (June 1971), pp. 40–49.

Warner, W. Lloyd, Marchia Meeker, and Kenneth Ealls. *Social Class in America*. New York, 1960.

Waterman, John D. *Perspectives in Linguistics*. University of Chicago Press, 1970.

Weinreich, Uriel. "Is a Structural Dialectology Possible?" *Word* 10 (1954), pp. 388–400.

————. *Languages in Contact: Findings and Problems*. New York, 1953.

————. *The Field of Yiddish—Studies in Language, Folklore, and Literature*. The Hague, 1965.

————. "Multilingual Dialectology and the New Yiddish Atlas." *Anthropological Linguistics* 4 (1962), pp. 6–22.

————, W. Labov, and M. Herzog. "Empirical Foundations for a Theory of Language Change." in W. P. Lehmann and Y. Malkiel (eds.). *Directions for Historical Linguistics*. University of Texas Press, 1968.

Welmers, William, and Warren d'Azevedo. *Some Terms from Liberian Speech.* 2nd Edition. U.S. Peace Corps in Liberia. Monrovia, 1970.

Whinnom, Keith. *Spanish Contact Vernaculars in the Philippine Islands.* Hong Kong University Press, 1956.

———. "The Origin of the European-Based Pidgins and Creoles." *Orbis* 14 (1965), pp. 590–627.

———. "Linguistic Hybridization and the 'Special Case' of Pidgins and Creoles." In Dell Hymes (ed.), *Pidginization and Creolization of Languages,* Cambridge University Press, 1971.

Whitten, Norman E. "Contemporary Patterns of Malign Occultism Among Negroes in North Carolina." *Journal of American Folklore* 75 (1962), pp. 311–25.

———, and John Szwed (eds.). *Afro-American Anthropology: Contemporary Perspectives.* New York, 1970.

Williams, Frederick (ed.). *Language and Poverty, Perspectives on a Theme.* Chicago, 1970.

Williams, Gomer. *The Liverpool Privateers and the Liverpool Slave Trade.* London, 1897.

Williamson, Juanita V. *A Phonological and Morphological Study of the Speech of the Negro of Memphis, Tennessee.* Publications of the American Dialect Society 50 (1961).

———. *The Speech of Negro High School Students in Memphis, Tennessee.* U.S. Office of Education OEC-6-10-207, Final Report.

———, and Virginia M. Burke (eds.). *A Various Language. Perspectives on American Dialects.* New York, 1971.

Willson, Minnie Moore. *The Seminoles of Florida.* Kissimee, Florida, 1910. (With a Glossary by "Mr." Willson.)

Winks, Robin. *The Blacks in Canada.* Montreal, 1971.

Wise, Claude M. "Specimen of Louisiana French-English: or Cajun Dialect in Phonetic Transcription." *American Speech* 8 (1935), pp. 63–64.

———. "Negro Dialect." *Quarterly Journal of Speech* 19 (1933), pp. 522–28.

————. *Applied Phonetics.* Englewood Cliffs, New Jersey, 1957.

Wissler, Clark. *The American Indian.* Oxford University Press, 1922.

Witherspoon, John. "The Druid," Numbers V, VI, and VII. *Pennsylvania Journal and the Weekly Advertiser,* 1781.

Wolfram, Walter. Review of Dillard, *Black English: Its History and Usage in the United States. Language,* 1973.

————, and Nona H. Clarke (eds.). *Black-White Speech Relationships.* Washington, D.C., 1971.

————, Marie Shiels, and Ralph Fasold. *Overlapping Influence in the English of Second Generation Puerto Rican Teenagers in Harlem.* Final Report, U.S. Office of Education Grant No. 3-70-033(508).

Wood, Peter H. *Black Majority: Negroes in Colonial Carolina from 1670 through the Stono Rebellion.* New York, 1974.

Wood, Ralph (ed.). *The Pennsylvania Germans.* 1942.

Wood, Richard. "New Light on the Origins of Papiamentu: An 18th Century Letter." *Neophilologus* LVI (1972).

————. "The Hispanization of a Creole Language." *Hispania* 55 (1972).

Woodson, Carter G. *The Negro in Our History.* 5th Edition. Washington, D.C., 1928.

Woodward, Thomas Simpson. *Reminiscences of the Creek or Muscogee Indians.* Montgomery, Alabama, 1851.

Wright, Joseph. *English Dialect Dictionary.* Oxford University Press, 1898–1905.

————. *English Dialect Grammar.* Oxford University Press, 1905.

Wright, Richard R. "Negro Companions of the Spanish Explorers." In August Meier and Elliott M. Rudwick (eds.), *The Making of Black America.* New York, 1969.

Wright, Thomas. *Dictionary of Obsolete and Provincial English.* London, 1857.

Wright, William. *History of the Big Bonanza.* Hartford, 1879.

Wyld, Henry C. *A History of Modern Colloquial English.* Oxford, 1920.

————. *A Short History of English.* 3rd Edition. New York, 1927.

Yule, Henry, and A. C. Burnell. *Hobson-Jobson. A Glossary of Colloquial Anglo-Indian Words and Phrases, and of Kindred Terms, Etymological, Historical, Geographical, and Discursive.* London, 1903.

Zettersten, Arne. *The English of Tristan da Cunha.* Lund, 1969.

INDEX

Acadians, *see* Cajuns

Achebe, Chinua, 15

Across America; or, the Great West and the Pacific Coast (Rusling), 118, 119

Adams, Rev. James, 57

Adams, Ramon F., 33, 39, 43, 126, 130, 133-34, 137, 140, 142, 143, 146

adstratum language theory, 195, 309 n.

Africanisms in the Gullah Dialect (Turner), 26-27, 93

Afrikaans, 285 n.

Alabama Indians, 106, 118

Algonquian Indians, 100, 139, 182, 290 n.

Alvarez Nazario, Manuel, 211

America by River and Rail (Ferguson), 26, 88

American Dialect Society, 21, 75

American English: dialect diversity, 50, 250-51 n.; dialect and geography, 155-90; frontier speech, 115-53; immigrants and, 77-113; koiné, 45-76; speakers of, 246-48; spread of, 191-92; verb with a preposition, 63-64

American English (Marckwardt), 3, 142

American Indian Pidgin English, 11, 14, 41, 73, 99-111, 266 n.; African transmission to, 102, 107; in the Northwest, 110-11; in the Southwest, 105-10

American Indians, 5, 42, 53, 56, 58, 78, 158; bilingual program, 109; church-dominated schools, 106-7, 108, 109; frontiersman's English contact with, 117-20, 136-37, 141, 144-47, 151, 153; lingua franca tradition, 119-20, 124; loggers' language from, 136-37; migration, 77-78, 102; progress of English among, 105-11; sign languages, 101, 102, 103, 104-5, 151; slavery, 99; trade languages, 280 n.; word forms, 13-14; *See also* names of tribes

American koiné, 45-76, 165, 175, 181, 186; Americanisms, 64-67, 271 n.; Anglophilic influences, 69; Appalachian and Ozark pioneers, 63; beginnings of, 50-51, 268 n.; of British-derived immigrants, 45-58, 59, 60; correct English and, 68-69, 74; efforts to maintain, 74-76; formation process, 60-68, 260 n.; frontier speech and, 70-74, 76;

geographic factors, 54; list of words, 66-67; Lyceum and Chautauqua movement, 76, 272-73 n.; maritime influences, 49; "pure," 59, 68, 71-72, 74, 76; schoolteachers' role in, 74-75, 76, 267 n.; slave population, 57, 58, 70; slave trade, 49; social class/caste relationships, 54, 58, 60, 62, 264-65 n.; unity of, 59, 75-76; variations from, 57- 58; verb with a proposition, 63-64
American Language, The (Mencken), 138
"American Linguistic Geography: A Sociological Appraisal" (Pickford), 160
American Notes (Dickens), 71
American Vulgate, 165
Americanisms, 64-67, 271 n.; British in origin, 65; of Italian origin, 83
Amish (religious sect), 86, 275 n.
Andrews, Charles M., 48
anti-Semitism, 140-41
Apache Indians, 105, 107, 110, 119
apostrophes, Spanglish, 203-4
Arawak Indians, 214, 315 n.
Asbury, Herbert, 112, 182-83
Aspillera, Paraluman S., 237-38
Atkins, John, 7, 21
Atwood, E. Bagby, 75, 142
Austin, Moses, 122-23, 129
Austin, Stephen F., 123, 131
Australia: aboriginal languages, 19; koiné-forming process, 61-62, 63

Bailyn, Bernard, 49
Bantu, 224
Barbary Coast, The (Asbury), 112, 182-83
Barbot, John, 21
Barrere, Albert, 12, 43
be (Irish durative), Black English and, 83, 90-94, 277-78 n.

Beach-la-Mar Pidgin English, 256 n.
Beadle, John H., 87-88, 106
Beck, Robert, 162, 163
Beginnings of New England, The (Fiske), 50-51
Bernard, J. R. L.-B., 62
Beschryvinge van de Volksplantinge Zuriname (Herlein), 24
Beyond the Mississippi (Richardson), 72, 124, 150
bilingualism, 4, 16, 70, 131, 132; American Indian program, 109; Puerto Rico, 191-222
Black Beaver, 73, 102-104, 105
Black English, 20, 36, 42, 43, 50, 82, 250-51 n., 279 n.; American geographic variations, 162-63, 164, 173-79, 180, 187-88, 298 n., 301-2 n., 303 n., 307 n.; *be* (durative), 83, 90-94, 277-78 n.; British regionalisms, 89-90; of Canadian Negroes, 41; of children, 174-75, 176, 177, 236, 301 n., 319 n.; folklore and beliefs, 98; frontiersman's contact, 148, 149-51; influence on Southern whites, 175-78, 300-1 n., 302 n., 308 n.; in Liberia, 226-27, 228, 237, 318 n.; in the Northern states, 96-98; and Spanglish, 206-7, 208, 217-18, 311-12 n.
Black English, 102, 112, 127, 175
Blacks in Canada, The (Winks), 28, 95
Blues People (Jones), 98
Boont, 183-84, 305-6 n.
Bossu, Jean-Bernard, 104, 146
Boucher, Rev. Jonathan, 56, 58-59
Boucicault, Dion, 120-21
Bourgeois Gentilhomme, Le (Moliere), 7
Bourke, John G., 72, 110, 119, 132-33
Brackenridge, Hugh Henry, 93
brand-name vocabulary, 173
British English, 159, 180, 186-87, 188, 247; "r-less" pronunciations, 69;

acquisition of, 192; *See also* Spanglish
Puritans, 77
Pyles, Thomas, 44, 84, 145, 152

Quakers, 55, 152

r-lessness, 69, 308-9 n.
r-pronouncing, 189
radio, 84-85; vocabulary of, 170, 171
Read, Allen Walker, 20, 51, 259-60 n., 270 n.
recorded music terms, 170
Reinecke, John, 17
Religious Intelligencer, The, 15, 16
rhyming slang, 298-99 n.
Richardson, Albert D., 72, 124, 140, 150
Robertson, Rev. W. S., 106
Roosevelt, Theodore, 192
Roucek, Joseph S., 242-43, 245
Rusling, Gen. James F., 118, 119, 125, 140
Russian, 166

Sabir, *see* Mediterranean Lingua Franca
Sand Pebbles, The (McKenna), 30, 37-39
Saramaccan, 120
savvy, 6, 126, 136
Sawyer, Janet B., 132, 169
Scandinavian immigrants, 77
Scotch-Irish immigrants, 77
Seminole Indians, 42, 137, 182, 290 n.
Shall I Try Australia? (James), 61
Shakespeare, William, 4, 74, 149, 224-25, 241
Shakespearean English, 251 n.
Sharpe, Granville, 25
Sheldon, George, 96-97
Shuy, Roger W., 156, 157, 158, 159, 161, 164, 165, 171, 175

sign language, American Indian, 101, 102, 103, 104-5, 151
Silverheels, Jay, 104
Six Months in the West Indies in 1825 (Coleridge), 25-26
skookum, 111, 134, 135
slave trade: language chronicle of, 21-29; maritime Pidgin English, 6-15, 20-29, 42, 49, 94-95; New York City, 95; triangular route, 12, 49
slavery, 77, 78, 99, 111; demographic movement, 95; frontier speech-ways and, 117-18, 120, 121, 126, 141; speech in Northern colonies, 96-97; *See also* Black English
Sledd, James, 177-78
Smith, Captain John, 3-4
Smith, William, 7, 21
Smyth, J. F. D., 27, 58
Social Stratification of English in New York City, The (Labov), 166
Sociological Inquiry (publication), 239
Southern white English, 58, 175-78, 250-51 n., 300-1 n., 302 n., 308 n.
Spanglish, 16, 191-222, 233-35, 241; Anglicization, 203-5; Black English vernacular and, 206-7, 208, 217-18, 311-12 n.; comparison between Curaçao and, 208-10; Condado resort area, 202-4; distinction between Spanish and English, 199-201; English verb-preposition compounds, 201-2, 310 n.; German and French words, 202-3; *germania* relationship, 198-99; inflectional endings, 198; language-mixing, 199-206, 208, 212-13, 215; of Neoricans, 216-17; New York City and, 205-6, 215, 216, 220-21; reasons for, 208, 210-13; street directions, 194-95; use of apostrophes, 203-4; vocabulary substitutions, 215-16; *See also* Puerto Rico

41, 58, 102, 227-28, 266 n.
Western Wilds (Beadle), 106
Western Words: A Dictionary of the American West (Adams), 33, 39, 43, 130, 133-34, 137, 140, 142, 143, 146
Western World, The, or, Travels in the United States in 1846–47 (Mackay), 27-28
Whinnom, Keith, 35
Whitten, Norman, 98
Williams, Roger, 5, 106
Williamson, Juanita, 176-77
Winks, Robin, 28, 95
Witherspoon, John, 71, 296 n.
Wolof, 36, 298 n., 301 n.
Woods Words (McCulloch), 39, 135, 136

Woodward, Thomas, 103
Woodward's Reminiscences of the Creek or Muscogee Indians, 103
Words and Ways in American English (Pyles), 84
World War I, 30
World War II, 30, 139, 166
Wright, Thomas, 54, 162-63

Yankee, 144-45
Yiddish, 81, 83, 84, 141, 267 n., 299 n.; contribution to American English, 84-85; importance of German in, 85
Yiddishisms, 165

ABOUT THE AUTHOR

J. L. DILLARD is a linguistics teacher, researcher, and writer who has taught in many universities in the United States and abroad, including Universidad Central in Ecuador, Université Officielle de Bujumbura in Burundi, and Ferkauf Graduate School of Yeshiva University in New York City. He now teaches at the University of Puerto Rico.